GOVERNMENT, SCHOOLS AND THE LAW

How have conflicts of interest between individual and state been affected by the 1988 Education Reform Act?

In recent years, education has become the scene of some of the government's most radical reforms. The principles of freedom of choice, accountability and 'market forces' all came into play in the drafting of the Education Reform Act of 1988. As the Act has been implemented, it has brought to the surface a whole range of tensions between central and local government and between individual interests and the interests of the community.

This book focuses on five areas of education in which the legal debate is complex and the implications are particularly wide-reaching for ordinary parents and children: school choice, the secular curriculum, expenditure constraints and their effects on educational provision, falling rolls and opting out. It looks both at the legislation in these areas and at specific challenges in the courts, and a final chapter sets the issues in their political context and considers possible future developments.

Paul Meredith is a lecturer in law at the University of Southampton and the author of numerous articles on education and the law. His other interests include the law relating to civil liberties generally, police powers and police governance.

GOVERNMENT, SCHOOLS AND THE LAW

Paul Meredith

London and New York

First published in 1992
by Routledge
11 New Fetter Lane, London EC4P 4EE

Simultaneously published in the USA and Canada
by Routledge
a division of Routledge, Chapman and Hall Inc.
29 West 35th Street, New York, NY 10001

Typeset by LaserScript Limited, Mitcham, Surrey
Printed and bound in Great Britain by
Mackays of Chatham PLC, Chatham, Kent

British Library Cataloguing in Publication Data

Meredith, Paul, 1950–
Government, schools and the law.
I. Title
379.0941

Library of Congress Cataloging in Publication Data

p. cm.

ISBN 0-415-03658-5

CONTENTS

PREFACE

The provision of education has become one of the most critically important and controversial areas of governmental activity in the past decade. It raises fundamental questions concerning the role of government, the relationships between the different levels of government, the interests of the individual and of the community, and the role of the law. This book sets out to explore in some detail a selection of the most notable areas of current controversy and conflict over the governance of schools in England and Wales. The process of selecting these major areas has inevitably involved the omission of many other issues deserving of study, but it was felt preferable to attempt treatment in greater depth of a limited number of areas of conflict rather than cover a wider range of issues in a more superficial way. It is probable that many of the lessons that can be derived from the discussion of the issues selected would apply with equal force to other areas of conflict over the governance of schools, and, indeed, to other areas of governmental activity. Discussion of those other areas would in many cases have involved probing the same types of issue, asking the same types of question and often coming up with similar conclusions. It is hoped, however, that the selection actually made can be justified as isolating issues of fundamental importance to the relationships between central and local government, between public authorities and the individual, and between collective and individual interests.

In the course of writing this book I have been supported and encouraged by my colleagues in the Faculty of Law at Southampton University, and to them I offer my thanks. In particular, however, I owe a considerable debt of gratitude to Alison Lampard who greatly assisted me through her considerable skills in the art of word processing.

I also wish to express my thanks to the editors of *Public Law*, the *Modern Law Review*, the *Journal of Social Welfare Law* and the *Journal of Education and the Law* for permission to incorporate, in a revised and updated form, some material which first appeared in their journals in article form.

Paul Meredith
Southampton

TABLE OF CASES

Page references are in italics.

Associated Provincial Picture Houses Ltd v. *Wednesbury Corporation* [1948] 1 KB 223. *44*

Bostock v. *Kay* (1989) 87 LGR 583. *162–3*

Brunyate v. *ILEA* [1989] 2 All ER 417. *178–9, 181–3*

Council of Civil Service Unions v. *Minister for the Civil Service* [1985] AC 374. *205*

Cumings v. *Birkenhead Corporation* [1972] 1 Ch. 12. *206*

Equal Opportunities Commission v. *Birmingham City Council* [1989] 1 All ER 769. *139–40, 175*

Gillick v. *West Norfolk and Wisbech Area Health Authority* [1985] 3 All ER 402. *7–9*

Harvey v. *Strathclyde Regional Council* (1989) SLT 612. *141–3*

Legg v. *ILEA* [1972] 3 All ER 177. *204, 210*

Meade v. *Haringey London Borough Council* [1979] 2 All ER 1016. *103–6, 108, 109*

Nichol v. *Gateshead Metropolitan Borough Council* (1989) 87 LGR 435. *132, 136–7*

R. v. *Brent London Borough Council, ex parte Gunning* (1986) 84 LGR 168. *127–32, 135–6, 137*

R. v. *Bromley London Borough Council, ex parte C, The Independent* Law Reports, 13 June 1991. *194*

R. v. *Croydon London Borough Council, ex parte Leney, The Times* Law Reports, 27 November 1986. *206*

R. v. *Governors of Bishop Challoner Roman Catholic School, ex parte C, The Independent* Law Reports, 1 August 1991. *195*

R. v. *Governors of John Bacon School, ex parte ILEA, The Independent* Law Reports, 29 March 1990. *209*

EUROPEAN COURT OF HUMAN RIGHTS CASES

APPLICATIONS BEFORE EUROPEAN COMMISSION OF HUMAN RIGHTS

UNITED STATES SUPREME COURT CASES

TABLE OF STATUTES

Education Act 1944

Sex Discrimination Act 1975

Race Relations Act 1976

Education Act 1980

Education (Scotland) Act 1980

Education Act 1981

Education (Scotland) Act 1981

Supreme Court Act 1981

Local Government Act 1985

Education (No. 2) Act 1986

Education Reform Act 1988

Local Government Act 1988

TABLE OF STATUTORY INSTRUMENTS

(Amendment) Regls 1990, SI 1990 No. 1109.
Education (National Curriculum) (Attainment Targets and Programmes of Study in Technology) Order 1990, SI 1990 No. 1531.
Education (Individual Pupils' Achievements) (Information) Regls 1990, SI 1990 No. 1381.
Education (National Curriculum) (Assessment Arrangements for English, Mathematics and Science) Order 1990, SI 1990 No. 1543.
Education (Grant-Maintained Schools) (Finance) Regls 1991, SI 1991 No. 353.
Education (National Curriculum) (Attainment Targets and Programmes of Study in Geography) Order 1991, SI 1991 No. 678.
Education (National Curriculum) (Attainment Targets and Programmes of Study in History) Order 1991, SI 1991 No. 681.

ABBREVIATIONS

AC	Appeal Cases
All ER	All England Law Reports
CA	Court of Appeal
Ch	Chancery Division
CO	Crown Office
DES	Department of Education and Science
EHRR	European Human Rights Reports
HMI	Her Majesty's Inspectorate of Schools
ILEA	Inner London Education Authority
KB	King's Bench Division
LEA	Local Education Authority
LGR	Local Government Reports (Knight's)
QB	Queen's Bench Division
SLT	Scots Law Times
TES	*Times Educational Supplement*
US	United States Supreme Court Reports
WLR	Weekly Law Reports

1

INTRODUCTION

SCOPE AND AIMS OF THE BOOK

This book sets out to explore the relationship between government (at both central and local level) and the law in the context of one of the most controversial areas of state activity directly affecting the community at large and individual citizens – the provision of education in maintained schools. This is an area of governmental activity where the policies adopted and the decisions taken inevitably have a significant social and political impact, whether it be at the level of the formulation of the national curriculum, decisions as to expenditure constraints or school closures, or more individualised decisions as to choice of school or individual curricular complaints. It is an area where there is a considerable tension not only between government and opposition, but between different levels of government – between central government and local authorities, LEAs often being of a different political complexion from the central government of the day, often operating under a very different social and educational philosophy and seeking to strike a very different balance between collective and individual interests. There has also been a tendency in recent years across a wide range of governmental functioning – education being but one example, although a very prominent one – for that tension to develop into a marked centralisation of power, with central government seeking to erode many local authority functions. The governance of schools thus offers in many ways an excellent case study of central and local government relations. It is also an area where the community interest is high: there is no doubt that schools are a significant community resource and that there is a strong community interest in the maintenance of the highest attainable standards for all pupils in a given area. That community interest may well at times conflict with the interests of individual parents and children, and the balance between these interests is indeed one of the most important considerations in educational decision-making today. The interaction between these several interests – central, local, community and individual – has often given rise to conflict, and this has led to frequent recourse to the courts as a means of resolution, though it has also led to the establishment of more informal means of dispute resolution, as for instance in the case of local appellate tribunals to determine disputes over choice of school and, very recently, the establishment of local curricular complaints machinery under the Education Reform Act 1988.

The aim of this book is to offer an examination of the way in which central and local government interacts in the context of school governance, the way in which law and policy are formulated and implemented, the way in which discretion is exercised; and to consider the impact of government policy and discretionary decision-making on the community and on individuals, and the means whereby the many disputes that arise in this area may be resolved. The whole of the governance of schools is, of course, a huge area, and cannot possibly be covered in a book of this length. No attempt has therefore been made to achieve comprehensive coverage of all areas of potential interest: this book is unapologetically selective in terms of its substantive areas of coverage. Rather, it has been sought to isolate a limited number of areas of the governance of schools where tension has been particularly high and where there has been a considerable volume of conflict, and to study these in greater depth than would have been possible in a wider study. These substantive areas should be seen essentially as examples: there is every reason to believe that closely analogous issues, interests, tensions, conflicts and modes of resolution would arise elsewhere within school governance.

The remainder of chapter 1 is devoted to examining some of the main reasons for the elevation of education in recent years as one of the foremost areas of political debate and legal importance; and then to examining some aspects of the several interests in education, notably the interests of the individual parent or child. We then go on to consider the manner in which those interests may be safeguarded both within our own domestic constitutional structure and legal system and through international protection. Chapters 2 to 6 form the main part of the book and are devoted to substantive studies of particular areas of school governance: in chapter 2 we will look at an issue very close to the heart of Conservative educational philosophy – parental choice of school; chapter 3 examines the way in which the law regulates the contents of the secular curriculum in schools; chapter 4 in a sense is a development from chapter 3 in that it considers the possible legal consequences of a breakdown in the substantive content of education as where economic constraints or other factors lead to the provision of what may be regarded as legally 'insufficient' education; chapter 5 examines some of the agonising disputes over the closure or amalgamation of schools as a consequence of falling rolls; chapter 6 is a development from chapter 5 in that it examines the possibility of schools forestalling the threat of closure, amalgamation or any other form of reorganisation by opting out of LEA control in favour of grant-maintained status. Chapter 7 offers a brief consideration of possible future developments.

THE PROMINENCE OF THE EDUCATION DEBATE

There are few who would seek to deny that the governance of education has in the past decade and more come to the very forefront of political, social and legal conflict. In part this is attributable to the level of concern felt by individual citizens over the scope and content of education provided by the state and over the attainment of the highest reasonably practicable standards of provision, in the realisation that education is fundamental to the development of children to their full potential as autonomous adults. In part it is attributable to conscious policy decisions by successive governments to elevate education policy to a prominent position on the political agenda: the then Prime Minister, Mr James Callaghan, in 1976 responded to widespread concern over declining educational standards by instituting a 'great debate' on educational issues, clearly in the realisation that there was a major problem in this context that merited extensive public discussion, but also, more cynically, in the realisation that there was a good deal of political capital to be gained from being seen very publicly to instigate considered measures to combat the problem. This, along with the issue of parental choice and the longstanding debate over comprehensive reorganisation, served to make educational issues a significant factor in the May 1979 general election campaign.

The successive Conservative governments which have held office since 1979 have maintained the prominence of educational issues in political debate by treating education as a central instrument of political and social reform, using it as a vehicle for the application of a range of principles which lie at the heart of the government's political philosophy. Among the most important of these principles are the *enhancement of individualism* and *freedom of choice*, seen particularly in measures to secure greater parental choice of school, though this often operates at the expense of the collective interest of the community as a whole. A second principle is that of *accountability* on the part of the providers of education to their 'consumers', represented in this context chiefly by parents, seen partly through increasing parental representation on school governing bodies and an enhancement of their powers, but perhaps more significantly through the application of a further principle central to government philosophy, namely the subjection of schools as far as practicable to *competitive market forces*. This is achieved through the linking of more effective parental choice of school with the funding of individual schools on the basis of a formula which treats the number of registered pupils as the predominant factor. Again, this may be beneficial to individual parents or individual institutions, but be highly detrimental to the collective community interest. Education has also been used as a vehicle for the implementation of policies seeking to reverse what the government perceives as a decline in moral standards, encouraging more *traditional 'family-orientated values'*, seen in the inclusion of certain important provisions in legislation concerning the school curriculum. And, very importantly, the government has used education along with several other important areas of governmental activity as a vehicle for achieving a fundamental shift in the balance of power between central and local government, seen in the erosion of LEAs' responsibilities over the management of schools, in the creation of new categories of school outside LEA control, and, most graphically, in the massive *centralisation of power* effected by the centralised prescription of curricular content under the national curriculum.

These are measures of the first importance and have served to bring educational issues and educational reform to the very forefront of political controversy in the past decade. They have been introduced through a series of statutes, culminating in the Education Reform Act 1988, many aspects of which were bitterly opposed in Parliament, by LEAs, by educationalists and by many others, and they have served in a single decade to bring about the most radical reshaping of both the structure and the content of educational provision since the Education Act 1944.

It is, however, not merely in the political arena that education has been prominent: since the late 1970s we have witnessed a considerable increase in the volume of litigation over educational issues. The closure, amalgamation or other reorganisation of schools necessitated by falling rolls has given rise to a steady flow of applications for judicial review of the procedures adopted by LEAs in drawing up their proposals for submission to the Secretary of State; there have been challenges to the procedures for balloting parents over opting-out of LEA control in favour of grant-maintained status, and over the subsequent determination by the Secretary of State of opting-out proposals; the proceedings of local education appeal tribunals set up to determine choice of school disputes have been challenged; and parents have sought to invoke the authority of the courts to compel LEAs to meet their obligation to provide a legally 'sufficient' education for their children, where expenditure constraints have brought about a decline in educational provision to a level which many regard as wholly unacceptable and a denial in some cases of what may truly be regarded as an education of the standard and scope that might properly be regarded as an entitlement in an advanced liberal democracy. These serve merely as some examples of the range of educational issues which have been brought before the courts in recent years, and to emphasise the increasing importance of the courts – particularly through applications for judicial review before the High Court – in the educational context.

INTERESTS IN EDUCATION

The majority of studies in this context focus largely on what may rather imprecisely be termed 'parental rights' or, in some cases where they are given a degree of recognition, 'children's rights'. It may be that these terms represent roughly what many would regard as reasonable and perhaps obvious – that parents and children have, or should have, a range of 'rights' in relation to education and that these should be reflected in the administration of the system and, in the event of conflict, ultimately be enforceable through recourse to the courts. It should, however, be emphasised from the outset that these terms are bedevilled with difficulty when examined from a legal standpoint, and that, in the sphere of education, it is rarely accurate to speak in terms of the legal 'rights' of parents or children in the sense of their being rights which are directly enforceable in the courts. It is probably better to regard these, rather, as in the nature of political assertions which may be met by qualified legal obligations on the part of the providers of educational services. As we will see below, the Education Acts do not confer any express 'rights' on parents or children, but, rather, impose duties on the education authorities to provide educational services, and even to have regard to 'parental wishes' in so doing, but these 'duties' are so hedged about by qualifications and provisos and vagueness of phraseology as to have their practical content seriously undermined.

It is for these reasons that the phrase 'parental rights in education' or 'children's rights in education' are largely avoided in this discussion as being essentially misleading. Parents' 'interests' or children's 'interests' in education, though still substantially unclear as to their meaning, are preferred as having at least the merit of avoiding any implication of clear enforceability in the courts.

Before going on in the following section to consider the rationale for parents' or children's interests in education, it should be stressed that these are not the only legitimate interests in the provision of education. It is perhaps obvious, but ought nonetheless to be mentioned at least in passing, that the state itself has an interest, seen primarily from the broader economic and social viewpoint, in education: the importance of education and training, research and technological advance to the good of the economy is frequently stressed, though arguably insufficiently recognised by the government. And the state's interest is not merely economic: there are undoubtedly important social, cultural and 'law and order' benefits to be gained from the promotion of an increasingly well-educated population. Of greater practical importance in the context of this book, perhaps, is the interest of the community: as has already been mentioned, there is often a need to strike a balance between collective and individual interests in educational decision-making and, particularly, the allocation of resources, and how that balance is struck lies at the heart of much of the debate about education, as indeed about much of government. Thus, the realisation of parental choice by a few might be extremely damaging for the collective whole through exacerbating the problem of falling rolls at certain schools in the area, leading to their further contraction and further depletion of their resources; one school opting out in favour of grant-maintained status may be perceived as highly desirable by those who instigated the move, but nonetheless be highly damaging to the interests of the schools in the area remaining within LEA control. These are merely two examples which will be explored further in the chapters that follow, but they serve to emphasise here that the individual interests of parents and children are not the only considerations, and that there is a constant need to temper individual interests by weighing them properly in the balance with countervailing collective interests. That is *not* to say that individualism is inherently wrong: it is utterly right that individual interests should play a constructive part in conditioning the decision-making processes, and it is thoroughly healthy that there should be effective mechanisms for individual voices to be heard and, where appropriate, to prevail. But it is essential that an appropriate balance be struck between those individual interests and the wider collective interests of the remainder of the community.

THE LOCATION OF INDIVIDUAL INTERESTS IN EDUCATION – CHILDREN OR PARENTS?

The recognition of *children's* (as opposed to parental) interests in education in English domestic law is negligible: the Education Acts merely assume that the interests of children are subsumed by those of their parents, and that parents will in all material respects represent the interests of their children. This is a manifestation in a sense of traditional parental authority over minor children. For example, it is upon the *parents* that section 36 of the Education Act 1944 imposes the duty, subject to criminal sanctions, to ensure that their children of compulsory school age receive 'efficient full-time education'; and section 76 of the same Act imposes on the Secretary of State and LEAs an obligation, subject to provisos, to have regard to the general principle that pupils are to be educated in accordance with the wishes of *their parents*. Section 6 of the Education Act 1980 imposes on LEAs a duty to make arrangements for *parents* to express a reasoned preference over which school their child should attend. Under section 3 of the Education (No. 2) Act 1986, provision is made for *parental* representation on school governing bodies, but no provision whatsoever is made for the representation of pupils (not even of those who have reached the age of majority).

The law thus assumes a coincidence of interests in the sphere of education between parents and children[1] and offers no real recognition of any autonomous interests in the child, although a glimmer of such recognition may in due course emerge in education by analogy with the relationship between doctors and minor patients in the context of the giving of medical advice: in *Gillick* v. *West Norfolk and Wisbech Area Health Authority*,[2] the mother of five daughters aged under 16 years challenged the legality of a Department of Health Circular advising doctors that they would not be acting unlawfully by prescribing contraceptives to a girl aged under 16, provided that they were acting in good faith to protect her against the harmful effects of sexual intercourse. The Circular had also stated that, while the governing assumption should always be that the parents should be involved and that their consent should be obtained, circumstances *could* arise where contraceptives could properly be prescribed without consulting the parents or obtaining their consent, on the basis of the principle of confidentiality between doctor and patient. The House of Lords held, by a majority and reversing the decision of the Court of Appeal, that a child grew increasingly independent as it grew older and that this brought about a corresponding dwindling in parental authority; parental rights were recognised by law only for as long as needed for the child's protection, and any such parental rights yielded to the child's right to make her own decisions when she had reached a sufficient level of understanding and intelligence.

The *Gillick* case represents a recognition of at least a degree of developing autonomy in older minors and that there may not be a coincidence of interests between a child and its parents. It is possible that there will in time develop an increased legal recognition in a range of contexts, including perhaps education, of children's rights in English law,[3] a recognition that has long been given through international treaties and conventions, as we will see below. In the meantime, however, this is barely discernible in the English law relating to education. This is so despite the fact that a clash of interests between parent and child may well arise in the educational sphere, for instance over choice of school or the decision to withhold a child from attendance at school at all (it is, of course, recognised that some parents very properly and effectively provide for their children's education otherwise than at school), or over the provision of sex education, or over personal counselling in relation to matters of considerable delicacy. In relation to personal counselling, teachers may as a final resort recognise this lack of coincidence of interests over delicate personal matters and be prepared to offer counselling without parental involvement or consent, and would not normally thereby be acting unlawfully. It is possible in some such circumstances that a teacher may owe an obligation of confidentiality to a pupil analogous to that between a doctor and a minor patient as recognised in *Gillick*, although the law here is far from certain.[4] In the main, however, excluding consideration of judicial proceedings relating to the welfare of children, for instance in the context of actions for divorce (which lie outside the scope of this book), there simply are no mechanisms within the administrative and legal structures for the voicing of children's interests independently of those of their parents, and the governing assumption that the interests of children and those of their parents merely coincide thus prevails. Thus, children substantially surrender to their parents the exercise of their interests in education rather than exercise any clear legally recognised autonomy and independence of judgment themselves. For those reasons the main focus of attention in the chapters that follow will be on the individual interests of parents rather than of children.

THE RATIONALE FOR INDIVIDUAL INTERESTS IN EDUCATION

Perhaps the essential rationale for individual interests in education, on the part of both parent and child, lies in the very fundamentality of education to the development of the child into a fully autonomous adult equipped to the optimum extent to take advantage of its life chances; and these life chances are seen in terms of the highest achievement of which that individual is capable in the context of leading an autonomous and fulfilled adult life. In realising this interest, children – particularly younger children – necessarily surrender either all or much of their individual freedom of choice and discretion to their parents, and parents thus assume a critical role in safeguarding their child's educational and social development through to maturity. The philosopher John Stuart Mill, writing in his essay *On Liberty* in 1859, emphasised that

> Hardly anyone indeed will deny that it is one of the most sacred duties of the parents... after summoning a human being into the world, to give that being an education fitting him to perform his part well in life towards others and towards himself.... To bring a child into existence without a fair prospect of being able, not only to provide food for its body, but instruction and training for its mind, is a moral crime, both against the unfortunate offspring and against society[5]

This powerful role has been called 'liberal paternalism',[6] and it places a weighty responsibility upon the parent to ensure that the child receives that education which will best equip it for eventual autonomy and fulfilment. This may well involve subjecting the child to disciplines and rigours against its will, and may well involve curbing its freedom. This is justified in the name of liberal paternalism if it is for the child's ultimate benefit as leading to its eventual 'rational independence'[7] as an autonomous adult.

It is obvious today that for practical reasons the vast majority of parents delegate this role substantially to the state, although it should be noted, firstly, that many educationalists consider the impact of the education and conditioning within the home environment as critical to the child's overall social and intellectual development, particularly in the early years; and secondly, that a significant minority of parents do *not* delegate educational functions to the state, preferring to have their children educated in the independent sector or within the parental home or otherwise. In the latter cases, however, it should be remembered that there is still a significant element of state involvement through inspection and control. For the majority of parents today, however, recourse to state provision of educational services is the only practical option, and it is broadly taken for granted that the state has a legitimate and important role not only in ensuring that children receive efficient full-time education within a given age-range, but actually in making that provision itself. By the same token, it is taken for granted today that the state should assume an extensive responsibility for further, higher and adult education and training; but this goes beyond the scope of this book.

Recognition of the legitimacy of the role of the state as an actual provider of education is in fact comparatively recent, and is the outcome of many delicate compromises, particularly with the Church authorities, culminating in the denominational settlement given statutory force by the Education Act 1944. Mill saw grave dangers in state provision (though not state *enforcement* of a compulsory system of private provision). In 1859 Mill wrote:

> That the whole or any large part of the education of the people should be in State hands, I go as far as anyone in deprecating. All that has been said of the importance of individuality of character, and diversity of opinions and modes of conduct, involves, as of the same unspeakable importance, diversity of education. A general State education is a mere contrivance for moulding people to be exactly like one another: and as the mould in which it casts them is that which pleases the predominant power in the government, whether this be a monarch, a priesthood, an aristocracy, or the majority of the existing generation; in proportion as it is efficient

> and successful, it establishes a despotism over the mind, leading by natural tendency to one over the body. An education established and controlled by the State should only exist, if it exist at all, as one among many competing experiments, carried on for the purpose of example and stimulus, to keep the others up to a certain standard of excellence.[8]

Such fears of state provision leading to a despotism over mind and body may perhaps have receded today, though there are many who are deeply critical of the level of centralised prescription of curricular content involved in the national curriculum under the Education Reform Act. Nonetheless, Mill's fears serve to emphasise that, although the vast majority of parents effectively delegate their role of ensuring the best possible education for their children to the state authorities, they *do not do so unreservedly*: while a liberal democratic view of education today would acknowledge the legitimacy of state provision (though not state monopoly), it would nonetheless regard it as essential that parents retain a significant element of personal discretion to ensure that their children are educated in such a way as to correspond with certain important aspects of their own personal conscience, convictions, religious and cultural beliefs and practices and social priorities. This would clearly have to be subject to some practical limitations in a system of mass state provision, and is very much a matter of striking a balance between practicality and individualism, but it can nonetheless be asserted that it is of central importance that there should exist a range of suitable statutory mechanisms for giving effect to the legitimate interest of parents in having their children educated in accordance with personal conscience. As we will see in the next section of this chapter, this is reflected in the European Convention on Human Rights, but it is doubtful whether domestic English law can be regarded as making more than a token gesture towards parental interests, given that the means of enforcing individual interests in English law in this context are far from clear.

THE LEGAL PROTECTION OF INDIVIDUAL INTERESTS

Within domestic English law

Within domestic English law the primary source of legal protection of individual interests in education is clearly statute law, as interpreted and enforced by the courts. The courts in England and Wales are bound to enforce the clear words of statutes duly enacted by Parliament (subject to the possible overriding supremacy of certain European Community measures which lie outside the scope of this book). Although our courts certainly enjoy a fairly wide measure of discretion in interpreting statute law, there are within our constitutional structure no fundamental rights – for instance, a right to free speech or a right to education – laid down in an entrenched constitutional framework which can be used as a yardstick by which to challenge the constitutionality of statutes. This is in marked contrast to most other states which have a written constitution which does incorporate entrenched rights – usually called a Bill of Rights – and where it *is* possible to challenge the constitutionality of ordinary legislation by alleging that it is in some way incompatible with one or other of the entrenched provisions of the written constitution.

The United States provides perhaps the best example of challenge to the constitutionality of legislation: one of the most celebrated challenges in the United States was in *Brown* v. *Board of Education of Topeka* in 1954[9] where a challenge was brought on behalf of black children to state laws permitting schooling segregated by race: the challenge was based upon a provision of the Fourteenth Amendment to the US Constitution to the effect that no state shall deny to any person within its jurisdiction the 'equal protection of the laws', with which the plaintiffs claimed that the state laws were inconsistent. In an historic judgment, the US Supreme Court overruled the earlier authority of *Plessy* v. *Ferguson* in 1896[10] concerning segregation on railroads which had permitted such segregation provided that the facilities for blacks and whites were of equal standard. In *Brown*, the Supreme Court held that the argument that the facilities were 'separate but equal' had no place in relation to schools, that, even if the physical facilities were equal, the very fact of segregation meant that the pupils were denied equal educational opportunities: separate educational facilities were by very definition unequal. Thus, the plaintiffs were able to have duly enacted state legislation struck down as in violation of an entrenched constitutional provision. There is no counterpart to this in English law, where the courts have no fundamental constitutional yardsticks by which to measure the constitutional propriety of statutes enacted by Parliament, subject, of course, to their exercise of a fairly wide measure of interpretative discretion where possible.

In the absence of any constitutionally entrenched rights in the sphere of education (or elsewhere), individuals must have recourse to ordinary statute and common law. Practically the whole of the law relating to education is statutory, though the statutory provisions have been substantially elaborated by judicial decisions. The courts have, however, applied common law principles of natural justice and legitimate expectations in the educational sphere, as we will see in the discussion of school reorganisation in chapter 5. Statute law is, however, the primary source of such protection of individual interests as may exist in English law.

As the chapters that follow will seek to demonstrate, however, the Education Acts and related legislation cannot possibly be regarded as providing a secure foundation for legally enforceable rights on the part of parents or children as to schooling. Repeatedly we will come across statutory provisions which are couched in extremely vague phraseology, conferring extensive discretionary powers on either the Secretary of State or LEAs; and, where express duties *are* imposed upon public authorities, they are commonly qualified by wide-ranging 'escape' clauses making their enforcement extremely difficult. Above all, nowhere are these statutory provisions expressed in terms of 'rights' vested in individuals: they are invariably drafted in terms of qualified statutory duties on the part of public authorities. Although it may be possible to discern a corresponding right flowing from the existence of a statutory duty imposed upon an LEA, this is only true in a limited and residual sense.

A fine example of vague phraseology conferring the widest element of discretion is to be found in the very first section of the Education Act 1944, which imposes upon the Secretary of State a duty 'to promote the education of the people of England and Wales' – a duty which plainly no individual could possibly enforce in legal terms, but whose enforcement lies purely in the political arena. In the context of expenditure cuts in chapter 4 we will look at the severe difficulties faced by parents in seeking to enforce the duty of LEAs to provide 'sufficient schools' within the meaning of section 8 of the 1944 Act: this difficulty is substantially attributable to lack of precision in the statutory phraseology.

Perhaps the most important examples, however, are two provisions which in a way come closest to the creation of individual rights, but nonetheless in the end shy away from doing so by permitting the public authorities concerned to shelter behind extensive escape clauses. The first, which we will meet below in several different contexts, is section 76 of the Education Act 1944, which provides that, in the exercise and performance of all their powers and duties under the Act, both the Secretary of State and LEAs

> shall have regard to the general principle that, *so far as is compatible with the provision of efficient instruction and training and the avoidance of unreasonable public expenditure*, pupils are to be educated in accordance with the wishes of their parents.[11]

This will be interpreted in more detail in chapter 2, but here it is sufficient to note that the proviso underlined offers the public authorities a generous escape clause and makes the section well-nigh unenforceable in the courts by individuals. The second example is section 6 of the Education Act 1980, which imposes on LEAs a duty to make arrangements for enabling parents to express a reasoned preference as to the school at which they wish education to be provided for their children, and places the LEA under a duty to comply with that preference, subject, however, to significant escape clauses, the most important of which relieves the LEA of this duty where compliance with the parental preference would prejudice the provision of efficient education or the efficient use of resources.[12] It is emphasised that section 6 is drafted from the viewpoint of the duty of the LEA and does not in anything approaching express terms confer a right on the parents concerned.

These brief examples, all of which will be explored further below, serve to illustrate that in domestic English law we *do not have a system of enforceable legal rights vested in individuals but, rather, one of qualified legal obligations on the part of the public authorities*. This is in fundamental contrast to the position in most other states where the individual does enjoy positive rights by virtue of the existence of entrenched provisions in a written constitution. In so far as rights can be discerned in the context of education within our jurisdiction as corresponding to duties imposed on public authorities, they are impoverished and residual in nature, dependent upon the rather improbable event of the individual succeeding in piercing the defensive shield of extensive discretion and of the qualifications which normally surround the statutory duties imposed upon the public authorities concerned.

By virtue of international recognition

In sharp contrast to English legislation, international treaties and conventions which have given recognition to individual interests in education *have* expressed them in terms of positive rights, but they tend, as is commonly argued to be the case where positive rights are asserted, to be couched in terms which are susceptible to wide interpretation; and only one such international treaty to which the United Kingdom is a signatory has an enforcement mechanism accessible by individuals – the European Convention on Human Rights and Fundamental Freedoms, which will be considered in more detail below. Nonetheless international treaties and conventions may be of considerable political significance, even in the absence of any means of individual enforcement.

The United Nations Universal Declaration of Human Rights, 1948, declares in Article 26(1) that:

> Everyone has the right to education. Education shall be free, at least in the elementary and fundamental stages. Elementary education shall be compulsory.

It goes on in Article 26(3) to stipulate that:

> Parents have a prior right to choose the kind of education that shall be given to their children.

The concern of the United Nations with the right to education was subsequently expressed in the Declaration of the Rights of the Child in 1959 and the International Covenant on Economic, Social and Cultural Rights in 1966.[13] Individual interests in education were subsequently expressed in greater detail when the United Nations adopted the Convention on the Rights of the Child in November 1989, though this has yet to be ratified by the United Kingdom government. This provides in Articles 28 and 29 a wide range of requirements as to the provision of education and as to its scope and nature. Article 29, for instance, provides that the

> States parties agree that the education of the child shall be directed to:
>
> (a) The development of the child's personality, talents and mental and physical abilities to their fullest potential;
>
> (b) The development of respect for human rights and fundamental freedoms... ;
>
> (c) The development of respect for the child's parents, his or her own cultural identity, language and values, for the national values of the country in which the child is living, the country

from which he or she may originate and for civilisations different from his or her own;

(d) The preparation of the child for responsible life in a free society, in the spirit of understanding, peace, tolerance, equality of sexes, and friendship among all peoples, ethnic, national and religious groups and persons of indigenous origin;

(e) The development of respect for the natural environment.

Significant though the United Nations Declaration, Covenant and Convention may be as political aspirations and statements of principle, it is to the European Convention on Human Rights and Fundamental Freedoms of 1950, promulgated under the auspices of the Council of Europe, together with its subsequent Protocols, that one must look for provisions incorporating individual rights in education which have the attribute of enforceability through the right of individual application to the European Commission on Human Rights and subsequently, if declared admissible by the Commission, to the European Court of Human Rights. Several Articles of the Convention may have a bearing on education – notably Article 8 concerning respect for private and family life, and Article 9 concerning freedom of thought, conscience and religion. The provision of primary importance in the sphere of education is, however, Article 2 of the First Protocol to the Convention, which came into force in 1954,[14] and which provides that:

> No person shall be denied the right to education. In the exercise of any functions which it assumes in relation to education and to teaching, the State shall respect the right of parents to ensure such education and teaching in conformity with their own religious and philosophical convictions.

This the United Kingdom government acceded to subject to the formal reservation, reflecting the terms of section 76 of the Education Act 1944, that the second sentence was accepted only so far as compatible with the provision of efficient instruction and training and the avoidance of unreasonable public expenditure.[15]

The interpretation of Article 2 will be examined in several contexts in the chapters that follow, notably in relation to choice of school and the secular curriculum and sex education. At this stage suffice it to say that its potential application is wide, given the open interpretation that *could* be given to the word 'education' in the first sentence and the phrase 'philosophical convictions' in the second. The first sentence *could* be interpreted as requiring the provision by the state (or supervision over private provision) of at least an elementary education free of charge to all children within a given age range, though whether it could also be interpreted as requiring the provision of nursery education or further and adult education is by no means clear. There is a real possibility that some LEAs are currently in breach of the first sentence by virtue of the impact of expenditure constraints, some children in inner London boroughs having to be sent home from school as there are no suitably qualified teachers available to teach them. It is possible that the second sentence could be breached through the denial of parental choice of school based on cultural convictions, or the inclusion of certain matters within the curriculum relating to religion, culture, politics or sex coupled with the absence of any parental right to withdraw children from classes. Recently, a small religious sect who regard television as abhorrent were denied their claim to have their children exempted from education in information technology which involved them working with video display units, the Minister claiming that no children should be permitted to opt out of what the government regarded as an essential component of the school curriculum:[16] it is perhaps improbable that the sect would succeed in a claim that the Minister's decision amounted to a breach of their right to respect for their religious and philosophical convictions, but a cogent argument to that effect could nonetheless be made, and it serves well to illustrate the potential difficulty of interpretation that would be involved.

The potential breadth of application of the concept of 'philosophical convictions' was demonstrated by the successful application brought by the mothers of two pupils at Scottish state schools on the basis of their objections to the use of corporal punishment: *Campbell and Cosans* v. *United Kingdom*.[17] The complaints were founded not only on the incompatibility of the use or threatened use of corporal punishment in schools with the mothers' philosophical convictions under the second sentence, but also on the denial of the pupils' 'right to education' under the first sentence, as the pupils had been suspended from school until such time as they submitted to the corporal punishment. A further claim was brought to the effect that the punishment (or its threat) constituted 'inhuman or degrading treatment or punishment' within the meaning of Article 3 of the Convention. The Court rejected the claim under Article 3, but found that the United Kingdom government was in breach of both sentences of Article 2 of the First Protocol. The Court rejected the government's submission that the disciplinary process in a school was merely a matter of internal administration which was ancillary to but not truly part of 'education and teaching', preferring the view that it was

> an integral part of the process whereby a school seeks to achieve the object for which it was established, including the development and moulding of the character and mental powers of its pupils.[18]

And it went on to hold that 'philosophical convictions' denoted

> such convictions as are worthy of respect in a 'democratic society' and are not incompatible with human dignity,[19]

and that the parents' views on corporal punishment related to

> a weighty and substantial aspect of human life and behaviour, namely the integrity of the person, the propriety or otherwise of the infliction of corporal punishment and the exclusion of the distress which the risk of such punishment entails.[20]

The Court thus interpreted 'philosophical convictions' as including the parents' abhorrence of the use or threat of corporal punishment, and thereby held the United Kingdom government to be in breach of the second sentence of Article 2. The pupils were also held to have been denied their 'right to education' under the first sentence as it had been made a condition of their readmission to school that they submit to a form of discipline that itself conflicted with a right enshrined in the Protocol: the pupils' return to school could only have been secured if the parents had acted contrary to their convictions.

The *Campbell and Cosans* case offers an excellent illustration of individual challenge to the legality of a practice adopted in state schools running counter to parental convictions within the meaning of Article 2 of the First Protocol. The United Kingdom government was forced as a consequence to introduce legislation bringing practice in state schools into conformity with the Convention: its first attempt, the Education (Corporal Punishment) Bill 1985, foundered in the House of Lords amid widespread criticism of its intention to divide pupils into two categories according to expressed parental wishes – those who could and those who could not be subjected to corporal punishment.[21] Many critics regarded the measure as educationally unworkable, socially undesirable and apt to lead to chaos in terms of its implementation, and the government decided to accede to pressure to drop the Bill. Corporal punishment in state schools was subsequently abolished for all pupils (not merely a category of pupils) by virtue of section 47 of the Education (No. 2) Act 1986.

The *Campbell and Cosans* case was thus a notable victory for opponents of physical punishment in British schools and led to an important change in the law. The European Convention, though of great importance as the one international treaty relating to education with a mechanism for individual enforcement, should not, however, be regarded as a regular mode of redress. As we will see below in the contexts of choice of school and the secular curriculum, it is not easy to bring a successful challenge based on the very wide wording of the Convention, and it should not be regarded in any way as an adequate counterbalance to the substantial absence of effective means of challenging the exercise of the extensive discretionary powers enjoyed by public authorities under domestic English law.

2

CHOICE OF SCHOOL

INTRODUCTION

Parental choice of school has been a prominent political issue in Britain particularly since the early 1970s, and is often seen as lying at the heart of parental interests or rights in education as a whole. It is concerned with the extent, scope and enforceability of the interest or right of a parent to select which school his or her child should attend, and not strictly with the interest or right of a parent to influence the content of the education or the circumstances in which that education is provided in the chosen school, although plainly the latter is likely to have a profound effect on the substance of parental choice.

It is clear that economic and demographic factors are likely to condition the extent to which parental choice gives rise to friction in a particular area: in the late 1970s, when pupil numbers were at a highpoint and the availability of school places was under greatest pressure, there was a high incidence of friction between individual parents and LEAs in this context. As pupil numbers have fallen during the 1980s the competition in demand for school places might have been expected to have eased through the emergence of a substantial surplus of available places, with choice of school assuming a lower place on the political and social agenda and the incidence of friction in this context substantially declining. Any such expectation has, however, been proved to be far from the reality of events as they have unfolded during the 1980s and now into the 1990s. As is explained in more detail in chapter 5, falling rolls have had a very uneven impact across the country, and LEAs, although reacting differently to the challenges they have presented, have all come under great pressure to remove surplus capacity. The uneven effects of falling rolls are attributable largely to disparate social and demographic factors:

pressures of unemployment have led to some shift in population from the north to the more economically favoured south of the country; inner-city areas have suffered a marked movement of population to the more socially favoured suburban areas; and rural communities have lost many younger families with children to the cities. These and other factors have led to schools in certain areas – mainly in the more socially favoured urban or suburban communities – coming under very strong parental demand for places, while others – mainly in the inner cities – have had a surplus of spare capacity. Above all, perhaps, parental demand has been distorted and channelled in new directions by closures and amalgamations of existing schools: thus, it is fully to be expected that closure of schools A and B and their replacement by a newly amalgamated entity, school C, will have a profound effect on demand for places at schools X, Y and Z as parents reassess their pre-existing assumptions and expectations as to the quality of educational provision on offer at each of these schools. These and other factors have contributed to making parental choice of school remain – even in times of falling rolls – an issue of acute controversy and considerable tension in many areas, though the level of friction remains dependent in each area on variable social and economic pressures.

It is clear that the Conservative governments in office since 1979 have treated individual freedom of choice in respect of school placements as close to the heart of their overall philosophy of individualistic freedom: the individual should enjoy the maximum practically achievable freedom of choice. The Conservative approach has, indeed, hardened during this period: now, as we shall see below, under the provisions of the Education Reform Act 1988, individual parents are placed in the position of consumers of a range of educational services provided by the state (and the independent sector), and given as much freedom as practically possible to choose between the providers of those services, who themselves are required to compete with each other in order to attract consumer demand. In this way economic principles of supply and demand are applied to the provision of education,[1] the aim being to force the providers of educational services to offer an efficient, economical and attractive educational product attuned to the optimum degree to parental wishes, and to be held continuously and comprehensively accountable for the provision they make. These desired aims are sought through the withdrawal of demand for places at particular schools under the open enrolment provisions of the 1988 Act in the event of failure by their providers to meet parental expectations and wishes, thereby leading to contraction of the schools concerned and, ultimately, to their closure. This consequence is now brought closer under the 1988 Act by directly linking the level of financial resources channelled to each school with the number of registered pupils on its roll.

This elementary statement of the underlying philosophy of the present Conservative government as to parental choice indicates that that philosophy goes considerably further than the stance on parental choice of school adopted by the Opposition, though it should be recalled that the Callaghan Labour government itself sought to introduce a degree of statutory protection for parental choice in its abortive Education Bill of 1978, which fell with the general election in 1979. The fundamental difference in approach between the Conservative and Labour parties lies in the manner in which the balance is struck between individual and collective interests, and this indeed is the essential dilemma which lies at the heart of the whole choice of school debate.

The *Conservative* philosophy places a considerably higher emphasis on individualistic freedom, exemplified particularly by the open enrolment provisions of the 1988 Act, even at the expense of the collective interest represented by the concern of LEAs to achieve rational long-term or even medium-term planning by spreading pupil intakes between schools to afford protection to contracting schools and achieve curricular balance. The approach adopted by the *Labour* party, on the other hand, while respecting the right of parents to express a preference as to the school their children should attend, broadly endorses the need for LEAs to impose an upper limit on the number of pupils to be admitted, even where this number is lower than the physical capacity of the school. This is seen by the Labour party as a critical element in achieving the goal of due respect for the collective interest in supporting schools under severe social and economic pressure which may be vital to the local community, while nonetheless as far as possible endorsing parental choice up to the planned admissions limits.

THE RATIONALE FOR PARENTAL CHOICE OF SCHOOL

Much of the rationale for parental choice of school lies in the basic interest of parents in bringing up their own children in accordance with their own conscience and in the very fundamentality of education to the individual's well-being and the critical importance of the very right to education (discussed in chapter 1). What then makes *choice* of school so important is the recognition that educational provision is not by any means of a uniformly excellent quality and that there is – partly by design – a wide diversity of types of education available and of types of school in which it is offered. *Diversity of educational provision* is, then, an essential element in the rationale for parental choice, a diversity which is unlikely to be greatly reduced by the introduction of the national curriculum. But even if there were far greater uniformity of educational provision, there would still be room for parental choice founded on such considerations as the denominational character of the school, the cultural mix of the area served by the school, geographical proximity of the school to the family home, siblings of the child in question already in attendance at the preferred school, other family connections with the school, medical or psychological factors, preference for single-sex or mixed education, and much more.

It is, however, the barely disputable factor of diversity of provision that gives parental choice of school its primary justification. Diversity of provision was, indeed, central to the structure of maintained schools established under the Education Act 1944: within the maintained sector, voluntary schools, established in the main by the Churches, would co-exist with non-denominational county schools, and the extent of the autonomy enjoyed by the governors of those voluntary schools would depend on the school's classification as voluntary aided, voluntary special agreement, or voluntary controlled.[2] Diversity of provision in terms of religious education (and ethos) has however in more recent years taken on a further dimension in areas with high proportions of pupils from ethnic minority family backgrounds. The religious, ethnic and cultural diversity of the population in many areas has undoubtedly led to a wide diversity in the ethos of schools,[3] even though under the terms of the Education Reform Act the religious education in schools serving such areas must remain predominantly Christian in character.[4]

Quite apart from religious diversity, the 1944 Act envisaged a diversity in the *academic* nature of schools, although this has now been substantially overtaken by the widespread adoption of the comprehensive (non-academically selective) system. The 1944 Act envisaged a tripartite structure of grammar schools for pupils who were deemed sufficiently academically able at the age of eleven plus, technical schools for those with an aptitude for a vocationally orientated technical education, and secondary modern schools for the majority of pupils who remained.[5] In the event, technical schools were never widely established, and so there developed in effect a bipartite structure of grammar and secondary modern schools, this having a profound influence on parental choice with parents keenly aware of the long-term educational and social advantages of a grammar school education. With widespread comprehensive reorganisation, particularly in the 1960s and 1970s, it might have been thought that much of the foundation for parental choice would have been lost, but this has proved to be far from true: there were – and are – perceived to be wide disparities of provision *between comprehensive schools*, and, indeed, there are substantial differences in the organisational structure of comprehensive schools themselves, including all-through schools catering for the full 11 to 18 years age range, middle and upper school systems, sixth form colleges, tertiary colleges, and more.[6] Another important consideration for many parents, particularly perhaps for some ethnic minority groups, has been the availability of single-sex education. And, most recently, these organisational differences have been extended yet further through the establishment under the Education Reform Act of new categories of school in the shape of grant-maintained schools[7] and city technology colleges, an important part of whose rationale in the government's eyes has undoubtedly been the expansion of parental choice through greater diversity of provision.

Diversity has, however, not been limited to the religious ethos, academic nature or organisational structure of individual schools. The underlying philosophy behind much of the Education Act 1944 – now much eroded, especially under the 1988 Act – was that the actual provision of education should be *at local level* and that there should be a good deal of *local autonomy* as to the style and substantive content of education. There was room for local curricular initiative, adaptation and experimentation, and for the implementation of local policy on curricular matters, and there was a high level of respect for the professional curricular expertise of the teaching profession who were expected to have a significant input into curricular content, approach and style. This whole ethos is now being radically altered with the highly centralised imposition and elaboration of the national curriculum with a negligible formulatory role for LEAs and the teaching profession,[8] but while it lasted it undoubtedly encouraged diversity of educational provision, subject always to a degree of overall coordination, in particular through HMI, through many central initiatives (for instance, through the Schools Council) and, at secondary level, through examination syllabuses set by the examinations boards.

A significant and distressing element of diversity has developed, furthermore, through the differential impact both between and within individual LEAs of expenditure constraints. LEAs have been under increasing pressure from central government since the 1970s to cut back on expenditure, and there have been widespread reports of seriously adverse effects on their capacity to provide sufficient staffing levels, books and equipment, or to provide for the adequate upkeep of buildings. The impact of expenditure constraints is discussed more fully in chapter 4. Suffice it here to say that their differential impact has undoubtedly served to accentuate the diversity of provision and standards and to act as a significant conditioning factor upon parental choice of school.

The government thus perceives a diverse range of choices available to parents as essentially healthy, an encouragement to individualistic freedom and a means of ensuring that the providers of educational services bear prominently in mind the need consistently to satisfy their consumers, the level of consumer satisfaction being manifested by the level of demand for places at individual schools. This is the absolute antithesis of the concept of collective provision and collective consumption where basic public services – including education, health care, environmental, social welfare, public housing, planning and transport services – are provided by state authorities on the basis of *established criteria of social need rather than by reference to market forces*.[9] Throughout the 1980s and now into the 1990s the collectivist attitude has been progressively eroded, and this erosion could hardly be better exemplified than by reference to the active expansion of parental choice of school.

PARENTAL CHOICE OF SCHOOL AS AN INTEREST WORTHY OF FUNDAMENTAL PROTECTION: THE EUROPEAN CONVENTION ON HUMAN RIGHTS

The previous section of this chapter has set out a range of basic justifications for parental choice of school. Before exploring the extent to which parental choice *is actually protected* in England and Wales in the next section, it is important to give some consideration to the protection afforded in this context under the European

Convention on Human Rights. Article 2 of the First Protocol of the Convention has already been discussed in general terms in chapter 1: here we are concerned with its specific application in the context of choice of school. The extent to which Article 2 may be used by parents before the European Commission and Court of Human Rights to attain their choice of school is in practice very limited, not least because the UK government accepted the second sentence of the Protocol subject to the reservation that it should apply only so far as is compatible with the provision of efficient instruction and training and the avoidance of unreasonable public expenditure, phrased in terms identical to the provisos contained in section 76 of the Education Act 1944 (discussed in the next section).

It would seem from the caselaw that the main operative context of this Protocol is the substantive content of what goes on within schools, especially in relation to religious and secular education, including sex education, political education, the language used as the medium of teaching, as well as modes of discipline. Parents have, however, argued that the Protocol should be so interpreted as to encompass an obligation, even if a qualified one, on the part of the state to admit children to the schools of their parents' choice. The European Commission and Court of Human Rights have, however, seen fit to apply a narrow interpretation of the Protocol in this context in the very few cases in which the issue has been raised before them. The Court has clearly stated that the Protocol imposes no obligation upon the state to establish at its own expense or to subsidise *education of any particular type or at any particular level*:[10] no parent or group of parents could insist on the establishment of a new school of a particular type, or a state subsidy for an existing school, providing an education consonant with a particular cultural or religious or denominational tradition, or with any particular academic specialisation. Once, however, the state has *embarked upon* the provision of education, it comes under certain positive obligations towards parents under the Protocol, chiefly in the context of the substance of what is taught, but which could conceivably have a bearing on choice of school, even though any such obligations may be difficult to enforce. In this context two applications from the UK have come before the Commission for consideration, both illustrating the difficulty confronted here by parents.

One challenge[11] was brought jointly by two pairs of parents: both pairs had been denied their choice of maintained secondary school for their children by the LEAs concerned, and had had their appeals to their respective LEA statutory appeals tribunals[12] rejected. Both pairs had expressed a preference for having their children educated at single-sex grammar schools, but both were denied their choice on the ground that there were no more places available in the schools concerned and that the admissions quota could not be exceeded without prejudicing efficient education at the schools and the efficient use and distribution of resources between these and other schools. The applicants alleged that the denial of a place at a single-sex, selective grammar school, obliging them to send their children to mixed comprehensive schools, constituted a breach of their right to have their children educated in accordance with their philosophical convictions under the second sentence of Article 2. The Commission considered the meaning of 'philosophical convictions', noting in particular that the duty to ensure respect for parents' philosophical convictions was not without some practical difficulty. The Commission took the view that the essence of the second sentence of the Protocol was 'the safeguarding of pluralism and tolerance in public education and the prohibition on indoctrination',[13] and it stressed that parents' philosophical convictions had to be *respected*, not necessarily *reflected* in the state school system.

Applying this interpretation to the facts of these two applications, the Commission noted that there was a dual system of selective and comprehensive secondary education in operation in the LEAs concerned, and that it would have been lawful for the children to be educated in the independent sector or at home. There was thus a diversity of types of educational provision available. The Commission then expressed the view that the reasons given by the LEAs for not acceding to parental wishes – the unavailability of places, efficiency of education and cost – could *not* be viewed as conflicting with the requirements of the Protocol, and it went on to observe that:

> there is no evidence in this case that the applicants' children are being indoctrinated in the respective comprehensive schools which they are attending or that the teaching of the children is not conveyed in an objective, critical or pluralistic manner. Moreover there is no allegation that the comprehensive system denies the applicants their major role in the education of their children, in particular the transmission of their values or philosophical convictions.[14]

Given their failure to establish that the fundamental principle of *objective, critical and pluralistic* teaching and education in the schools available in the LEAs concerned had been breached, the parents were unsuccessful in their attempt to apply the Protocol to the question of choice of school. While it would appear to be theoretically applicable in this context, it would take a much stronger case than this to invoke the Protocol.

The other challenge was even less likely to succeed: this application[15] was brought by parents aggrieved over the refusal by their LEA to provide financial support for the education of their children at an independent school, the Rudolf Steiner School. They complained that, despite the fact that they were paying for education through the state (and local) taxation system, the government and LEAs would not contribute towards the cost of their children's independent education which, they claimed, was in accordance with their religious and philosophical convictions. Any such obligation was roundly rejected by the Commission in ruling the application to be inadmissible: to require the provision of such financial support would have been to require the state to provide support for a particular educational establishment serving particular religious or philosophical beliefs or convictions, and no state was under any such obligation. It was sufficient that the state 'evidence respect for the religious and philosophical beliefs of parents within the existing and developing system of education'.[16] It was further noted that the government had 'shown respect' for the Rudolf Steiner School by granting it charitable status and bringing it within the government's assisted places scheme.

Although Article 2 of the First Protocol has not been successfully invoked in the context of choice of school, it remains of considerable importance as a fundamental statement of principle supporting parental choice of school as an interest worthy of protection. The phraseology of the Article is more apt for the context of curricular content, and it will be more extensively considered in chapter 3. Its application in relation to choice of school was bound to be limited, given the government's express reservations when acceding to the Article, and it is therefore to the domestic law of England and Wales that one must turn to establish the practical extent and nature of legal protection of parental choice of school.

THE DOMESTIC LEGAL FRAMEWORK FOR SECURING PARENTAL CHOICE OF SCHOOL

The Education Act 1944

In the absence of any constitutional protection of basic rights in the United Kingdom, it is necessary to look to such ordinary statutory or common law protections as exist to establish the extent and nature of the right of parental choice of school.[17] The Education Acts did not intentionally and explicitly offer legislative support for parental choice *between schools of the same type* before the enactment of the Education Act 1980. It should, however, be recalled that a most important element in the Education Act 1944 was the religious settlement struck in particular with the Anglican and Roman Catholic Church authorities, enabling their schools to come within the maintained school framework as voluntary controlled, aided or special agreement schools[18] and with substantial financial support from the state. Furthermore, as has already been noted in this chapter, the 1944 Act established a tripartite structure of grammar, technical and secondary modern schools, children being allocated on the basis of availability of provision and of ability and aptitude. Given this multiplicity of types of school – both denominational and academic – it was seen as important to incorporate into the 1944 Act a provision which, though couched in highly generalised terms, would nonetheless afford legislative acknowledgement of the principle of parental choice as between the *different types* of available school, particularly on the basis of religious preference.[19] Lord Butler, who, as President of the then Board of Education, was the Minister responsible for the passage of the 1944 Act, recalled in a House of Lords debate on parental rights in 1974 that he himself had drafted the provision – section 76. He emphasised that it had been drafted in the particular context of the *religious settlement*:

> The origin of section 76 was rather different from what some people imagine. It originated in the first place out of what was known as the religious settlement of the Act of 1944, which took me three years to negotiate. The object of that settlement and of section 76 was to give Roman Catholic and Anglican parents a choice of school.[20]

Section 76,[21] however, rapidly came to be prayed in aid by many parents on many different grounds, frequently with no bearing on religious preferences, in order to secure their choice *between schools of the same type*. That this happened in relation to section 76 should come as no surprise, given particularly that its phraseology is wide open to a multiplicity of interpretations: it sought to impose a broad duty upon both LEAs and the Secretary of State[22] in the performance of all their functions under the Act to 'have regard to the general principle' that pupils are to be educated in accordance with their parents' wishes, in so far as is compatible with

(i) the provision of efficient instruction and training; and
(ii) the avoidance of unreasonable public expenditure.

To interpret this as imposing a clear-cut duty on LEAs to allocate children to the schools of their parents' choice would, however, have led to administrative chaos,[23] and regular judicial review of executive action on the strength of this interpretation of the section would have imported an unacceptable element of uncertainty into the allocation process. The Court of Appeal roundly condemned any such interpretation in *Watt* v. *Kesteven County Council* in 1955,[24] a case still regularly cited in this context despite the passage of years. The LEA – as was then not uncommon – did not itself maintain a secondary grammar school, but instead had a standing arrangement with an independent secondary school (in Stamford), under which the LEA would take up places in that school for pupils deemed to be of grammar school ability, and pay their full tuition fees. Mr Watt's twin sons passed the LEA's selection examination, and the authority duly offered them free places at Stamford; but Mr Watt refused this offer, preferring that they attend Roman Catholic schools elsewhere with which the LEA had no standing arrangements. The LEA refused to pay the full tuition fees at the preferred schools, even though they were lower than at the school in Stamford, but did offer to make a means-tested contribution towards those fees in accordance with a scale which they operated for this purpose. Mr Watt argued that the LEA was in breach of its duty under section 76 to have regard to parental wishes by failing to pay the full tuition fees at the preferred schools. The LEA argued that it had fulfilled its statutory duty by offering free places at Stamford and a means-tested contribution towards the fees at the schools of Mr Watt's choice. A unanimous Court of Appeal held that the LEA had not failed to carry out its duty under section 76: section 76 imposed a broad duty on the LEA in carrying out its many functions under the Act (in this case, its duty under section 8 to secure the availability of suitable secondary education) to 'have regard to the general principle that' children are to be educated in accordance with parental wishes, subject to the two provisos. That did not in all cases mean that the LEA must *give effect* to parental wishes. Lord Justice Denning stressed:

> Section 76 does not say that pupils must in all cases be educated in accordance with the wishes of their parents. It only lays down a general principle to which the county council must have regard. This leaves it open to the county council to have regard to other things as well, and also to make exceptions to the general principle if it thinks fit to do so. It cannot therefore be said that a county council is at fault simply because it does not see fit to comply with the parents' wishes.[25]

The LEA had been greatly concerned as to the consequences of giving effect to Mr Watt's choice: it argued that it would have been absurd if every parent could come to the LEA asking for payment in full of tuition fees at any school he chose. The LEA had been prepared to pay only according to the parents' means.

The Court of Appeal took the same view in *Cumings* v. *Birkenhead Corporation* in 1972.[26] Parents of children transferring from Roman Catholic (RC) primary schools to secondary schools in Birkenhead claimed that circulars issued by the LEA had unwarrantably confined their choice to RC secondary schools. This the LEA had done in the light of lack of accommodation in its secondary schools: it could comfortably accommodate all the children from RC primary schools in RC secondary schools; but there was inadequate room for non-RC children in non-RC secondary schools let alone for RC children too. The parents' principal contention was that, by operating this policy, the LEA had been in breach of section 76. The unanimous Court of Appeal again stressed the limitations on the LEA's duty to give effect to parental choice:

> The wishes of the parents are only one thing. There are many other things to which the education authority may have regard and which outweigh the wishes of the parents. They must have regard, for instance, not only to the wishes of the parents of one particular child, but also to the wishes of the parents of other children and of other groups of children. In this particular case the education authority were having regard to the wishes of those parents who had had their children at Roman Catholic primary schools, and also the wishes of those whose children

> had been at other schools. The education authority were doing the best they could to allocate places as between the various groups of parents for whom they had to cater. That is quite legitimate. There is no warrant for the suggestion of a breach of section 76.[27]

A later instance of refusal by the courts to give effect to a claim of parental choice based on section 76 – before enactment of the Education Act 1981 dealing with special educational needs – arose in the context of parental preference for the education of a physically and mentally handicapped child in a local primary school which had no special facilities for pupils with special educational needs, rather than at a school some two miles distant which had a special class for the mentally handicapped.[28] Although there was conflicting medical evidence as to the degree of mental disability,[29] the court concluded that the school chosen by the parents was not, and could not reasonably become, one in which the child would receive an education suitable to his age, ability and aptitude within the meaning of section 8 of the 1944 Act; and that there was no basis for the parents' claim that the LEA was bound by section 76 to give effect to parental choice.[30]

It is clear from these attempts by parents to invoke section 76 that that section imposes a far from absolute duty on LEAs to succumb to parental choice of school. The courts have in this context been disinclined to intervene, in view particularly of the administrative confusion and uncertainty that would flow from a stronger interpretation of section 76. As will be seen below, it was not until the Education Act 1980 that parental choice was given any effectively enforceable statutory endorsement.

Before considering the detail of the 1980 Act, however, one further provision of the 1944 Act which was frequently invoked in this context – though with a remarkably low incidence of success – should be mentioned.[31] Aggrieved parents frequently wrote letters of complaint directly (or through their MP) to the Secretary of State, and these were, as a matter of course, treated as complaints under section 68. Under that section – which is still in force, though rarely used in this context following the 1980 Act – if the Secretary of State is satisfied that an LEA (or school governors) have acted or are proposing to act *unreasonably* in respect of any of their functions under the Act (including admissions), he may give such directions to the LEA (or governors) as appear to him to be expedient. Over 1,000 parents per year would commonly appeal to the Secretary of State over secondary school allocations, but intervention by the Secretary of State was exceptional: almost invariably, following a closed, informal dialogue between central department officials and officials of the LEA concerned, the complaint would be rejected. For example, during 1977, the Secretary of State for Education and Science received 1,124 complaints (treated as complaints under section 68) over secondary school allocations, giving rise to a mere *two* directions to LEAs.[32] Although non-intervention by the Secretary of State was primarily explicable by a strong reluctance on the part of the central department to be regarded as a regular mechanism of appeal on the merits of individual cases, a further explanation lies in the narrow interpretation of the scope for legitimate intervention under section 68 by the Court of Appeal and the House of Lords in the *Tameside* case in 1976.[33] It was held, in essence, that the Secretary of State could properly issue a direction to an LEA only if satisfied that the action taken or proposed was based on a view that was '. . . not only wrong, but unreasonably wrong, so wrong that no reasonable person could sensibly take that view'[34] – a legal test of irrationality which is hard to satisfy.

The 1980 Education Act, however, represents the first major statutory underpinning of parental choice, recently greatly extended by the open enrolment provisions of the Education Reform Act 1988. Aspects of these measures will now be considered.

The Education Act 1980[35]

The crucial provisions of the Act relating to choice of school were the creation for the first time of a parental right to express a reasoned preference as to which school his or her child should attend, the establishment of a system of locally organised appeal tribunals against admissions decisions running counter to parental preferences, and a new duty on LEAs and schools to provide specified information about schools and the admissions process. There is little doubt that these measures were a highly political gesture, choice of school being high on the political agenda in the 1979 general election, and parental choice being central to Conservative philosophy.[36]

Section 6: the right to express a reasoned preference

Under section 6, LEAs (or the governors in the case of voluntary aided schools) became duty bound to make arrangements enabling parents to express a reasoned preference as to the school they wished their child to attend, and to give reasons for their preference (if they so wished), and the LEA (or governors) became legally obliged to comply with that preference unless:

(i) compliance would prejudice 'the provision of efficient education or the efficient use of resources';[37] or
(ii) if the preferred school was a voluntary aided or special agreement school, and compliance would be incompatible with any arrangements between the governors and the LEA in respect of admissions;[38] or
(iii) if the preferred school was academically selective, and compliance would be incompatible with the operation of the selection process.[39]

It was seen as important that, in expressing their reasoned preferences, parents should have at their disposal a range of information concerning the LEA's arrangements for admitting children, and, in particular, the policy established by the authority for making decisions in this context. The latter could be of critical importance in informing parents' expression of choice of school, as it would include an elaboration of the LEA's *priority ranking criteria* – the criteria upon which the LEA would set about distinguishing between competing applications for places in the event of a given school being oversubscribed. These would commonly include such criteria as distance between home and school, the presence of siblings in the school, other family connections with the school, medical or psychological factors, and others; but each LEA is free to adopt its own criteria and to rank them in accordance with its own perception of need. Hence, under section 8(1) to (4), LEAs are obliged to publish such information concerning their admissions procedures and criteria. Far more controversially, however, the Secretary of State was empowered under section 8(5) to require the publication by LEAs of 'such information as may be required by regulations' concerning each individual school.[40] This gave the Secretary of State a wide discretion to legislate by Regulations on issues of considerable controversy: while there was wide agreement about much of this information, at the heart of the issue here lay the heated debate over the wisdom of publication of the results of public examinations in the case of secondary schools. Many felt their publication to be potentially misleading in the absence of detailed contextual statements elaborating the socio-economic background of the pupils concerned and any relevant special educational factors that may have had a bearing on the pupils' performance in a given year; but the pressures in favour of publication of public examination results prevailed and provisions requiring this were duly incorporated into the Regulations.[41]

On the basis of this information – and any other factors they see fit to take into account – parents are free to express their reasoned preference in accordance with section 6(1); and LEAs are duty bound to comply unless they can resist the parental choice by reference to one of the three provisos in section 6(3). Before we examine section 6(3), a note of caution should be sounded as to the foregoing statement, in the light of an important dispute that arose in Middlesborough within the area of Cleveland LEA during 1990, involving the co-existence of section 6 of the 1980 Act with the Race Relations Act 1976 which prohibits discrimination on grounds of race in the provision (among other services) of education. The Middlesborough dispute, which was raised by the Commission for Racial Equality with the Secretary of State, arose where the parents of a child who had been allocated to a particular school requested that she be transferred to a different school on what the press publicity described as racial grounds. The parents' reasons were elaborated in an *Independent* leading article as follows: it was reported that the mother had complained

> that her daughter . . . was put in a class of 24 children, including only four who were white, and came home 'reciting songs in Hindu and drawing Pakistani vegetables'.[42]

The legal question is whether the Race Relations Act, read in conjunction with section 6 of the Education Act 1980, imposes any limitation upon the grounds on which a parent may express a choice of school. The LEA took the view, supported by the Secretary of State,[43] that, given that there was available capacity in the school to which the parents had requested their daughter to be transferred, there was no legal basis for opposing the reallocation. It was emphasised that section 6 does not *require* parents to offer any reason for their preference, and it would seem wrong for a parent who has expressed a reason to be in a worse position than one who has remained silent as to the reasoning. Until this issue is resolved in the courts, the better view would appear to be that there is no legal limitation on the reasons parents may express – if any – for their choice of school, and that LEAs are confined in their rejection of a parental preference to the three provisos elaborated in section 6(3).[44]

Our concentration will be upon the first proviso, which is generally taken to refer to the school concerned being oversubscribed, and has proved to be by far the most important in practice. As might have been expected, it has been used extensively by LEAs as their reason for non-compliance. The phrases 'efficient education' and 'efficient use of resources' are open to widely divergent interpretations, and could, indeed, be said to undermine the essential policy of the whole of section 6, rendering it little more than a political gesture. This first proviso was regarded by many on the Conservative right as an odious escape clause for LEAs unsympathetic to the cause of parental choice and more concerned with their own administrative convenience, and thus ripe for amendment. As we shall see in the discussion of open enrolment below, this proviso has now been significantly amended by the 1988 Act.[45]

The particular technique used by LEAs to defeat parental choice by virtue of the first proviso lay strangely hidden in section 8 – the section which imposes on LEAs obligations with respect to the publication of information about their schools and their admissions arrangements and policies. This provided – before it too was amended by the 1988 Act[46] – that the particulars to be published shall include particulars of the number of pupils that it is intended to admit in each school year.[47] This gave LEAs a highly significant discretion over establishing an *admissions quota* for each school, and provided them with a potent (though not conclusive) argument, in the event of parental demand which exceeded the admissions quota, that the admission of further children (even just one more child) would run counter to efficient education or the efficient use of resources. In effect, it enabled the LEAs themselves to *define oversubscription* for each school. The establishment of admissions quotas – which might well be below a school's actual physical capacity – was, indeed, a central feature of LEAs' resolution of the problem of falling rolls. As is discussed more fully in chapter 5, it was their policy in many cases to spread pupil intakes in order to prevent pupil numbers dwindling excessively in certain schools, as a means of securing effective deployment of resources and ensuring educationally viable teaching groups. This is the clearest example of rational planning for the collective good being used as a limiting factor on individual choice.

Even before the 1988 Act, however, the discretion enjoyed by LEAs to set admissions quotas was not unlimited: it was circumscribed by section 15 of the 1980 Act, under which the Secretary of State exerted an element of control. The essence of section 15 was that each year group in a school had a 'standard number' of pupils, which was deemed to be the number admitted in September 1979 – when, broadly, school rolls were at their highpoint. Any LEA which intended[48] to reduce the number of pupils in any age group to four-fifths or less than four-fifths of the 'standard number' had first formally to publish its proposals for so doing, and submit them for determination by the Secretary of State following the consideration of objections.[49] Subject to that statutory limitation, however, LEAs exercised a wide discretion over admissions quotas, and in many areas their use dominated the admissions process until the introduction of open enrolment. Nowhere was this more clearly illustrated than in Dewsbury in the Metropolitan Borough of Kirklees during 1987 and 1988.

The Dewsbury dispute[50] arose through the denial by Kirklees Borough Council of preferences expressed by parents of some 25 children through the council's strict adherence to its settled admissions quota. The parents had expressed preferences for allocation of their children to either Thornhill or Overthorpe Schools in Dewsbury, where the majority of children were white and both of which had a predominantly Christian ethos, but the LEA instead, on the basis of oversubscription at those schools, allocated their children elsewhere, mainly to Headfield School, where some 85 per cent of the children came from Asian backgrounds. The parents emphasised in the strongest terms throughout that their preferences were based *on cultural and not on racial grounds.* The parents' complaints to the LEA and then their appeals to the local education appeals tribunal were rejected on the basis that the admissions quotas at Thornhill and Overthorpe had clearly been reached and that admission of any further pupils would have fallen clearly within the proviso in section 6(3)(a) as constituting prejudice to efficient education and the efficient use of resources. The parents' subsequent complaint to the Secretary of State under section 68 of the Education Act 1944 against the reasonableness of the LEA's position was also rejected on the basis that the Minister – though politically committed to parental choice as a concept – could not regard the LEA's actions as irrational; and the LEA was acting in accordance with the terms of the 1980 Act in establishing and adhering to an admissions quota and was thus not in breach of its statutory obligations.[51] The parents were outraged by the LEA's and the tribunal's decisions (reluctantly confirmed by the Secretary of State) claiming that there was spare capacity at the preferred schools, and presented their children at the gates of those schools for admission at the start of the school term. They were, however, denied admission by the headteachers. In the event, the children were educated privately on the premises of a public house in Dewsbury, pending settlement of the dispute following an application for judicial review.[52]

A great deal of the considerable press publicity attracted by this dispute related to the question of multi-cultural education, the desirability of bringing different cultural, racial, ethnic and religious groups of children together for the purpose of schooling in pursuit of enhancing their understanding and appreciation of other groups than their own, rather than educating children separately along with children of their own group. A considerable volume of specialist literature has grown up on multi-cultural education, an issue of immense difficulty and importance which goes beyond the scope of this book.[53] Some of the most important competing separatist and integrationist arguments were however, put in an *Independent* leading article at the time:

> The Dewsbury dispute has forced on to the agenda some awkward issues about the implications of all-Asian, all-white or all-black schools. The standard argument is that such schools would be unhealthy and divisive and 'reinforce community separation'. But is this so when the separation is voluntary? It is possible that, for one generation at least, some children from ethnic minorities might benefit from doing things on their own. They gain experience and confidence and avoid the deadening pressures of being in a permanent minority. It is, further, possible to argue that enforced integration breeds resentment. There is, finally, something rather patronising about the implication that children from ethnic minorities need the uplifting presence of white children in order to achieve academically.
>
> On the other hand, schools clearly should play an important 'socialising' role in a society assimilating large numbers of immigrants and their children. For their own sake they should emerge from school with a clear grasp of the English language and of the culture into which they have migrated.[54]

The aggrieved parents in Dewsbury powerfully expressed their view on educational and cultural grounds that their children's educational interests would be best served by their being educated at the predominantly white and Christian Overthorpe and Thornhill Schools; the LEA, on the other hand, anxious to avoid excessive numerical imbalance among its schools and the longer-term educational and administrative problems that this would create, adhered to its established admissions quotas and refused to accede to the parental demands. The dispute was only resolved following the parents' application to the High Court for judicial review: the Council settled the case by agreeing to meet the parents' demands, after admitting that there had been procedural defects in the application of its admissions quotas and in publication of those quotas as part of the formal information required to be published by it under section 8.[55] The parents' ultimate victory was on purely procedural aspects of the LEA's admissions practices and unrelated to the parents' substantive challenge to the rationality of the LEA's decisions. The LEA's insistence that the admission of the 25 extra children to Overthorpe and Thornhill schools would have caused educational and financial prejudice within the meaning of section 6(3)(a) remained intact, and would, indeed, have been extremely hard to challenge on substantive grounds.[56] We will see below in the context of open enrolment that strict adherence to an admissions quota by an LEA as in Dewsbury would not now be possible. Under open enrolment, the parents would, subject to the school's physical capacity, have been bound to be granted their choice from the outset. Given that a similar ethnic, racial and cultural profile pertains in many other parts of the country, one consequence of open enrolment is likely to be a greater incidence of separatism in schools between different groups within society.

One other highly significant aspect of section 6 requires elaboration before going on to examine the newly created appeal procedures: by virtue of section 6(5), LEAs were placed under the same duty of compliance with parental wishes in relation to children living in the area of another LEA as they were in relation to children living in their own area. 'Extra-district' preferences were thus safeguarded statutorily. This might seem rather technical and exceptional, but in fact was – and remains – of considerable significance in relation to the scope for choice of school enjoyed by parents living close to the boundaries of two or more LEAs, in whose case it might well make sound geographical sense to send their children to school in a neighbouring authority, or where one LEA operates a comprehensive and another a selective system and parents have a strong preference for one or the other system. This has assumed even greater importance in London following the abolition of the ILEA on 1 April 1990 and the transfer of its functions to the Inner London borough councils and the Common Council of the City of London.[57]

A major dispute arose in this context recently in Lewisham and Greenwich when the governors of John Ball Primary School applied for judicial review of a decision by Greenwich Borough Council to *give priority* in allocating places in oversubscribed schools to children living within its own area, with the consequence that neighbouring Lewisham children would be unlikely to obtain places in Greenwich schools: *R.* v. *Shadow Education Committee of Greenwich London Borough Council, ex parte Governors of John Ball School* [58] The John Ball School governors argued that, while it was quite proper for Greenwich to adopt certain policy criteria in order to establish a ranking order for competing claimants for scarce places, for instance sibling connections with a school, or distance between home and school, it was unlawful in the light of the policy underlying section 6(5) – which expressly provided for cross-border placements – to adopt a policy giving priority to children in its own area, thereby discriminating against children living in another. To do this would thwart the policy behind section 6(5), which was that extra-district children should rank on an equal footing with children from within the borough. There had, indeed, been a 'two-way traffic' of children between the boroughs for many years under ILEA: children living near the border might well attend a primary school in one borough and a secondary school in the other. Both the Divisional Court and the Court of Appeal upheld the governors' argument: an LEA was free to adopt any lawful policy it thought fit in establishing ranking, but one which – as here – conflicted with the policy of section 6(5), which was that extra-district pupils should be treated on an equal footing, was illegal. At first sight it would indeed seem wrong to permit discrimination against extra-district pupils, though the equality-of-treatment policy may give rise to difficulties, especially in the case of selective schools for whose places there is likely to be heavy competition from children both within and outside the relevant area,[59] and, indeed, of any schools with a good reputation where parental demand is high and where this decision may well give rise to grievance among parents of children denied places granted to extra-district pupils.[60]

Section 7: education appeal tribunals

The government sought to complete this package of reforms in the

1980 Act with the establishment under section 7 and Schedule 2 of local tribunals to which aggrieved parents could appeal.[61] They must be established by each LEA (and by the governors of voluntary aided or special agreement schools). Section 7(5) appears at first sight to give these tribunals real power by providing that their decisions shall be binding on the LEA (or governors) concerned: it should, however, be noted that, in the case of tribunals set up by LEAs, the central feature of the composition of these tribunals[62] is that the LEA will always be in a position to ensure that a majority of the tribunal's members will also be members either of the LEA itself or of its education committee.[63] It is not argued that LEA or education committee members will by any means always be compliant followers of the LEA's line of argument, but the very fact of a statutorily guaranteed LEA majority undoubtedly casts a shadow of scepticism over the independence of these tribunals in the minds of many appellants. The remaining tribunal members will be chosen from among non-members with experience in education, or parents of registered pupils.

The actual procedures to be followed by the tribunals are laid down[64] only in the most skeletal form: a great deal was left to the discretion of the LEA (or governors) concerned.[65] It is, however, provided that the appeal must be by notice in writing, setting out the grounds on which it is based;[66] the tribunal must allow the appellant an opportunity to appear before it in person, but there is no *right* to be accompanied or represented, let alone *legally* represented, although there is a discretion to allow this.[67] The tribunal is required to take into consideration any preference expressed by the parent under section 6 as well as the LEA's (or governors') arrangements (including any priority ranking criteria for distinguishing between competing claimants for scarce places) as published under section 8. Beyond those mandatory considerations, the tribunal may take into consideration such other factors as it sees fit, subject always to the generally applicable legal principles of reasonableness, relevancy, propriety of purpose and good faith. It is provided that the appeals shall take place in private 'except when otherwise directed by the authority or governors':[68] this escape clause plainly permits the LEA (or governors) to group like cases and to hear them together.

The tribunal's reasoned decision must be communicated in writing to the appellant and to the LEA (or governors). The decision may be reached, in the event of disagreement, by a simple majority of the members: it should be noted here that the tribunals are required to comprise three, five or seven members[69] – always an odd number – and that an arithmetical majority should thus normally emerge; but, in the event of an abstention[70] and an equality of votes being cast, the chairperson has a second or a casting vote.[71]

The Council on Tribunals[72] in 1985 issued a (revised) *Code of Practice* amplifying these skeletal statutory provisions: although this has no legally binding effect, it offers helpful guidance and could be of evidential importance in the event of any legal challenge to the procedural propriety of a tribunal's action.[73] This is a wide-ranging and important document dealing with such matters as the importance of arranging hearings at such times as to maximise the opportunities of appellants to attend,[74] of giving at least 14 days' written notice of the date of a hearing,[75] of holding hearings, where possible, other than on LEA premises in order to underline the tribunal's impartiality.[76] It emphasises that it may be appropriate for the committee to group appeals together and to hear the arguments *of the LEA (or governors)* in relation to all of the appeals together; thereafter, *unless any parent objects* in relation to his or her own appeal, the appeals may be heard in the presence of other parents;[77] and it may be necessary to adjourn all the decisions until all the appeals have been heard.[78]

This non-statutory *Code of Practice* offers important guidance to these tribunals faced, as they often are, with most intractable problems of distinguishing between competing claims for a very finite resource – a limited number of as yet unallocated places at an oversubscribed school – where individual parents may be putting forward virtually indistinguishable arguments. Beyond the skeletal procedural provisions of the Act, the guidance offered by the *Code of Practice*, and the guidance (but *not directions*) of their own LEA issued either generally or through their clerk (who will be appointed by the LEA or governors),[79] education appeal tribunals have operated largely unaided. This is subject, however, to an important High Court decision in 1984 – the only authoritative legal ruling on the working of these tribunals – which will be considered below. It is also subject to a limited though regular flow of reports issued by the Commissioners for Local Administration (Local Ombudsmen) following complaints by aggrieved parents: the Local Ombudsmen have, indeed, assumed a significant role in monitoring the operation of education appeal tribunals.[80]

The major danger of this rather limited degree of guidance and control is the emergence of a disparate and uneven attitude and approach by education appeal tribunals up and down the country, given especially that the incidence of appeals in some areas is high. The Council on Tribunals, indeed, noted in a 'progress and problems' report in its *Annual Report for 1987–1988* that it was this very lack of clear statutory guidance and the consequent delegation to individual LEAs and governing bodies of the responsibility for determining the large part of the procedural arrangements that was the major problem, leading to an unwelcome diversity.[81] Furthermore, although the Council on Tribunals keeps local education appeal committees under scrutiny in so far as its limited resources allow, the true extent and scope of this diversity cannot be accurately stated. Nor is it even possible precisely to state the incidence of appeals, as there is a manifest lack of central organisation and collation of statistical information in this context. The 1988–1989 *Annual Report* of the Council on Tribunals is unable in its statistical analysis to offer precise figures. It noted merely that:

> An informal biennial survey, by means of a telephone trawl, is conducted by the Department of Education and Science. The last survey suggested that in 1989 there were about 10,500 admission appeals in England. Of these, there were 8,250 appeals against decisions of Local Education Authorities and 2,250 against governors' decisions . . . . The figures can only be regarded as indicative of the actual total number of admission appeals in England in that year.[82]

This inadequate statistical information is a direct result of the absence of central coordination of education appeal tribunals; and it is regrettable that they should have been permitted to develop such a diversity of practice and approach, given that they are charged with the taking of decisions of such acute importance to the individual parents involved.

As mentioned above, however, this lack of coordination and procedural guidance has been tempered by one important decision of the High Court in 1984: *R.* v. *South Glamorgan Appeals Committee, ex parte Evans*.[83] This was the first opportunity for authoritative legal guidance as to how the tribunals should set about their task. The applicant, Mr Evans, was the father of two young children and had expressed a statutory preference for places at a particular (Welsh-medium) Cardiff primary school for his children. His preference was based on the facts that he had heard well of the school and that it was the nearest Welsh-medium school in the area to the family home. The LEA, however, refused to meet Mr Evans' preference on the basis that the chosen school was oversubscribed, and offered places instead at a more distant Welsh-medium school.

Mr Evans exercised his right of appeal under section 7, but initially only in relation to his older child, the younger not at that time having a statutory right of appeal as she was not yet within six months of her fifth birthday. The appeal in relation to the older child was successful, and he was admitted to the chosen school. Subsequently, when the younger child attained the age of four and a half, Mr Evans appealed on her behalf, and it was the rejection of this appeal by the tribunal that gave rise to this application for judicial review.

The rejection was based essentially on the tribunal's acceptance of the LEA's argument that the school was oversubscribed (some 36 pupils already in a class whose designated number was 30) and that this prejudiced the provision of efficient education within the meaning of the proviso in section 6(3)(a), discussed above.

Among the facts to be taken into account by the tribunal are the expressed parental preference and the arrangements published by the LEA for allocating children. The published arrangements in this case had indicated that the priority ranking criteria would be geographical factors, place of residence, exceptional medical or social factors, and children with older brothers or sisters in the school.

The two most important submissions by counsel for Mr Evans were, first, that no reasonable tribunal could have reached the conclusion that the admission of this child would have prejudiced the provision of efficient education in this school – an argument based on the generally applicable administrative law principle of reasonableness,[84] and secondly, if the tribunal had in fact properly determined that there would be prejudice to the provision of efficient education, it had failed thereafter to go on to what was *procedurally the proper next step*, namely to balance the weight of that prejudice against the strength of the parental preferences, as required by the Act.

The applicant's first submission – the *Wednesbury* reasonableness argument – was to the effect that the tribunal had come to a conclusion that no reasonable tribunal in these circumstances could have reached. Mr Justice Forbes had no difficulty in accepting that a reasonable tribunal on the evidence led might well conclude that 36 children in a class designed for 30 might produce a state of educational prejudice; but for the tribunal therefore, without further evidence at all on the point, to conclude from that that the addition of *this one further child under consideration* would necessarily 'prejudice the provision of efficient education' could possibly be regarded as unreasonable. It was clearly necessary for the tribunal to go further and *to direct its attention singly to the educationally prejudicial impact of the addition of this one child*. It was not enough to be satisfied that there was *a pre-existing state of prejudice*. This one child had to be shown to *aggravate* that state of prejudice – a significantly different matter. The judge declined, however, to hold that this tribunal had in fact acted unreasonably in this matter, although the evidence led before the tribunal had related to establishing the pre-existing prejudice rather than the aggravation that the admission of this child would bring about, on the ground that this was a tribunal of educational experts who might be taken to have satisfied themselves as to the aggravation factor on the basis of their own knowledge and experience rather than the evidence led before them. It would, indeed, probably be very difficult in practice to show unreasonableness on the part of a tribunal comprising educational experts making a complex educational assessment, in the narrow sense that they had acted in a way in which no reasonable tribunal could act, but tribunals would perhaps be wise always to make it explicit that they have directed their attention to the additional aggravating impact of the addition of the particular child under consideration, ensuring that evidence is before them on that very point, rather than just reach a broad conclusion that a state of prejudice existed.

The second submission related to a procedural matter of the greatest importance. It was accepted by the Court and has now been elaborated by the Council on Tribunals in its *Code of Practice*.[85] It is that the tribunal's task ought properly to be separated into two identifiable stages: first, it must consider whether there is evidence on which it can conclude that the admission of the child in question would cause prejudice (either to the provision of efficient education or the efficient use of resources); and secondly, if it concludes that this is so, it must then go on to perform a discretionary balancing exercise to determine whether the *degree of prejudice* is sufficient to outweigh the 'parental considerations' – the reasoned preference expressed together with the authority's priority ranking criteria set out in its published arrangements. The 'parental considerations' are irrelevant to the establishment of prejudice, but they are an essential ingredient in the balancing exercise that then follows. The judge wholly accepted this analysis of the functions of the tribunal into a two-stage process, and concluded on the evidence in this case that this tribunal had indeed confined its attention to the question of whether prejudice would be involved and had taken the parental considerations into account at that one composite stage, rather than adopting the two-stage process.

One further point of general importance to arise from Mr Justice Forbes' judgment related to the location of the burden of proof in such appeals: the judge concluded that it was clearly the LEA which bore the burden of proof at stage one – the establishment of prejudice to efficient education; at the second (balancing) stage it was less clear, but the judge felt that there was a very strong argument that it lay on the LEA here too, given that the primary object of the provisions was the enhancement of parental choice. It is noteworthy that, as a result of this judgment, the Council on Tribunals' *Code of Practice* now clearly suggests that the LEA's case should be submitted *before* the parent's case rather than after, thereby reflecting the correct location of the burden of proof.[86]

It may be that the significance of this case for education appeal tribunals is more procedural than substantive: perhaps it is improbable that any different *conclusion* would emerge from consideration of the issues in two stages rather than one. Nonetheless the view expressed by the judge that, in order to establish prejudice to efficient education or the efficient use of resources, it is necessary to consider the *additionally prejudicial impact of the single child* whose appeal is at this moment under consideration could be regarded as placing tribunals very often in a virtually impossible position of having to distinguish between like or even identical cases. It is noteworthy though, that, although the judge phrased the test in this way, he declined to hold that this educationally expert tribunal had erred on this point, and the difficulty of successfully challenging any such tribunal's finding here on grounds of unreasonableness should not be forgotten. In order to avoid possible challenge on the more fruitful ground of defective procedure, however, tribunals would be well advised explicitly to follow the two stage procedure outlined in the *South Glamorgan* case and subsequently endorsed in the *Code of Practice*.

Open enrolment under the Education Reform Act 1988[87]

The fundamental shortcoming of the parental choice provisions of the 1980 Act as perceived by the Conservative government was undoubtedly the ability of LEAs to establish what the government regarded as substantially artificial admissions quotas. Pleas by LEAs that this was essential in order to spread pupil intakes between schools and thereby achieve rationally coordinated, educationally efficient and socially acceptable planning against the background of falling rolls went largely unheeded. The government firmly expressed its dissatisfaction with the existing state of affairs in its 1987 consultation paper on *The Admission of Pupils to Maintained Schools*,[88] claiming that this was seriously inhibiting parental choice and declaring its intention to introduce provisions in the forthcoming Education Reform Bill requiring schools, if there were a demand for the places, to admit pupils up to their physical capacity.[89]

The essence of the 'open enrolment' provisions under sections 26 and 27 of the 1988 Act is that the LEA (or governors in the case of an aided or special agreement school) may not fix an admissions quota below the school's 'standard number', defined generally as the number of pupils admitted in the school year beginning in September 1979 (as under section 15 of the Education Act 1980), or in September 1988 (before section 26 of the 1988 Act came into force), whichever is the greater. Standard numbers will be subject to variation by the Secretary of State.[90] Proposals by an LEA (or governors) for *reducing* a standard number will be subject to formal procedures under section 28 analogous to those for school closures under sections 12 and 13 of the 1980 Act, but, very significantly, the only legitimate legal basis for his approval of such proposals will be his satisfaction that the reduction is 'necessary, having regard to any reduction in the school's capacity to accommodate pupils'.[91]

The link between these provisions and parental choice is sealed by section 26(9) which provides that, in the first proviso to the duty of an LEA to comply with the expressed parental preference under section 6 of the 1980 Act – prejudice to efficient education or the efficient use of resources – *no such prejudice* shall be taken to arise until the standard number has been reached. These provisions seek in this way to provide for pure parental choice – 'open enrolment' – up to the limit of a school's physical capacity, even though the consequence may be the running down of certain schools to a point where there will be little option but to close them, or the need to maintain staffing at a disproportionate level at certain schools in order to meet the needs of the national curriculum. If this does lead to school closures, the open-enrolment policy may, paradoxically, serve to inhibit rather than expand parental choice.

The full consequences of this for schools cannot be properly understood without making the link between these provisions for open enrolment and the closely connected provisions establishing new budgetary arrangements for schools under the local management provisions of the 1988 Act. It is, indeed, the linking of these two sets of provisions under the Act which ensures that schools, as far as possible, will be driven for their very survival by market forces. The essential point is that, not only are schools now required by virtue of open enrolment to admit as many, or as few, pupils as parental demand dictates, subject to the limit of their standard number, but the public money they receive under the new budgetary arrangements will be directly related to this number. They will have to attract pupils or face the possibility of closure.

Under the new system of local management of schools, the formula for determining the budget share for each school will be required to take into account the number and ages of registered pupils,[92] though it may include other variable factors affecting the needs of individual schools – in particular, the number of registered pupils with special educational needs.[93] There will be no uniform model formula, but guidance offered by the DES indicates clearly that age-weighted pupil numbers are to be the 'central determinant'.[94] The practical impact of the adoption of age-weighted pupil numbers as the primary determinant is not clear. One factor which it leaves out of account is staffing costs, which may vary considerably according to the age profile of staff. This may have a particularly distorting impact on small schools, which also frequently face disproportionate staffing costs in order to maintain a balanced curriculum. The guidelines suggest that this consideration should be built into the formula for small schools,[95] but that average costs should be used for larger schools, and, indeed, the governors of larger schools are likely to face acute difficulties in this context.

This new system for open enrolment and allocating resources according to pupil numbers is, indeed, very close to what has often been called a 'voucher' system for school education, under which parents would receive a voucher worth a certain amount of money to be encashed at the school of their choice. A voucher system would operate on a different administrative basis, though many of its effects would be the same as open enrolment; but perhaps the most important difference is that it may be possible for parents to 'top up' their vouchers from their own resources and to encash them at independent schools: any such scheme would involve massive state subsidy for private education.[96] At the time of writing, the Secretary of State for Education has indicated that education vouchers are not on the agenda.

The combined effect of the reforms under the 1988 Act concerning choice of school will thus be to undermine the capacity of LEAs for rational planning of educational provision through controlling pupil intakes – critical in times of falling rolls – and to replace this with the unpredictability of parental demand. The schools themselves will be unable to make long- or even medium-term plans, given the budgetary uncertainty inherent in the new system, and will be forced to compete directly with one another for pupils and thus for resources; and those that fail for whatever reason to attract these resources may be forced to close, thereby, paradoxically, *restricting* parental choice which might well otherwise have existed. These consequences are justified by the government in the name of parental choice, individualistic freedom and sensitive accountability of schools to their consumers through being required to compete in an educational market place.

CONCLUSIONS

The provisions of the Education Act 1980 and the Education Reform Act 1988 concerning choice of school have been hailed by their supporters as a charter for parental rights. It is, however, doubtful whether this is a true description except in the narrow sense of their being a parents' charter for a minority of strong-willed, articulate, middle-class parents with the time, inclination and knowledge of the system required to pursue *their* claims to what they see as a satisfactory conclusion. In exerting pressure on LEAs and taking their claims to local education appeal tribunals under the 1980 Act, these parents – as a very broad generalisation – are successful in achieving their goal; but the majority of claimants without these attributes may well fare less well. This is due in large part to structural and procedural shortcomings in the appeal tribunals themselves: structurally, they are – and are seen to be – essentially under the control of the LEAs which established them. This is not attributable merely to the in-built LEA majority, although that is certainly at the heart of the matter, but also to the fact that they are established and administered by the LEA, that they are served by LEA officials as clerks and that they may meet on LEA premises. These structural defects are compounded by the breathtaking procedural discretion enjoyed by the LEA in establishing the tribunals, admittedly now guided by the Council on Tribunals' *Code of Practice* and the *South Glamorgan* decision, but nonetheless remaining very wide indeed. Appellants – with no absolute right to representation – faced by an LEA-dominated tribunal, where the LEA's case is presented by an experienced LEA official well-versed in the administrative complexities of the admissions process and the relevant legislation and well-accustomed to the proceedings of the tribunal itself, must often have the impression that their chances of success are remote.

The solution to these problems ought to have been in a careful and systematic re-examination of the operation of the appeal tribunals themselves: the government, however, made no attempt in the 1988 Act to introduce greater safeguards into the tribunal procedures, but instead opted to legislate for what it saw as greater parental choice in the shape of open enrolment. In seeking to introduce parental choice qualified only by schools' standard numbers – in effect, their maximum physical capacity – it has in reality eradicated the critical element of *balance* which had previously existed through the capacity of LEAs to impose admission quotas: LEAs, acting in the collective interests of the areas served by them, had been able by imposing quotas to *counterbalance* absolute freedom of choice exercised by the individual. It was very much in the public interest that that element of balance should have been retained, but it has been swept aside by open enrolment with social and educational consequences for the collective community which are likely to prove unpredictable, but which will almost certainly include the contraction and ultimately the closure of schools which ought to have been retained as collective resources serving important elements of the community as a whole.

3

LEGAL CONTROL OVER THE CONTENTS OF THE SECULAR CURRICULUM

INTRODUCTION

The rationale for individual interest – represented chiefly by parental interest – in the substantive contents of the secular curriculum in schools, and the methods and style of teaching, is perhaps relatively easy to see, and it may be that there is a rather greater degree of political consensus in this context than in the other major areas of controversy examined in this book (though political conflict here is by no means absent). As a starting point one should certainly consider the centrality of the impact of the nature and substance of the curriculum upon the entire development of the child, as discussed in chapter 1. It is this central role of the substantive education provided at school which is the essential foundation for parental concern in this context, a concern which may be argued to have the attributes of a fundamental human right to exercise at least some degree of involvement in or even control over the content of the education provided in accordance with the parent's personal conscience. On grounds of practicality, however, few would argue that this right should be absolute, although some would certainly argue in favour of an absolute right in a liberal democracy to 'alternative' education outside the state sector, either in independent schools or at home, subject to suitable inspection by state agencies.[1] Given the fundamental nature of parental concern here, it is to be expected that the provisions of Article 2 of the First Protocol to the European Convention on Human Rights requiring education in conformity with parents' religious and philosophical convictions would have some real force in this context, and we shall examine some of the relevant caselaw in the context of sex education below. The Protocol has also been invoked in the context of religious education, though that falls outside the scope of this discussion.

One underlying rationale for concern in this context which is frequently invoked in arguments over the location of decision-making power as to the school curriculum ought to be identified at the outset. It is a concern which can be exaggerated, or at least couched in emotive phraseology, but is one which anyone concerned with the preservation of democratic values ought to recognise and respect. It is the background possibility of state 'indoctrination' – a concept which is all the more potentially dangerous as it eludes precise definition. There is always in the background the possibility that a state may seek through the assumption of excessively centralised powers over the curriculum to abuse its position through the inculcation of certain social, political, economic or other tenets, and the censorship of material of a countervailing nature, in order to attain certain goals which it perceives as desirable. Arguments along these lines were invoked against the national curriculum, and against section 28 of the Local Government Act 1988 concerning the promotion of homosexuality by local authorities, as we shall see below; and the fear of indoctrination was undoubtedly an element in the thinking behind the adoption of the First Protocol to the European Convention. Although emotive and easily exaggerated or raised in inappropriate contexts, it is an argument which should not be forgotten.

The scheme of this chapter will be to examine the location of decision-making power over the curriculum established under the 1944 Education Act; then to identify some of the pressures for change which emerged particularly during the 1970s and 1980s; then to examine the major reforms under the Education (No. 2) Act 1986, with a particular consideration of the problems of political education and sex education; and finally to consider the move towards centralised prescription of the secular curriculum under the Education Reform Act 1988.

THE EDUCATION ACT 1944 AND RELATIVE CONSENSUS IN THE EARLY POST-WAR PERIOD

The most striking feature of the 1944 Act's very sparse provisions concerning the secular curriculum was local discretion and the total absence of prescription: this may have been partly in response to an inherent fear of centralised control, direction or even indoctrination in the light of the experience of pre-war Germany, but was probably more substantially attributable to a genuine belief that local government and the teaching profession had and ought to have an important contribution to make to curricular content and that, within limits, diversity of provision was inherently desirable. The White Paper which preceded the 1944 Act stressed that it was

> just as important to achieve diversity as it is to ensure equality of educational opportunity,[2]

and this emphasis on diversity may be seen no less in section 23 of the Act concerning the secular curriculum than in the provisions setting up the new organisational structure of schools. Under section 23, control over the secular curriculum in all maintained schools (except voluntary aided secondary schools) was vested in the LEA, except in so far as otherwise provided in the school's articles of government; in the case of aided secondary schools, control was vested in the governors. Section 23 was thus highly permissive in its nature: it permitted LEAs to enjoy the widest possible discretion over the curriculum, subject to schools' articles of government, and subject to the very general duty of the Secretary of State under section 1 to 'promote the education of the people', and

> to secure the effective execution by local authorities, under his control and direction, of the national policy for providing a varied and comprehensive educational service in every area,[3]

and to the largely unenforceable general principle in section 76 of respect for parental wishes already discussed in the context of choice of school in chapter 2. Section 1 admittedly gave the Secretary of State a wide-ranging overall concern with all educational matters, but there is no doubt that the real discretion over curricular matters was deliberately vested in LEAs and governors. Articles of government varied, though many followed the model articles issued by the central department,[4] giving the LEA a general supervisory role but placing determination of day-to-day curricular matters essentially with the headteacher subject to consultation with and direction as to matters of general policy from the governing body. There is little doubt but that the driving force in the majority of schools in practice was the headteacher, leaving governors as a relatively compliant consultative body and the LEA with a broader overall policy concern with education in its area as a whole.

PRESSURE FOR CHANGE UP TO 1979

This broad consensus structure established under the 1944 Act remained for over a decade reasonably intact, but school education then came under a highly complex range of different pressures for change, one of the most important of which was the introduction in the 1950s and then the widespread adoption in the 1960s and 1970s of comprehensive reorganisation, which was followed by a fundamental reappraisal of curricular arrangements during the 1970s and 1980s, culminating in the establishment of the national curriculum under the Education Reform Act 1988. In part arising out of comprehensive reorganisation, but also with many other social and educational causes, there arose during the 1970s a significant concern about the curriculum and educational standards. This took many forms and gave rise to many different inquiries, reports and central and local initiatives. It is impossible to identify a starting point for this concern, but perhaps the catalyst was the ILEA Report into events at William Tyndale School in Islington, published in 1976.[5] This report arose out of what was perceived by many parents of children attending the school to be a collapse of educational standards and discipline through the application by the head and some other teachers of radical educational theories and methods involving a minimum of formal structure and discipline and a maximum degree of personal autonomy, and learning through experimentation and self-discovery on the part of the pupils. This led to what many parents saw as a substantial educational and disciplinary breakdown at the school, and many withdrew their children in protest. The impact of these events and the report, given extensive press publicity, was wide and was reflected in considerable disquiet over the curriculum and standards as a whole nationwide.

This widespread disquiet – which had many causes other than the William Tyndale affair – led the then Prime Minister, Mr James Callaghan, on 18 October 1976 to make his famous speech at Ruskin College, Oxford calling for a 'great debate' on education, attacking the view that the curriculum was a 'secret garden' open only to those with professional expertise in the area, and exhorting everyone with an interest in the subject to contribute:

> I take it that no-one claims exclusive rights in this field. Public interest is strong and will be satisfied. It is legitimate. We spend £6 billion a year on education, so there will be discussion. But let it be rational. If everything is reduced to such phrases as

> 'educational freedom versus state control' we shall get nowhere. I repeat that parents, teachers, learned and professional bodies, representatives of higher education and both sides of industry, together with the government, all have an important part to play[6]

This speech led to the holding of a series of regional conferences on education during February and March 1977, and some aspects of these deliberations were crystallised in a Government Green Paper, *Education in Schools: A Consultative Document*, issued in July of that year.[7] The elements of the national curriculum concept are very clearly discernible in this Green Paper:

> The Secretaries of State will therefore seek to establish a broad agreement with their partners in the education service on a framework for the curriculum, and, particularly, on whether, because there are aims common to all schools and to all pupils at certain stages, there should be a 'core' or 'protected' part.[8]

Following this Green Paper, the government sought to gather in detailed evidence as to curricular practice, and to this end issued a circular requiring all LEAs to report in detail as to their curricular arrangements.[9] The responses disclosed what the government subsequently described as 'substantial variations within the educational system in England and Wales in policies towards the curriculum'.[10] The government's conclusions from the Circular 14/77 review were that

> not all authorities have a clear view of the desirable structure of the school curriculum, especially its core elements. They [the government] believe that they should seek to give a lead in the process of reaching a national consensus on a desirable framework for the curriculum and consider the development of such a framework a priority for the education service. They recognise that this is a complex and difficult task. Such a framework will need to relate to the broad shape of the whole curriculum for the various stages of school education, and be capable of flexibility in accordance with changing perceptions over time of individual and social needs.[11]

The government's first step in 'giving a lead' towards a national consensus on a curricular framework would be to invite HMI to 'formulate a view of a possible curriculum on the basis of their knowledge of schools',[12] with a view to the issuing of a draft circular for consultations which the government hoped to hold in 1980.

This tentative statement endorsing the general principle of a nationally coordinated curriculum at least as to an essential framework encapsulates the position reached by the then Labour government by the time of the general election in 1979. That position had, however, also been informed by an important report commissioned by the DES on the role and composition of school governing bodies chaired by Councillor Tom (later Lord) Taylor: *A New Partnership for Our Schools*.[13] The Taylor Report advocated a more positive role for governors in curricular matters, defining the curriculum broadly as the totality of the child's experiences within school, and in particular it advocated the view that the governing body should be given the responsibility for

> setting the aims of the school, for considering the means by which they are pursued, for keeping under review the school's progress towards them, and for deciding upon action to facilitate such progress.[14]

The Taylor Report also recommended significant structural changes in the composition of governing bodies: it advocated what it called the 'four equal shares principle' under which governing bodies would comprise equal numbers of LEA representatives, school staff, parents and community representatives.[15] As might have been expected, the Taylor recommendations were strongly resisted, in part by the teachers' unions and professional associations jealous of their professional standing,[16] and in part by LEAs anxious not to have their representation on governing bodies diluted. What is important today about the Taylor recommendations is that we can discern in them very clearly the concept of *accountability* or, put less delicately, *consumerism*, concepts which, paradoxically, though espoused in a report in 1977 commissioned by a Labour Secretary of State, came to the forefront of the subsequent Conservative government's educational philosophy in the 1980s. Indeed, important elements in the Taylor recommendations were enacted, as we shall see below, in the Education (No. 2) Act 1986.

On the Conservative government's assumption of power in 1979, therefore, two very clear and fundamental curricular trends were already well in motion – the adoption of a closer consensus as to the contents of the secular curriculum, and the greater involvement of school governors, with enhanced parental representation – in curricular decision-making. It by no means follows from this, however, that the legislative initiatives actually adopted in these contexts by the incoming Conservative government bore much resemblance to those envisaged by the outgoing Labour administration.

RADICAL CHANGE AFTER 1979

The Conservative government which came to power in 1979 seized on the secular curriculum in schools as a major political and social issue, and has transformed legal regulation in this context almost beyond recognition – from the negligible provisions of the 1944 Act to a structure of detailed regulation at a level of precision which few would have envisaged during Mr James Callaghan's 'great debate', involving a radical *centralisation of power* over curricular matters, in addition to a range of highly controversial *measures of prohibition as to what may be taught* in the schools, in the contexts of political issues, sex education and, in particular, homosexuality. From the legislation introduced in this context since 1979 may be discerned three highly significant trends which will be developed in the discussion below: first, there was a great concern that LEAs should be held in check by the 'consumers' of education – the parents – evidenced by measures to increase parental representation on governing bodies and enhance their powers; secondly, there emerged a highly traditional and family-orientated moral attitude to social and, in particular, sexual values, coupled with an obscure fear that traditional values were being systematically undermined by radical factions in society which had infiltrated local government in general and the teaching profession in particular, and were in danger of corrupting children through the promotion of their various causes; and thirdly, there was the trend towards the radical centralisation of power in the hands of the DES with a consequential loss of power by LEAs. We will now go on to examine some of the ways in which these trends have been manifested in legislation.

Increasing consumerism

The government has repeatedly emphasised its commitment in a range of educational contexts to securing effective accountability on the part of those who provide education – meaning, in this context, LEAs and teachers – to the consumers of educational services, represented here by parents. Accountability is central to the subjection of schools to market forces and is manifested perhaps most clearly by the imposition upon governing bodies of the obligation to hold an annual parents' meeting under the Education (No. 2) Act 1986,[17] and in the open enrolment provisions of the Education Reform Act 1988;[18] but it may also be seen clearly in the context of the school curriculum by the vesting in governing bodies of enhanced curricular responsibilities under sections 17 to 19 of the Education (No. 2) Act 1986. Underlying its public commitment to principles of accountability and market forces, however, it may be that there was a further element in the government's thinking, namely the desirability of restraining what it perceived to be eccentric and in some cases abhorrent curricular excesses by a number of left-wing LEAs, through granting enhanced powers to governing bodies and ensuring stronger parental representation on those bodies. It by no means follows that parental representatives would necessarily oppose radical LEA curricular policies, but there was a feeling that a strengthened parental voice would, as a broad generalisation, operate as a restraining influence.

The first legal technique for ensuring enhanced consumer orientation adopted in the Education (No. 2) Act 1986 was the reconstitution of the governing bodies themselves. In the Act itself are to be found the essential requirements as to the composition of schools' governing bodies, and these must then be translated into practice through the amendment of schools' instruments of government. The critical section of the Act here is section 3, which increased the number of elected parent representatives on school governing bodies, the actual membership in each group of governors depending on the size of the school. Thus, in a school with 600 or more registered pupils, the governing body must comprise:

(a) five elected parent governors
(b) five governors appointed by the LEA
(c) two elected teacher governors
(d) the headteacher (unless he or she declines to serve)
(e) six co-opted governors (four foundation and two co-opted governors in the case of a controlled school).[19]

Enhanced consumer orientation is not, however, ensured only by increased parental representation: section 6 provides explicit statutory endorsement of the involvement in the running of schools of the '*local business community*'. In the process of selecting suitable persons as *co-opted* governors, the other members of the governing body are under a duty to have regard to the extent to which the local business community is already represented on the governing body. In the event of there being no local business community representative already on the board, or where it is felt desirable to increase its representation, the governors are under a duty to co-opt someone who 'appears to them' to be a member of 'that community'. The last provision thus makes co-option of at least one local business community member mandatory. That section 6 should isolate one aspect of the local community, the business community (a phrase which defies clear definition), setting it apart from the remainder of the community as meriting express mandatory representation, could be construed as a highly political gesture, indicative of the government's perception that the curriculum – and all other aspects of the conduct of schools in relation to which governors have concern – should be influenced or even moulded in a given direction, perhaps with an emphasis on vocational training and the needs of business, but certainly directed away from any curricular trends that might be regarded as radical. Thus, consumer orientation has been significantly strengthened through the reconstitution of school governing bodies with a clearly discernible emphasis on both parental and local business community representation.

The second technique was to elaborate in statutory form the respective curricular responsibilities of LEAs, school governors and headteachers, requiring schools' articles of government to be amended in such a way as to reflect these statutory requirements. This statutory elaboration goes considerably beyond the provisions which previously existed in schools' articles of government, and significantly emphasises the role of governors. By virtue of section 17, LEAs are under a duty to determine, and to keep under review, their policy in relation to the secular curriculum and to formalise it in the shape of a written statement;[20] and, in doing this, they are required to give particular consideration to the *range* of the secular curriculum and the *balance* between its different components.[21] Governing bodies are in turn, by virtue of section 18,[22] duty bound to consider the LEA's stated curricular policy;[23] to consider what, in their opinion, should be the *aims* of the secular curriculum for the school;[24] and to consider how, if at all, the LEA's statement of policy should in their opinion be *modified* in relation to the school.[25] The governors must then formulate a written statement of their conclusions. The governors' power to modify the LEA's formulation emphatically empowers them to override any aspects of LEA curricular policy from which they dissent. We shall look expressly at sex education below, but it should be noted here that the governing body is required by section 18 to consider the issue of sex education separately from all other aspects of the secular curriculum, making a separate written statement of their policy as to the content and organisation of the curriculum in this context after having considered the LEA's statement.[26] It is even open to the governors to conclude that sex education should form *no part* of the curriculum (subject to meeting the requirements of any public examination syllabuses).

In the process of considering and deliberating on these issues, the governing body is statutorily required to consult the school's headteacher[27] and the LEA,[28] and, furthermore, to 'have regard to' any representations in this context by persons connected with *the community served by the school*,[29] and any representations by *the chief officer of police*.[30] The requirement to have regard to community representations again reflects the atmosphere of consumer orientation running throughout these provisions; and the requirement to have regard to any representations from the chief constable could again be interpreted as a highly political gesture, with an emphasis on 'law and order', and social and political conformity.

The headteacher, finally, is given express statutory responsibility for the 'determination and organisation' of the secular curriculum and for ensuring that 'that curriculum' as determined is indeed followed.[31] In so doing, the headteacher is required to consider the LEA's and the governing body's respective statements[32] and must have regard, in terms identical to those applying to the governors, to any representations from community members or the chief constable.[33] The critical provision is, however, the requirement that the headteacher must ensure that the curriculum as followed in the school is 'compatible with' the LEA's policy 'as modified by the governing body's statement':[34] this plainly emphasises the intention that the governors' statement should be given *priority* over the LEA's policy statement in the event of any inconsistency. The headteacher is also duty bound to ensure curricular compatibility with the governors' statement of policy as to sex education, except to the extent that the policy statement is inconsistent with any public examination syllabus;[35] and overall curricular compatibility with 'enactments relating to education',[36] a phrase which is all-embracing but which is clearly intended to encompass other provisions of the 1986 Act (for instance, those relating to political and sex education, discussed below), and subsequent enactments, of which the most prominent are the provisions of the Education Reform Act 1988 concerning the national curriculum (discussed below).

These provisions of the Education (No. 2) Act 1986 have for the first time given school governing bodies a potential role of real significance in respect of curricular formulation, thereby eroding the predominant position in this context enjoyed hitherto by LEAs and professional teachers, and inserting what the government perceived as a much needed element of direct consumer involvement at the formative stage of curricular planning and of subsequent accountability for the manner of delivery of the curriculum in the schools. This should not be categorised merely as marginal fine tuning of the system but as a radical legislative initiative seeking to bring about a significant political and educational reform by effecting a fundamental shift in the balance of decision-making power over the contents of the secular curriculum. As we shall see below, however, it may be that this potential role of real significance has been substantially eroded by the highly prescriptive nature of the national curriculum.

Curbing political indoctrination

A second trend during the period from 1979 has been the perception by the government of a need to impose an element of restraint on certain aspects of the substantive contents of the curriculum. This was to counterbalance what it saw as a tendency on the part of some LEAs and some elements within the teaching profession to abuse their position by incorporating into the curriculum issues of a highly controversial political nature which were presented in a manner which lacked political and social balance, and which in some cases could be identified as proselytising on the part of known factions in society. The latter might represent an extreme form which would be difficult to substantiate on any widespread basis, but the government nonetheless perceived this as a sufficiently significant phenomenon to require positive action – over and above increasing parental representation on governing bodies as a restraining factor – in the form of a legislative requirement that political issues be presented in a 'balanced' manner – yet another phrase which defies clear definition and which would make any attempt to *enforce* the legislation in this context substantially impracticable. Before we examine the introduction and the detail of this legislation, it should be recalled that the state – represented here by LEAs, school governors and headteachers – was already obliged by virtue of Article 2 of the First Protocol to the European Convention on Human Rights to respect parents' religious and philosophical convictions, and that the European Court has in the curricular context interpreted this as requiring that issues should be presented in an 'objective, critical and pluralistic' manner.[37]

Governmental concern over what may loosely be called 'political indoctrination' has been manifested in a range of contexts, but perhaps the clearest was the attack by the then Secretary of State for Education, Sir Keith Joseph, on the inclusion in the curriculum as a separate topic of 'peace studies'. Sir Keith Joseph in a speech in 1984 expressed his regret at the use of the phrase 'peace studies', and went on to comment:

> There will be occasions – in history, in religious studies, in physics, in English, for example – when questions of the morality of war, the conditions which lie behind war and other aspects of international affairs will crop up. As pupils mature they ought to be encouraged to apply their reasoning powers to these and other important issues of the day. These might include topics such as closed societies and open societies, such as one-sided or two-sided disarmament. The approach in the classroom should be rational and not emotional. Since such subjects will come up naturally in the curriculum there seems to be no need to make special space for subjects labelled 'peace'. And when the subject does arise it seems to me essential that the teacher should deal with it in a proper professional way as he ought to deal with any other topic involving facts, their interpretation and value judgments. His presentation needs to be as objective as he can make it, in the sense that he ensures that what is offered as a fact is indeed true; that the selection of facts gives a picture which is neither unbalanced nor superficial; that facts and opinions are clearly separated; and that pupils are encouraged to weigh evidence and argument so as to arrive at rational judgments.[38]

This plea for balance and for the treatment of controversial political issues as and when they arise in the course of the teaching of other subjects rather than as separate subjects perhaps reflected a fairly widespread concern about courses on 'peace studies' in schools. A far more vitriolic attack on LEAs and the teaching profession was, however, launched by Baroness Cox in a House of Lords debate on 'Education: Avoidance of Politicisation' in 1986,[39] in which she referred to what she perceived as educational practices which represented

> a violation of education as it is understood in a free society. I refer to deliberate attempts to undermine and to destroy our cultural heritage, our traditional beliefs and values and our democratic freedoms.[40]

Baroness Cox went on to offer instances of inclusion in the curriculum in ILEA schools of what she categorised as 'anti-racism', in addition to some material which she described as 'essentially anti-heterosexual' and some as 'anti-police'.[41] She referred to 'anti-police propaganda' promulgated by the Greater London Council and the Hackney branch of the National Union of Teachers as

> grossly distorted, only showing the police as brutal, racist and incompetent. There is no adequate account of their merits or of attempts they are making to respond to legitimate criticism. The material – posters, booklets and a video – are indoctrinatory in their gross bias and appear calculated to stir up hatred, conflict and contempt: classic ingredients for revolution.[42]

These words may reflect a view held by some critics on the far right, fearful of the activities of a minority of 'subversive socialist teachers',[43] rather than the view of the government, but the government was nonetheless sufficiently sympathetic to the view that there was a real and significant danger of abuse – albeit abuse by a small minority of radical factions within LEAs and the teaching profession – to support the inclusion in the Education (No. 2) Bill 1986 of clauses relating specifically to political education.

Section 45[44] imposes on LEAs, governing bodies and headteachers an obligation to 'take such steps as are reasonably practicable' to secure that, where political issues are brought to the attention of pupils at school, they are offered 'a balanced presentation of opposing views'. The Secretary of State, in guidance issued to LEAs offering his own interpretation of this section, stressed his view that section 45

> should not inhibit schools from dealing with controversial issues within the curriculum. Schools play an essential role in developing and teaching the attitudes, knowledge and skill which are necessary for the proper appreciation of our society's

> fundamental values, notably its commitment to parliamentary democracy, the freedom of the individual within the law, and the equality of all citizens under the law . . .
>
> LEAs, governors and headteachers should be ready to encourage schools to tackle issues that are politically controversial . . . . How this is best done for pupils of varying maturity and understanding is a matter of professional judgment by the teacher and calls for the exercise of professional responsibility within the duties imposed by this Act.[45]

This interpretative guidance goes little distance towards clarifying in any practical sense what section 45 actually means: indeed, the stress placed upon 'professional judgment' and 'professional responsibility' tends to obscure the meaning even further. It will be immediately obvious that the obligations created under section 45 are in reality so weak as to be virtually unenforceable: not only is the requirement to take 'such steps as are reasonably practicable' far from an absolute obligation, but there is room for wide divergence of opinion as to what is meant by a 'balanced presentation', or, indeed, an 'opposing view'. Judicial review here would therefore be a hazardous prospect.[46] It should also be noted that no enforcement mechanism was built into the 1986 Act itself, although, as we will see below in the context of the national curriculum, LEAs are now under an obligation by virtue of section 23 of the Education Reform Act 1988 to establish curricular complaints mechanisms to hear complaints as to unreasonable conduct or breach of statutory duty on the part of LEAs or governing bodies (but not individual teachers) concerning either the implementation of the national curriculum or 'any other enactment relating to the curriculum'.[47] This would certainly cover complaints concerning alleged abuse in the context of political education, and section 23 would be the anticipated means of redress, though the nature of the remedy remains obscure. Following complaint under section 23, further complaint could be lodged with the Secretary of State under section 68 or 99 of the 1944 Act: the Secretary of State does have power to issue legally enforceable orders to LEAs or governors under those sections, and this would appear in this context to be the ultimate remedy, albeit an extremely remote prospect, short of judicial review.

In view of the imprecision of the language used in section 45 and the improbability of legal challenge, it may be best to view it as a gesture of contempt by the government for LEAs and for the activities of a limited number of politically motivated teachers, and as a public gesture by the government wishing to be identified as staunch upholders of political purity in educational matters.

Sex education[48] and the promotion of traditional family values

The government's concern with the possibility of political indoctrination was paralleled closely by its concern with the possibility that, in some LEAs, the treatment within the curriculum of issues relating to sex might run counter to certain traditional values, or, in particular, might be offensive to certain religious or ethnic groups. As in the case of possible political indoctrination, there was wide press coverage of a small minority of specific cases of alleged abuse in this context, and this served only to exaggerate the issues and to encourage the expression of extreme views. Nonetheless although there was wide recognition that much of the publicity here had been exaggerated, the government considered that the potential for abuse here was sufficiently great and that there was sufficient public concern over the issue, or that there was sufficient political capital to be gained by being seen to take a stance on the issue, to justify taking positive steps to limit the freedom of LEAs, governors and headteachers in formulating the curriculum in this context. We have already seen that school governors were required by section 18(2) of the Education (No. 2) Act 1986 to consider their policy on sex education separately from all other aspects of the secular curriculum and then to formulate a separate written statement on sex education; and there is little doubt that the rationale for enhancing parental (and perhaps local business community, though this is less certain) representation on governing bodies was the promotion of traditional family values in these deliberations. But this reform did not, in the government's view, go far enough: all this did was to lay the structural foundations (with a more securely guaranteed family orientation) for the determination of policy on this matter. It was necessary, in the government's view, to go further and to seek by law actually to delimit the substantive content of any such policy statements emanating from governing bodies.

Before we go on to examine how the government has approached this perceived need for more positive intervention through departmental circular and legislation, however, it is necessary to consider the pre-existing obligations of the state in this, as in other, curricular contexts under the European Convention. Sex education is, indeed, one context where individual parents have challenged state action before the European Commission and Court of Human Rights. There would be wide agreement that the nature, scope and content of sex education raise issues of greater potential sensitivity than almost any other area of the secular curriculum and may raise acutely the extent of the individual's right to challenge state action: the second sentence of Article 2 of the First Protocol, requiring respect for parents' religious and philosophical convictions, would thus appear to be of great potential significance in this context.

The leading challenge was brought by parents of children attending state primary schools in Denmark and related to the imposition of compulsory sex education integrated into the teaching of other subjects in the curriculum of state primary schools under an Act of the Danish Parliament of 1970: *Kjeldsen, Busk Madsen and Pedersen* v. *Denmark*.[49] The parents objected to the nature and content of the sex education and to the fact that, under the 1970 statute, it would be *integrated* into the teaching of other subjects in the curriculum, thus making any question of the withdrawal of their children impracticable. Although it would have been possible to educate their children at private schools (to which the statute did not apply), or to educate them privately at home, neither course was practicable. They asserted not only a lack of respect for their religious and philosophical convictions under the First Protocol, but also that the statute violated their right to respect under Articles 8 and 9 of the Convention itself for their private and family life and their right to freedom of thought, conscience and religion. The Court in the event did not separately consider the complaints under Articles 8 and 9, but simply stated that it had taken them into account in their interpretation of Article 2 of the First Protocol.[50]

In its judgment, the Court stressed that Article 2 did not prevent states from imparting in schools 'information or knowledge of a directly or indirectly religious or philosophical kind'.[51] Indeed, it concluded that it would be very difficult for many subjects taught at school not to have, to a greater or less extent, 'some philosophical complexion or implications'.[52] What the second sentence of Article 2 did require, however, was that the state must ensure that information or knowledge included in the curriculum was conveyed in an 'objective, critical and pluralistic manner',[53] and that the state must avoid anything which could be regarded as constituting indoctrination. The Court found as a matter of fact that the Statute in question was intended to ensure that the children in schools were given better *factual information* about sexual matters rather than permitting the information to be conveyed in such a manner as to further support for any particular opinion as to moral attitudes or behaviour. This clearly the Court regarded as of central importance, although it recognised that 'appraisals of fact easily lead on to value judgments'.[54] The Court found that:

> the Danish State, by providing children in good time with explanations it considers useful, is attempting to warn them against phenomena it views as disturbing, for example, the excessive frequency of births out of wedlock, induced abortions and venereal diseases.
>
> . . . These considerations are indeed of a moral order, but they are very general in character and do not entail overstepping the bounds of what a democratic state may regard as the public interest. Examination of the legislation in dispute establishes in fact that *it in no way amounts to an attempt at indoctrination aimed at advocating a specific kind of sexual behaviour.* It does not make a point of exalting sex or inciting pupils to indulge precociously in practices that are dangerous for their stability, health or future or that many parents consider reprehensible. *Further, it does not affect the right of parents to enlighten and advise their children, to exercise with regard to their children natural parental functions as educators, or to guide their children on a path in line with the parents' own religious and philosophical convictions.*[55]

The Court thus concluded that the Danish government was not in breach of Article 2 of the First Protocol, or of Articles 8 and 9 of the Convention itself. It is clear that it is in no way inconsistent with the Protocol or the Convention for a state to pursue a positive policy of incorporating sex education into the school curriculum, and there is no requirement to permit parents to withdraw their children from sex education, even where this is provided in separate classes rather than integrated within the curriculum as a whole. What matters under the Protocol is that an 'objective, critical and pluralistic' approach should be adopted, thereby deflecting any accusations of indoctrination.[56]

Despite the obligations of LEAs and governors by virtue of the European Convention, as interpreted in the *Kjeldsen, Busk Madsen and Pedersen* case, to ensure that any sex education in their schools was provided in an objective, critical and pluralistic manner, the British government nonetheless felt constrained to supplement these obligations with legislation, in the shape of section 46 of the Education (No. 2) Act 1986, together with detailed policy 'guidance' addressed to LEAs, governors and teachers offering the government's interpretation of the section and its wider perception of the appropriate content of the curriculum relating to sexual matters. In formulating their policy statements on sex education under section 18(2), governors are bound by section 46 but are free to depart from the DES guidance, in the sense that it has no statutory force, though they should bear in mind that that guidance is likely to be treated as of strong evidential significance in the event of any challenge to the governors' policy statement by an aggrieved parent to the curricular complaints body set up by the LEA under section 23 of the 1988 Act, to the Secretary of State, or by way of an application for judicial review.

The government's eagerness to adopt a positive stance over sex education was informed by its conviction that sex education 'cannot be morally neutral'[57] and that there existed a consensus throughout the community about certain broad moral principles, the critical element of which was recognition of 'the value of a stable family life'.[58] In formulating their guidance on sex education, the DES was strongly influenced by a report by HMI on *Health Education from 5 to 16* in 1986:[59] this stressed the need to recognise the differing attitudes to aspects of sex education taken by different ethnic and religious groups in society and the need for parents to be fully informed as to the school's policy and practice.[60] It nonetheless made no suggestion that issues of major controversy should be avoided at the appropriate age level in *secondary* schools:

> Schools need to deal sensitively with such issues as contraception, sexually transmitted diseases, homosexuality and abortion . . . . All these issues involve not only knowledge, but moral and legal questions, are of concern to parents, and may prompt pupils to seek advice from the teacher, either in the classroom or more informally. How the school approaches these issues may also be affected by its legal status and the principles on which it was founded. *Nevertheless it remains necessary to include all these issues* as part of the secondary school's programme of sex education since they are brought to pupils' attention in a variety of contexts both inside and outside school.[61]

Not only did it unequivocally advocate inclusion of these major issues of controversy within the curriculum, subject to sensitivity of handling, but the HMI report was clearly against any right on the part of parents to withdraw their children. It stressed that

> consultations with parents should make it clear that a programme of sex education is part of the school's provision; the participation of pupils is as much a requirement for this as for other parts of the secular curriculum.[62]

The government's response was to incorporate within the 1986 Act a requirement which could be said to be as vague and unenforceable as section 45 concerning the balanced treatment of political issues, but which enshrines what the government viewed as the critical element of 'family values', and thus statutorily endorses the view that sex education in schools should *not* be 'morally neutral'. Section 46 imposes on LEAs, governing bodies and headteachers the duty to

> take such steps as are reasonably practicable to secure that where sex education is given . . . it is given in such a manner as to encourage those pupils to *have due regard to moral considerations and the value of family life.*[63]

The Act does *not* incorporate any right of parental withdrawal, but it is open to the governing body to determine that *no* sex education shall be given, subject to any incompatibility of this determination with public examination syllabuses. Although limiting the obligation to 'such steps as are reasonably practicable', and although couched in terminology which is susceptible to many differing interpretations as to the meaning of 'moral considerations' and 'family life', section 46 nonetheless seeks to be *morally positive* rather than *morally neutral*. It seeks to promote a mode of living, of personal and sexual behaviour and relationships which exalts stable family relationships. This view is strongly supported in the government's interpretation of the section as expounded in its Circular on *Sex Education at School* in 1987:[64]

> The Secretary of State considers that the aims of a programme of sex education should be to present facts in an objective and balanced manner so as to comprehend the range of sexual attitudes and behaviour in present day society; to know what is and is not legal; to consider their own attitudes, and to make informed, reasoned and responsible decisions about the attitudes they will adopt both while they are at school and in adulthood. *Teaching about the physical aspects of sexual behaviour should be set*

> *within a clear moral framework* in which pupils are encouraged to consider the importance of self-restraint, dignity and respect for themselves and others, and helped to recognise the physical, emotional and moral risks of casual and promiscuous sexual behaviour. Schools should foster a recognition that both sexes should behave responsibly in sexual matters. *Pupils should be helped to appreciate the benefits of stable married and family life* and the responsibilities of parenthood.[65]

Not only does this further and emphatically emphasise the desirability of inculcating a non-promiscuous moral code – with which few would take issue – but it again explicitly promotes the traditional concept of the family and of marriage. This may well accord with the views of a majority within our society, but it is not without controversy: it *could* be regarded as promoting a single type of social and sexual behaviour contrary to the requirement of Article 2 of the First Protocol to the European Convention, as interpreted in the *Kjeldsen, Busk Madsen and Pedersen* case, that education in schools be presented 'objectively, critically and pluralistically'. It may be majoritarian (legally irrelevant under the Protocol), but it is arguably neither objective nor pluralistic as it promotes a *single* mode of living within one particular type of social unit – the traditional concept of the family – without recognising that there is a significant minority within our society that *prefers* to live outside the traditional family unit, and a further significant minority which does so by virtue of personal circumstances while not necessarily *preferring* to live in that way. In the latter category is the substantial and growing number of single-parent families; in the former are many who opt to live singly or communally but without a partner, or who live with a partner, either of the opposite or the same sex, but outside the traditional married state envisaged by the DES Circular in its reference to 'the benefits of stable married and family life'.[66] What the Circular emphatically does *not* do is commend the inclusion in school curricula of even the most objective, critical and pluralistic consideration of such alternative lifestyles. On the question of homosexuality it explicitly states that:

> There is no place in any school in any circumstances for teaching which advocates homosexual behaviour, which presents it as the 'norm', or which encourages homosexual experimentation by pupils. Indeed, encouraging or procuring homosexual acts by pupils who are under the age of consent is

> a criminal offence. It must also be recognised that for many people, including members of various religious faiths, homosexual practice is not morally acceptable, and deep offence may be caused to them if the subject is not handled with sensitivity by teachers if discussed in the classroom.[67]

This statement can confidently be interpreted as not in any sense prohibiting the inclusion of the topic of homosexuality within sex education – no more than other controversial issues, including contraception or abortion;[68] and the Circular goes on to emphasise the importance of including the topic of AIDS and other sexually transmitted diseases which may raise some aspects of homosexual (as well as heterosexual) behaviour. But the interpretation of the first sentence of the statement is nonetheless likely to give rise to considerable difficulty for governors in formulating their policy statements, and for teachers in implementing them. Most would readily agree that it would be wholly wrong to 'encourage homosexual experimentation by pupils', though this would also be true of any encouragement of heterosexual 'experimentation'. The concept of presenting homosexual behaviour as 'the norm' is obscure, in view of the fact that homosexuals are clearly in a numerical minority within our society as a whole. The *real* difficulty lies in the interpretation of the phrase 'advocates homosexual behaviour': in this context one would expect a considerable divergence of legitimate opinion as to what might constitute 'advocating' homosexual behaviour. This difficulty of interpretation has, indeed, been accentuated by further legislative intervention in the shape of section 28 of the Local Government Act 1988 which now stands alongside section 46 of the 1986 Act and the more informal government statement in its Circular. We must now turn to consider section 28 in the educational context.

Section 28 was tabled as an amendment to the Local Government Bill by a backbench Conservative MP, Mr David Wilshire, amid a considerable public outcry, but it was given government support and was thus ensured a safe passage and incorporation into the Act, though in a slightly amended form.[69] The introduction of the clause was a highly public reaction to widespread publicity that had been given to a very limited number of examples of the inclusion of some gay literature in materials regarded as suitable in restricted circumstances for use by pupils in a small number of LEAs, notably ILEA. A great deal of the publicity focused on *Jenny Lives With Eric and Martin* by Susanne Bosche,[70] which had been included in material made available in ILEA schools, though not as suitable for open library access but accessible only in exceptional circumstances by pupils and under adult guidance.[71] *Jenny Lives With Eric and Martin* is a book with simple text and photographs depicting the life of a young girl living with her father and his homosexual lover, portraying the relationships between them as happy and loving and promoting the view that her personal development was well-adjusted and balanced. Much attention also focused on *The Milkman's On His Way* by David Rees,[72] a novel relating the adolescent development and young adulthood of a homosexual youth and including some explicit sexual references in descriptions of his social encounters.[73]

The evidence as to the precise circulation and availability of these and other materials in schools is conflicting: what matters is that the press coverage of the issues was so extensive and, in some cases, so exaggerated as to give rise to a considerable public outcry. A *Times* leading article commented in relation to events in the London borough of Haringey that:

> When people of influence fail to stand against malignant causes, ordinary men and women will found their own resistance movement. That is what is now happening in the London borough of Haringey. A group of parents there is fighting against the extremists in charge of the local council who have been promoting 'positive images' of homosexuals in schools. It should provide no offence to adult homosexuals to argue that adolescent and younger children do not deserve to be subjected to what amounts to sexual propaganda.[74]

This article went on to describe the Haringey 'campaign' as 'designed to subject the school curriculum to homosexual proselytising'.[75] The education authority in Haringey has since gone on to publish the report of a working party on *Lesbian and Gay Issues in Education*[76] putting forward a range of recommendations as to the promotion of equality of respect and esteem for heterosexual and homosexual relationships, emphasising the diversity of types of family in which children within the borough live and stressing the need for accurate information and understanding. In a critical paragraph, the report concluded that:

> We strongly suggest that it would be unethical (and misguided) to attempt to persuade adolescents who are establishing their

> own identities that there is only one possible set of social, emotional and sexual experiences which are 'real'. We believe it is part of the task of the Education Service, in partnership with parents, to encourage young people to develop the confidence to manage their relationships with integrity, to establish friendships and other relationships *which have equality and respect as their basis*, and which are not exploitative. *That should apply whether they are between people of the same sex or different sexes.*[77]

This type of positive policy encouraging equality of respect and of treatment together with appreciation and accurate factual understanding of the existence of modes of living other than the traditional nuclear family is, however, exactly the type of 'positive images' policy which *could* conceivably be regarded now as falling foul of section 28 of the Local Government Act 1988. Section 28 provides that:

> (1) A local authority shall not
> (a) intentionally promote homosexuality or publish material with the intention of promoting homosexuality;
> (b) promote the teaching in any maintained school of the acceptability of homosexuality as a pretended family relationship.
>
> (2) Nothing in subsection (1) above shall be taken to prohibit the doing of anything for the purpose of treating or preventing the spread of disease.

Section 28 applies to local authorities generally, and much of the controversy generated by it related to local authority support for the arts and support for gay organisations or helplines such as the nationwide Gay Switchboard network. We are concerned here solely with the interpretation of section 28 in the context of the school curriculum. It would, indeed, be difficult to envisage a provision containing phraseology less susceptible to clear, precise and readily recognisable interpretation than that contained in section 28. The words which cause particular difficulties of interpretation are 'intentionally', 'promote', 'acceptability', and 'pretended family relationship'.

Before examining some of the difficulties involved in discerning any rational meaning in the section, however, it should be noted that it can certainly be argued that the section substantially fails to achieve its object of conditioning the contents of the school curriculum as it is expressly directed towards the activities of local authorities, which, as we have seen, have by virtue of sections 17 to 19 of the Education (No. 2) Act 1986 *only limited functions* in relation to the curriculum in general and sex education in particular. Although the LEA must formulate its policy on the curriculum under section 17, the governors must then go on under section 18 to consider the school's aims and to make any *modifications* they see fit to the LEA's stated policy; and, with respect to sex education, the governors must make a separate written statement of their policy, which may well be at variance with any statement on sex education in the LEA's policy formulation. Thus, in so far as in the exercise of their independent statutory functions, the *governors formulate* and the *teachers deliver* curricular policies which may be regarded as involving the 'intentional promotion of homosexuality' or teaching of the 'acceptability of homosexuality as a pretended family relationship', section 28 has no application as it is in its terms restrictive only of the *LEA's* activities and *not* those of the governors or teachers. This was stressed in a Circular issued by the Department of the Environment in May 1988 offering the Department's interpretation of the section:

> It specifically prohibits a local authority, in exercising its statutory functions, from promoting the teaching in any maintained school of the acceptability of homosexuality as a pretended family relationship. The effect of this will be that a local education authority will be prohibited from promoting homosexuality in the expression of its policy on sex education. Responsibility for sex education continues to rest with school governing bodies, by virtue of section 18 of the Education (No. 2) Act 1986. *Section 28 does not affect the activities of school governors, nor of teachers.*[78]

It is therefore debatable whether section 28 as presently drafted has any practical application to schools as it explicitly fails to impose any restrictions on either governors or teachers, the persons with the true statutory responsibility for formulating and delivering policy on sex education.

Despite this hesitation as to whether the section has any practical application to schools, it is nonetheless important to consider some aspects of its interpretation. The critical difficulty is to establish what type of curricular initiative might be regarded as prohibited. The word 'promote' in the first limb of the prohibition leaves quite unclear just what extent of active advocacy or positive portrayal of homosexuality would be required, except that the promotion must be 'intentional', a requirement which in this delicate context where all parties are acutely aware of the intensity of the controversy involved would appear to add little. In the second limb, the requirement of intention is omitted, and thus *any* promotion of the teaching of the 'acceptability' of homosexuality as 'a pretended family relationship' is prohibited: promotion here is again wholly undefined, and we also have to contend with the virtual impossibility of defining 'acceptability'. Still more obscure at a time when there are so many diverse forms of 'family' within our pluralist society is the phrase 'pretended family relationship'.

Before offering some examples of curricular initiatives which could possibly give rise to real interpretational problems, it should be noted that section 28 may also have the effect of inhibiting the *individual counselling* of pupils by teachers (as opposed to the taking of curricular initiatives). DES Circular 11/87[79] strongly emphasises the need for teachers not to trespass on the proper exercise of parental rights and responsibilities,[80] but there clearly could be cases in the context of pupils with doubts or problems relating to their sexual orientation where they are extremely reluctant to discuss the matter with parents and where responsible, caring and professional counselling by an experienced teacher might be appropriate and, arguably, very necessary.[81] This may be made an even more acute need in the light of the recognised health dangers of promiscuous sexual activity, be it homosexual or heterosexual.[82] No-one doubts that teachers must tread very warily when faced with difficulties of this nature, but section 28 may have an adversely inhibitory effect on personal counselling in this context which might otherwise have been appropriate and perhaps badly needed.

Difficulties of interpretation over curricular initiatives, as opposed to personal counselling, can perhaps best be illustrated by example. How far would each of the following curricular initiatives be prohibited under section 28? Let us assume that the pupils concerned are fifth-form pupils aged 16 years and that the teacher leading the discussion is at all times scrupulously careful to present the issues in a wholly objective, critical and pluralistic manner, above all avoiding any reference to his or her own sexual orientation:

(1) Discussion of well-documented professional psychiatric evidence of the statistical incidence of homosexuality;
(2) Discussion of the causes of homosexuality; whether it is an innate

factor latent within the human personality at birth, or whether it is acquired at some particular stage of human development; whether, if it is acquired rather than innate, people are in any way susceptible to influence or have any degree of personal choice in the matter;

(3) Discussion of the problem of discrimination in society on the grounds of race, religion, disability and sex and of the importance of tolerance and understanding of other groups generally, and the introduction of the idea that discrimination against homosexual people is no less an abuse of those basic principles of tolerance and understanding than other forms of discrimination more generally accepted;
(4) Discussion of whether homosexual practice (as opposed to the state of homosexuality) should be regarded as necessarily sinful where based on a loving, monogamous relationship;
(5) Discussion of whether loving, monogamous homosexual relationships should be regarded as forming no less valid a type of lifestyle than loving, monogamous heterosexual relationships;
(6) Discussion of whether loving, monogamous homosexual couples should be permitted to foster or adopt children;
(7) Discussion of whether homosexual females should be permitted artificial insemination by a donor.

These examples provide a range of possible curricular initiatives which conceivably *could* be regarded as prohibited by section 28, but, in the absence of authoritative legal guidance by a series of judicial decisions, nothing more than a speculative and highly subjective view could be offered. No such direct legal challenge in the courts has occurred at the time of writing, and, indeed, it may well be improbable that such a challenge will be brought in the courts.[83] It may in practice be that a complaint to a locally established complaints body under section 23 of the Education Reform Act would be more probable. However, if a judicial remedy were sought, the appropriate mode of challenge would be by way of judicial review in the High Court of the action or decision of the LEA concerned in formulating a curricular policy statement under section 17 of the 1986 Act: as we have seen, this challenge would be essentially misdirected. No application for judicial review based on non-compliance with section 28 would succeed against a governing body (still less a headteacher). In essence, the section is practically unenforceable in the courts, but it would be wholly wrong to underestimate its consequences in terms of practice. It is likely to have a substantial inhibitory effect on both governing bodies and on teachers through the fear of adverse criticism and publicity in the event of any controversial curricular initiative being adopted. In the case of teachers, that fear could turn to reality through their status as employees of their LEA and the possibility that they could be subject to disciplinary action. It is, indeed, its substantially unquantifiable inhibitory effect which is perhaps the most insidious aspect of section 28 in the educational context, rather than any real likelihood of judicial review. In the case of local authority activity outside the educational sphere, this inhibitory effect is coupled with a rather greater likelihood of legal challenge, though there too the problem of interpretation faced by the court would be enormous. In whichever sphere the political reality is that the ultimate decision as to interpretation would be vested in the court, comprising one or more judges representative of no-one, rather than in the elected representatives of the local population on the local authority.

The establishment of the national curriculum and the massive centralisation of power in the hands of the Secretary of State

It has already been noted in the section on 'Pressure for change' above that there had by 1979 already emerged some degree of consensus about the desirability of establishing an 'agreed' or 'core' or 'national' curriculum, but few could have envisaged at that date the scale of the centralisation of power in the hands of the Secretary of State and the level of precision with which its contents would be elaborated that has now emerged under sections 1 to 25 of the Education Reform Act 1988. A considerable transformation in the government's attitude took place between taking office in 1979 and the introduction of the Education Reform Bill in November 1987: this transformation is evident from the words of the then Secretary of State for Education and Science in 1982 in his Department's response to a report by the Parliamentary Select Committee on Education, Science and the Arts in which the Select Committee had put forward a recommendation favouring a nationally agreed minimum standard of provision in schools in terms of both facilities and of substantive educational content. The Secretary of State responded as follows:

> In the Government's view, the provisions of the 1944 Act on

> schools are based on a carefully judged division of powers and duties between the Secretary of State; the local education authorities; school governors, heads and teachers; and parents; and the Government believe that the terms of this recommendation conflict with that allocation of responsibilities. The Committee appears to take 'a nationally agreed guaranteed provision' as embracing a national minimum standard for both the provision of educational facilities, and for coverage of the curriculum. That concept seems to the Government to be alien to the variety of locally-determined provision which Parliament envisaged for England and Wales in the 1944 Act; *and to give the Secretary of State additional powers to prescribe curricular provision in detail would be an undesirable shift in a well-tried and well-understood distribution of functions.*[84]

This loyal declaration of adherence to the distribution of functions under the 1944 Act and apparent reluctance to accept centralisation of powers over curricular provision could hardly contrast more sharply with the Conservative government's subsequent conversion to extreme centralisation of curricular planning. That conversion may well have been brought about by a marked growth in political tension between central government and local authorities over a whole range of governmental functions and a realisation that, through the establishment of a national curriculum, there was a heaven-sent opportunity further to erode LEA functions. These considerations arise largely out of the increasingly polarised political relations which developed between the government and many Labour-controlled LEAs during the 1980s; but the government appears also to have been converted on educational grounds to the desirability of achieving consensus on the aims and content of the curriculum. Perhaps the most obvious manifestation of this conversion came in an important White Paper in 1985, *Better Schools*,[85] in which the government sought to set out a programme for the establishment of a clearer consensus over the objectives and content of the curriculum and for reform of the system of examinations and assessment. By 1987 in its Consultation Document, *The National Curriculum 5–16*,[86] one of a series of consultation papers preceding the Education Reform Bill, the government reported its view that 'a substantial measure of agreement has already been achieved'.[87] It continued:

> 5. Many LEAs and schools have made important advances towards achieving a good curriculum for pupils aged 5–16,

> which offers progression, continuity and coherence between its different stages. There is much agreement too about the subjects which should be included in the secular curriculum for 5–16 year olds; and valuable progress has been made towards securing agreement about the objectives and content of particular subjects.
>
> 6. But progress has been variable, uncertain and often slow. Improvements have been made, some standards of attainment have risen. But some improvement is not enough. We must raise standards consistently, and at least as quickly as they are rising in competitor countries.[88]

Accordingly it proposed the establishment, with the fundamental underlying purpose of raising standards, of a national curriculum – based on statute, not merely on guidance and exhortation – but which the government stressed would operate as 'a framework not a straitjacket', a framework which would leave room for 'the imaginative application of professional skills at all levels, within a statutory framework which sets clear objectives'.[89] The government went on to stress that it

> intends that legislation should leave full scope for professional judgment and for schools to organise how the curriculum is delivered in the way best suited to the ages, circumstances, needs and abilities of the children in each classroom . . . . There must be space to accommodate the enterprise of teachers, offering them sufficient flexibility in the choice of content to adapt what they teach to the needs of the individual pupil, to try out and develop new approaches, and to develop in pupils those personal qualities which cannot be written into a programme of study or attainment target.[90]

It is the gulf between this emphasis on room for manoeuvre in terms of the exercise of professional discretion and the application of professional expertise as stated emphatically in the Consultation Document, and the actuality of what has subsequently emerged in the Education Reform Act, as elaborated by the curricular Orders and the supporting documents referred to in those Orders, that has been at the heart of the controversy over the implementation of the national curriculum. As has already been noted, there had been a fair measure of progress towards developing curricular consensus under the Callaghan government up to 1979; the Thatcher government's own

White Paper, *Better Schools*,[91] noted evidence of further progress towards such consensus; and many educationalists would not have been averse to the introduction of a statutorily based national curriculum which was *balanced* by an appropriate degree of flexibility, which emphatically supported the importance of genuine involvement by LEAs and professional organisations at all formative stages, and which fully respected the professional expertise of the teaching profession. What, however, in the event was presented to Parliament, with an astonishingly brief consultation period,[92] and pushed through Parliament by use of the government's considerable majority[93] in the Commons,[94] was a statutory basis for a major shift in the balance of decision-making power over the secular curriculum from local to central government. And this has led the way to curricular prescription by the centre at a level of precision few outside government circles would have contemplated. Any view that the national curriculum as it has emerged is no more than a statutory endorsement and implementation of the consensus which had emerged over the curriculum during the previous 10 years or so, and thus a welcome, timely and uncontroversial tidying-up measure bringing our practice more into conformity with many of our European partners, is essentially flawed. It is, rather, a massive exercise in centralisation of power and a serious undermining of the role of the LEAs and the professional autonomy of teachers.

Section 1 of the Education Reform Act imposes a basic duty in respect of all maintained schools[95] upon the Secretary of State, LEAs, school governors and headteachers to exercise their functions 'with a view to securing that the requirements of the national curriculum are met'.[96] The curriculum must be 'balanced and broadly based' and must promote the 'spiritual, moral, cultural, mental and physical development of pupils at the school and of society' and prepare such pupils 'for the opportunities, responsibilities and experiences of adult life'.[97] These wide aspirations are perhaps of limited practical significance, but the Act goes on to spell out more explicit requirements in sections 2 and 3. There are two essential curricular components: first, provision for religious education and worship for all registered pupils *irrespective of age*; and second, for pupils *of compulsory school age*, a secular curriculum which meets stated requirements. Religious education and worship (with which this book is not concerned) are thus given a distinctly high profile. The stated requirements for the secular curriculum are that it shall include as a minimum the listed core and other foundation subjects, and in respect of each of these subjects it shall accord with specified 'attainment targets', 'programmes of study' and 'assessment arrangements'.[98]

The *core* subjects are mathematics, English and science (and Welsh in the case of Welsh-speaking schools in Wales).[99] The *other foundation* subjects are history, geography, technology, music, art and physical education; for children aged 12 and over, a modern foreign language; and Welsh in the case of non-Welsh-speaking schools in Wales.[100] For each of these core and other foundation subjects, the Secretary of State was placed under a duty to establish a 'complete' national curriculum as soon as reasonably practicable, and to revise it whenever he considered it necessary or expedient;[101] and to that end he was empowered to specify by Order for each listed subject such *attainment targets, programmes of study and assessment arrangements* as he considered appropriate.[102] Each of these would be geared to four age ranges or *key stages* – 5 to 7, 8 to 11, 12 to 14, and 15 to 16 years.[103] The *attainment targets* would specify the 'knowledge, skills and understanding which pupils of different abilities and maturities are expected to have by the end of each key stage'. The *programmes of study* would specify the 'matters, skills and processes which are required to be taught to pupils of different abilities and maturities during each key stage'. And the *assessment arrangements* would specify the 'arrangements for assessing pupils at or near the end of each key stage for the purpose of ascertaining what they have achieved in relation to the attainment targets for that stage'.[104]

The procedure for promulgating Orders specifying attainment targets and programmes of study (but not assessment arrangements) involves referral of the proposals to a new body corporate, the National Curriculum Council (or the Curriculum Council for Wales).[105] The Council comprises between 10 and 15 members, *all appointed by the Secretary of State*,[106] and has a wide remit to keep all aspects of the curriculum for maintained schools under review and to offer advice to the Secretary of State either at his request or of its own motion, and to conduct programmes of research and development.[107] A parallel body, the School Examinations and Assessment Council, has been established with a similar role in the context of examinations and assessment.[108] *Again, all members are appointed by the Secretary of State.*[109] The *dominant position* of the Secretary of State is further emphasised by the requirement that each Council in exercising its functions shall 'comply with any directions given, and . . . act in accordance with any plans approved, by the Secretary of State'.[110]

In respect of promulgating attainment targets and programmes of study, the National Curriculum Council has an explicit statutory role, in addition to its broader reviewing function already mentioned: formal 'proposals' are submitted by the Secretary of State to the Council,[111] and the Council is obliged to consult LEA associations, bodies representing the interests of school governors and school teachers, and any others it considers desirable to consult[112] before reporting its conclusions back to the Secretary of State.[113] The Secretary of State then publishes the draft Order, together with a reasoned statement in the event of his departing from the Council's recommendations.[114] After the elapse of one month for further representations, the Secretary of State may make the Order, with or without modifications.[115]

In practice the Secretary of State has superimposed upon this procedure a further and wholly non-statutory stage – the initial drawing up of 'proposals' for reference to the Council by *subject working groups*. It is apparent that *this initial stage is critical to the whole process*, and successive Secretaries of State have not hesitated to exert their influence over the fruits of the working group deliberations either before their formal submission to the Council under section 20 or while under consideration by the Council. For instance, greater emphasis on basic skills of multiplication and division was incorporated by the Council into its mathematics consultation paper against the initial recommendations of the mathematics working group;[116] and the Secretary of State sought greater emphasis on reading and writing skills for 11-year-olds than initially suggested by the working group on English.[117] Perhaps the most celebrated clash related to the recommendations of the history working group, chaired by Commander Michael Saunders Watson, which had placed a good deal of emphasis on the acquisition of skills and had argued that acquisition of purely factual knowledge of events and dates should play a less prominent part. This more progressive view of historical study, however, ran counter to the more traditional views of the Prime Minister and the Secretary of State, then Mrs Thatcher and Mr John MacGregor, and the History Curriculum Association. Mr MacGregor *decided* that the traditionalist view should prevail,[118] and this indeed was subsequently endorsed by the National Curriculum Council.[119]

The very fact that Mr MacGregor's and the Prime Minister's view prevailed in this way over the reasoned recommendations of the history working group illustrates graphically the dominance in this process of the Secretary of State. What was perhaps surprising was that his working party had produced recommendations so far out of line with the Secretary of State's views, given that the working groups are purely informal, non-statutory bodies (they appear nowhere in the Education Reform Act) appointed purely by the Secretary of State as individuals and representative of no-one. What was not surprising was that the Secretary of State could change the emphasis and content of the proposals sent up to the National Curriculum Council for formal statutory consideration. And, even if the Ministerially nominated Council should see fit to refashion proposals submitted to it by the Secretary of State in a way which the Secretary of State finds unpalatable, section 20(5) permits the Minister to depart from the Council's recommendations, although he must publish a statement of his reasons along with his draft Order in this event.

In this entire process – both at the non-statutory working group stage and the subsequent statutory stages – LEAs and the teachers' associations have a negligible role: the Council must give 'such associations of local education authorities . . . as appear to it to be concerned' a 'reasonable opportunity of submitting evidence and representations as to the issues arising';[120] and it must afford teachers' representative bodies a similar opportunity. Beyond this, the process is entirely centralised in the hands of the Secretary of State and his nominees on the Council. Closely parallel criticisms as to the absence of formal statutory involvement on the part of LEAs and teachers' associations may be made in respect of the promulgation by the School Examinations and Assessment Council of the detailed arrangements for the assessment of children at each key stage.[121]

The relegation of LEAs, governors and teachers to the curricular sidelines is, however, not absolute: LEAs, governors and headteachers will still have a formulatory role to play in respect of the curriculum by virtue of their duty to formulate and, in the case of headteachers, implement, curricular policies under the Education (No. 2) Act 1986,[122] but these must, of course, be consistent with their overriding duty under section 1 of the 1988 Act to satisfy the requirements of the national curriculum. Their duty so to comply with the national curriculum will be underlined by extensive requirements to publish information concerning the curriculum, including assessment results, at individual schools;[123] and by the requirement (which we have already noted in the context of political and sex education) that every LEA establish a complaints machinery to consider complaints that either the LEA or school governors have acted unreasonably or in breach of a statutory duty in relation to a curricular matter.[124] Further complaint may then be made to the Secretary of State under section 68 or 99 of the Education Act 1944.

The outcome of these new statutory arrangements for the national curriculum has now been a flow of Orders – which are themselves extremely brief and substantially uninformative – accompanied, however, by formal 'Documents' referred to in the Orders, and given legal force by them, in which the real substance of the prescription of the attainment targets and programmes of study is to be found.[125] And these are accompanied by extensive non-statutory guidance. The level of detail in the formal 'Documents' accompanying the Orders is such that one is driven to view with considerable scepticism the government's assertion that the national curriculum should be a 'framework not a straitjacket',[126] and to wonder what room remains for the exercise of professional judgment and expertise on the part of the teachers who have been so manifestly excluded from the formative processes. It comes as little surprise that the content of the proposed curriculum as well as the assessment arrangements – particularly at key stage 7 – have been the target of a mass of criticism on the basis of excessively detailed prescription, inflexibility, impracticality and, very importantly, inadequacy of resources for their implementation. This criticism has come from many informed sources, including no less a figure than HM Senior Chief Inspector of Schools in his Annual Report for 1988–1989:

> 24. There is a risk that some aspects of the implementation of the NC (National Curriculum) and its related assessment and reporting may undermine teachers' job satisfaction and morale. That risk arises not from the amount of work and the pressing timescales involved, but from too much detail and prescription in external instructions and guidance, and an undue insistence upon cross-checking everything that teachers are called upon to do.
>
> 25. If actually carrying out assessments, recording and reporting outcomes and accounting for what has been done do turn out to be overly prescriptive and inquisitorial, not only will the quality of teaching and learning be adversely affected, but the competence, professionalism and creativity of the teaching force may be undermined. Ultimately, the effective implementation of the ERA (Education Reform Act) will depend upon the work of teachers who are trusted to use their pedagogical skills and experience in the interests of their pupils and the nation,

> with a minimum of external checks and balances, but who are properly accountable for what they do. Too much prescription and too detailed an external scrutiny of the work of teachers will lead to impossible work loads, bureaucratic inflexibility, and a de-skilled teaching force.[127]

At the time of writing, the outcome of these pressures for modification is hard to predict, although a measure of respite was announced during 1990 by the then Secretary of State, Mr John MacGregor. In August 1990, Mr MacGregor announced that he was asking the National Curriculum Council to examine the possibility that pupils might be permitted to drop art, music and physical education, and possibly also history and geography, at 14 years of age. This he justified on the basis of his wish to retain flexibility in order for such optional subjects as economics, classics and further modern languages to be realistically available. He also hinted at this stage, in the light of widespread complaints from primary school teachers who had been involved in pilot studies of testing during the preceding school year, that the testing programme for seven-year-old pupils would be reduced in volume and complexity.[128] The simplification of the process of testing of seven-year-olds was subsequently confirmed by Mr MacGregor in October 1990: the tests would be confined to the basics of English, mathematics and science, and would be substantially reduced in terms of the amount of time they would involve.[129] Early in January 1991, Mr MacGregor's successor as Education Secretary, Mr Kenneth Clarke, confirmed that pupils would be required to study only English, mathematics and science up to the age of 16, while pupils would from the age of 14 be permitted to drop some other foundation subjects in order to achieve greater flexibility of choice between 14 and 16. Pupils would still be required to study technology and a modern foreign language to 16, but short courses combined with other subjects and examined by vocational bodies would now be offered in addition to GCSE courses.[130] And in May 1991 Mr Clarke announced a further streamlining of testing in Mathematics and Science.[131] As was to be expected, much political capital has been made by the Opposition out of these proposed modifications. They have been hailed as a major dismantling of the national curriculum and as an overt recognition that it was seriously ill-thought-out, grossly inflexible, grossly over-prescriptive, and involved the imposition of an impossible burden on the teaching profession without a substantial injection of extra resources – mainly in the form of appropriately paid teachers. This view is amply borne out by the considerable disruption to the testing of seven-year-old children during the summer term of 1991. It is almost certainly true that the current proposals, even given the modifications proposed by Mr MacGregor and Mr Clarke, are seriously out of balance and in need of carefully considered modification in addition to significant extra funding. There are, however, serious educational dangers in permitting particular subjects to be dropped at a given – and somewhat arbitrary – age.[132] Indeed, such Ministerial announcements of modifications as recently witnessed graphically illustrate the *institutional* shambles established by the Education Reform Act for the formulation of the national curriculum: a grossly over-centralised process where all the formative exercises are carried out by a limited number of hand-picked Ministerial nominees representative of no-one, and involving seriously inadequate consultation, particularly with LEAs and teachers' associations, was always likely to produce a prescription which would lack balance. A fundamental reconsideration not only of the prescription, but also of the institutional processes by which it is produced, is needed.

CONCLUSIONS

We have witnessed during the past decade and more a radical transformation in the legal regulation of the contents of the secular curriculum, from arguably the most non-centrally-prescriptive and discretionary to arguably one of the most highly centralised and inflexible; we have seen an attempt by the government through reforming the composition and functions of school governing bodies to instil a greater element of consumer involvement and control over the running of schools – including curricular decision-making – in the name of accountability and raising standards, but arguably with the less explicit but nonetheless important aim of imposing a degree of restraint on certain curricular policies pursued by some LEAs which the government found unpalatable; and we have seen an attempt at direct legislative intervention over the content of political and sex education.

Given the extent and sensitivity of individual concern with the contents of the curriculum, emphasised by Article 2 of the First Protocol to the European Convention, it is clearly vital that the process of formulation should be based upon an institutional framework in which the individual citizen – represented here essentially by parents – has an effectively articulated voice. This is especially important in relation to the curriculum, as it is widely recognised that it would be impracticable and possibly undesirable to meet each individual's curricular preferences with absolute precision: this must clearly be so in any large-scale public provision of compulsory education, and, indeed, it is clearly reflected in the absence of effective individual remedies for parental complaints in relation to the curriculum. As we have seen in the context of sex education, there exists no legal right of parental withdrawal of their children on the basis that the parents object to aspects of the sex education curriculum in the school concerned (though governors would have a *discretion* to permit withdrawal), and this absence of the right of withdrawal indeed applies throughout the secular curriculum.[133] There is no parallel to the right of withdrawal that exists in relation to religious education. Having entrusted their children's education to the state, parents are not permitted to pick and choose between aspects of the curriculum available: they must accept all or none. The right of parents to challenge curricular provision through making complaints under section 23 of the Education Reform Act 1988 remains untested at the time of writing, but it is very doubtful whether this would operate as an effective remedy for aggrieved parents on a wide-scale basis.[134] And judicial control in this context, as we have seen in relation to section 28 of the Local Government Act 1988, is a remote prospect.

It is this very absence of effective individual *control* which makes it all the more important that the individual should be effectively incorporated on a representative basis into the institutional process *at the formative stages*. Furthermore, those participating in that institutional process require the guidance of a range of fundamental principles which should be reflected in curricular decisions. The European Court of Human Rights has sought to elaborate some guiding principles through its interpretation of Article 2 of the First Protocol, notably the requirement of objective, critical and pluralistic presentation and treatment of issues; and the government has sought to establish more substantial parental representation on governing bodies in the Education (No. 2) Act 1986, while giving them somewhat stronger curricular responsibility. For the government to have gone further in terms of specific legislation on political and sex education was essentially unnecessary: effective representation at the formative stages, the formative body being guided by appropriate and accepted principles, should have been enough. The effect of the further specific legislation on political and sex education – particularly section 28 of the Local Government Act 1988 concerning homosexuality – is likely to be an undesirable inhibition upon proper, informed and constructive discussion of these important issues in schools, and possibly also upon the individual counselling of pupils.

Effective individual parental representation, however, presupposes the existence of an effective role for LEAs, governors and teachers in formulating the school curriculum. The reformed composition and functions of governors brought about by the 1986 Act have no real meaning unless there truly is such a role. The advent of the national curriculum under the Education Reform Act 1988, however, casts considerable doubt upon the continuing existence of any such genuine role for governors or LEAs in this context: through an excessive centralisation of power in the hands of the Secretary of State it has not only emasculated LEA functions in respect of the curriculum but it has also had the effect of undermining the 1986 Act's attempts to achieve a degree of effective representation and participation on the part of the individual. It is highly regrettable that we see two important statutes enacted by the same government within two years of each other yet pulling in such radically different directions from the viewpoint of individual involvement.

4

EXPENDITURE CONSTRAINTS AND THE LEGAL SUFFICIENCY OF EDUCATION

INTRODUCTION

In chapter 3 we examined aspects of the secular curriculum, including the introduction of a national curriculum, heralded by the government as a major force behind raising standards in education. It is, however, abundantly clear that these aspirations for raising standards, and indeed, even the capacity of LEAs, governors and headteachers to meet their legal obligations under the national curriculum provisions of the Education Reform Act 1988, may be seriously undermined by the impact of expenditure constraints on schools. It is quite possible to envisage schools being unable to meet their commitments to pupils of compulsory school age across the full range of core and other foundation subjects as a consequence of their being unable over a substantial period to fill teaching staff vacancies; or unable to afford the relevant text books or other equipment needed to meet the requirements of the prescribed programmes of study. It is quite possible that aggrieved parents will in time seek to activate the enforcement mechanism in section 23 of the Education Reform Act 1988 concerning the national curriculum, although the likelihood of subsequent intervention by the Secretary of State under section 68 or 99 of the 1944 Act in the context of shortcomings brought about by centrally imposed expenditure constraints is remote.

Of wider significance than failure to meet the requirements of the national curriculum is the possibility that expenditure constraints may so lower the quality of education in some LEAs or in some schools as to raise the question as to whether the pupils concerned are truly being provided with what may properly be regarded as a legally 'sufficient education' at all. This would, if substantiated, amount to a failure by the state to meet its essential obligation under our public system of education to provide for all pupils a sufficient education, and would amount to a serious denial of a basic human right – the right to a fully sufficient education. This denial of the right to education may come about in many different ways, some being more obviously educational than others: the non-availability of properly qualified teachers or lack of appropriate text books or other equipment are clearly factors with directly educational consequences; but school buildings which are crumbling through inadequate maintenance and repair, though less obviously an educational factor, may nonetheless contribute significantly to the type of dispiriting and hopeless environment which seriously undermines children's educational attainments and may quite properly be regarded as contributing to the denial of legally sufficient education.

Individual concern over the legal sufficiency of education may be expressed in terms similar to concern over the substance of the secular curriculum, discussed in chapter 3. Clearly it is based on the central importance of the educational experience to a child's entire development. As a fundamental right recognised and given legal force by the European Convention on Human Rights, however, it may be categorised rather differently: in relation to the contents of the secular curriculum, we focused on the *second* sentence of Article 2 of the First Protocol – the requirement that the state should respect parents' religious and philosophical convictions. In relation to legal sufficiency the argument is, rather, as to the denial by the state of the very right to education itself – the *first* sentence of Article 2 – although plainly there is likely to be an overlap between the two, and it is not possible to draw any clear-cut line between the right to education and the right to respect for one's views as to its content. In terms of the European Convention, though, our focus here is rather on the first sentence – 'No person shall be denied the right to education'.

In this chapter we will first examine some of the evidence as to defective provision of education in England and Wales, notably by reference to recent reports from Her Majesty's Inspectorate of Schools; and we will then go on to establish the legal basis for challenging allegedly insufficient provision of education by the state and examine the several legal mechanisms that may be available for this purpose and some attempts already made to invoke such mechanisms of challenge.

EVIDENCE OF INSUFFICIENT PROVISION

Throughout the past decade and more there has been growing evidence of severe financial strain being suffered by LEAs, and this has in turn been reflected in actual provision at the level of individual schools. The most authoritative evidence of this is to be found in the annual reports of HMI on the effects throughout England of LEA expenditure policies (HMI *Effects Reports*), published from 1980/81 to 1986/87, which have been superseded by the annual reports of HM Senior Chief Inspector of Schools from 1987/88.[1] HMI have also produced numerous reports based on their inspections of individual schools, and between autumn 1988 and spring 1990 carried out an extended programme of inspection visits to inner London schools – where the problems are widely perceived to be at their most acute – as part of the process of advising the Secretary of State as to the progress of the transfer of educational responsibilities from ILEA to the 13 new inner London LEAs under the Education Reform Act. This programme gave rise to the publication of a disturbing report on provision in schools in the London borough of Hackney[2] which will be examined below. And the question of the supply of teachers has recently been given widespread publicity in the context of children in inner London boroughs having to be sent home through there being insufficient teachers available to teach them, and has also come under the scrutiny of the House of Commons Select Committee on Education, Science and the Arts.[3]

The 1988–89 annual report by HM Senior Chief Inspector,[4] based on inspection visits throughout England during 1988–89, drew an overall picture of an education service in which 'what is done is of reasonable quality or better',[5] but nonetheless went on to stress specific issues which gave rise to 'serious concern'.[6] Three significant areas of concern isolated by the report were educational standards; standards of accommodation, equipment and materials; and the supply of teachers. It categorised about one-third of educational standards across all levels of schooling (and further education) as 'good or very good', but continued in terms which gave no grounds for complacency:

> That overarching picture must not hide the fact that there are serious problems of low and under-achievement; of poor teaching, and of inadequate provision. It is particularly troubling that in schools some 30% . . . of what HMI saw was

> judged poor or very poor. Those figures, if replicated throughout the system, represent a large number of pupils and students getting a raw deal. Furthermore, and sadly, less able pupils and students are much more likely to experience the poor and the shoddy than are the more able: a worryingly persistent feature of English education at all levels.[7]

In *primary* schools,[8] the report found that basic skills work in mathematics and English was 'satisfactory or better' in some 90 per cent of cases, but that that picture 'deteriorates markedly' when more advanced language and mathematical skills and applications are considered. It found the quality and range of work in science to be a problem, and that many primary schools have 'hardly made a start on technology, have little idea how to do so, and are ill-prepared in terms of teacher competence, accommodation and equipment and materials.'[9] History and geography, it found, 'hardly exist' in many primary schools, and teaching and learning in art, music, drama and physical education were found often to be 'shallow'.[10] In the *secondary* sector,[11] it found that some of the same areas gave rise to cause for concern: in mathematics, science and English, the teaching and learning of more advanced and applied understanding and skills were poor; and technology was regarded as a 'serious problem', being judged 'inadequate' in two-fifths of the secondary schools visited.[12]

In the context of accommodation, equipment and materials, the report found provision at primary school level to be reasonably satisfactory, though it identified an increasingly pressing need for more suitable accommodation and equipment for practical and applied work in science and technology that would in the coming years be required under the national curriculum.[13] In the secondary sector, however, the state of school buildings was regarded as problematic: some two-thirds of the schools inspected were judged to have unsuitable accommodation, and in about half of those the problems were described as 'serious and adversely affecting the quality of the work in one way or another'.[14] This was compounded by a lack of suitable specialist accommodation and equipment for science, home economics and craft, design and technology, and shortcomings in the availability of books brought about in part by the fact that book price inflation was in many cases outstripping rises in capitation allowances.[15]

A third major issue identified by the report was that of teacher supply where the report referred to 'complex and worsening problems'.[16] Many factors were seen as having a bearing on this issue, including demography, recruitment problems in certain parts of the country and actual shortages of certain kinds of expertise. These problems were in no sense novel. The report found that:

> There have been shortages of qualified science, CDT, modern languages, mathematics, music, religious education (RE) and even English teachers for many years. The system has got by by ignoring them; using teachers poorly qualified or not qualified to teach the subject in question; or more commonly, by simply not offering some subjects to all pupils, or not offering some subjects at all in some schools.[17]

These shortages would, furthermore, inevitably in many cases be exacerbated – though not initially be caused – by the implementation of the national curriculum, which would require the injection of extra teacher resources. The possibility of failing to meet the requirements of the national curriculum as a direct consequence of the inadequate supply of suitably qualified teachers was real:

> In whatever specific ways shortages or recruitment problems are tackled, a crucial difference between now and the past may turn out to be that there are now national, statutory requirements about the curriculum for all pupils during their compulsory schooling. Perhaps that will concentrate minds on reducing teacher shortages and minimising recruitment difficulties.[18]

The Senior Chief Inspector's report reflected findings based on inspections conducted throughout England, and thus inevitably involved wide generalisations and failed to reflect the level of difficulty faced within certain areas – notably in inner London – where the problems are often at their most acute. Inner London boroughs are not unique, but there is wide agreement that their problems are severe, and they were graphically described in the HMI special report, *Schools In Hackney: Some Issues* in 1990.[19] In terms of its socio-economic context, the HMI report described Hackney as an inner-city borough 'high on all the indices of deprivation',[20] with extensive municipal estates comprising high-density, 'high-rise' dwellings with a multitude of social and economic problems. Some 20 per cent of the population were unemployed, and unemployment among the substantial ethnic minority population in the area was considerably above this figure. It found that over two-thirds of pupils in the borough came from groups whose families originated outside the UK, and one-tenth of Hackney pupils spoke a language other than English at home, and among these some 100 languages were represented. It also noted that several hundred children in the borough were living in bed and breakfast or other 'temporary' accommodation.[21]

In the *primary* sector, the report categorised some 42 per cent of classes as less than satisfactory (compared with an overall national rate of 30 per cent, as stated in the Senior Chief Inspector's report, discussed above). Although there was undoubtedly evidence of effective and constructive work in some classes, the report concluded that:

> In a large majority of primary classes in the Borough and over the curriculum as a whole, teachers expect far too little of their pupils. *They ask no more than that they should achieve a basic minimum standard in a limited range of skills. In a significant minority of classes effective learning has broken down.*[22]

In the *secondary* sector the picture was similar: the report found that some 40 per cent of lessons were 'less than satisfactory or poor', and 10 per cent 'displayed serious shortcomings'.[23] These shortcomings were reflected in public examination results, although the report was careful to qualify its findings in this context by the acknowledged fact that it is extremely difficult to draw conclusions from examination results as to the educational 'success' of a school, given the complexity of the relationship between educational achievement and socio-economic background. Nationally some 25 per cent of pupils entered for GCSE examinations in 1989 obtained five or more passes at the higher grades (A–C), but in the Hackney secondary schools visited the figures ranged from 7 to 13 per cent.[24]

In both primary and secondary schools a significant factor was found to be the standard of teaching accommodation and equipment. The report commented that:

> Over half the primary schools visited provide a dismal setting for teaching and learning; untidy classrooms, poorly organised resource rooms and a low standard of cleaning contribute to the shabby environment. In some schools the quality of facilities such as the toilets raises questions about the attitudes which are conveyed, consciously or unconsciously, to pupils by the school.[25]

Similar shortcomings were found in the premises of secondary schools.[26]

Of central importance, however, was the question of teacher supply: the report found that most Hackney schools were unable to recruit and retain sufficient teachers 'of any kind' and had even more difficulty in attracting teachers of the experience and quality required to teach effectively, given the difficulty of the conditions in the area.[27] Advertisements for posts frequently elicited no response at all. These problems were partly caused by the high cost of housing, expensive and inefficient public transport and the unattractive nature of some parts of the borough. Recruitment problems were, indeed, extremely hard to reverse as 'potential applicants are deterred by the constant turnover of teachers and the sorry procession of stop-gap supply teachers'.[28] There was also found to be a considerable reliance upon teachers from overseas. The report drew the depressing conclusion in the context of teacher supply and retention that:

> Some of the teachers who have remained in Hackney schools have given up the struggle; others face the day to day disappointment and disillusion of working in a system that is under great strain. Their hopelessness is demonstrated in the indifferent quality of lesson planning, preparation and pace, and sometimes in high levels of teacher absence. For a number of teachers who have stayed, somewhat reluctantly in such dispiriting circumstances, their endurance and survival have become more important than professional initiative.[29]

The overall picture in Hackney was thus one where the schools were

> at a low ebb and in need of a concerted effort to help them gain new enthusiasm and a spirit of optimism before present circumstances conspire to crush all hope for the future.[30]

This picture of depression, disillusionment and deprivation is very likely to be closely paralleled in other inner London boroughs, and, indeed, in many other inner-city areas across the country. The problem of teacher supply in particular has been widely publicised,[31] and was recognised by the House of Commons Education Select Committee in its report on *The Supply of Teachers for the 1990s*.[32] This report emphasised that the *overall* problem of teacher supply was not particularly acute, noting that vacancies in secondary schools in England in 1989 numbered just under 2,500 or 1.2 per cent of the relevant teacher force,[33] but that there was undoubtedly evidence of shortages *in certain regions* and in certain subjects. It reported a picture of high teacher wastage, vacancies and turnover in the London area: in London, it noted that some 24 per cent of newly qualified teachers leave within two years, and 42 per cent within five years.[34] And it concluded that the implications for the long-term stability and experience of the teaching force were serious, and that the evidence suggested that the shortages currently affecting London were beginning to spread to other areas.[35]

The most graphic evidence of the problem of inadequate teacher supply, was, however, perhaps to be found in the London borough of Tower Hamlets, where several hundreds of pupils were required to remain out of school altogether as a direct result of the inadequate supply of teaching staff.[36] These children were thus wholly denied access to a state school, bringing into sharp focus the legal obligations of LEAs to make available for every pupil in their area a sufficient education. In relation to deteriorating and depressing buildings, adverse staff–pupil ratios, the inadequate supply of up-to-date textbooks and suitable equipment and the availability of experienced teachers properly qualified in the subjects they are actually required to teach, assertions as to insufficiency of educational provision would rarely be clear-cut, as the line of division between sufficient and insufficient education involves a substantial element of evaluation and doubt. In relation, however, to actual exclusion from school, as in the case of some children in Tower Hamlets, there might be a strong expectation on the part of the parents concerned of some form of effective means of redress against the LEA concerned with a view to compelling the authority to carry out its legal obligations. In the next section we will go on to examine the possible legal basis for such parental challenge.

LEGAL BASIS FOR CHALLENGING SUFFICIENCY OF EDUCATION

The fundamental difficulty faced by parents seeking to challenge educational provision on the basis of legal insufficiency is one of definition and evidence. It is true that we now have in the Education Reform Act 1988, and the delegated legislation promulgated under it, a defined national curriculum, and it is possible to envisage recourse to section 23 of the 1988 Act[37] by aggrieved parents where an LEA or governors fail to meet their obligations in that context, followed perhaps by subsequent complaint to the Secretary of State, although judicial enforcement is less likely. It is very likely that expenditure constraints may be one of the factors which bring about defective compliance with the requirements of the national curriculum, and thus it is quite possible that parents aggrieved over the consequences of expenditure constraints may use section 23 as an additional or an alternative means of recourse to those considered below. In the context of expenditure constraints and their educational consequences, however, the assertion by aggrieved individuals is often more basic than merely failure to meet the national curriculum: it is that the LEA is failing to meet its essential obligation under section 8 of the Education Act 1944 to provide 'sufficient schools'. It should be noted that the duty imposed by section 8 is upon the LEA and *not* the governors of individual schools: the delegation of school budgets and of school management, including the appointment and dismissal of staff and of extensive decision-making powers in relation to expenditure, under the Education Reform Act 1988,[38] will not relieve LEAs of their obligations under section 8, and thus any legal action based upon defective compliance with section 8 would have to be directed against the LEA concerned and not against the governors of an individual school or schools. Section 8 requires every LEA to secure the availability for its area of sufficient primary and secondary schools, and it is provided that:

> the schools available for an area shall not be deemed to be sufficient unless they are sufficient in number, character and equipment to afford for all pupils opportunities for education offering such variety of instruction and training as may be desirable in view of their different ages, abilities and aptitudes, and of the different periods for which they may be expected to remain at school, including practical instruction and training appropriate to their respective needs.

We will examine below the extent to which the duty in section 8 to provide sufficient schools is enforceable in the courts at the instance of individuals, but for the moment it should be noted that it is a very general duty involving a wide measure of discretion on the part of the providing LEA and that the phraseology of the section is extremely imprecise. Perhaps the most imprecise phrase of all is the word 'education' itself: before the introduction of the national curriculum, statute law did not seek to lay down with any level of precision what the content of secular education in maintained schools should be, beyond the largely unhelpful wording of section 8. This lack of any clear legal definition of education was illustrated in a legal challenge brought by a parent in 1981 against the decision of an LEA to impose charges for the provision of instrumental musical tuition in its schools: *R.* v. *Hereford and Worcester LEA, ex parte Jones.*[39] This was not a direct challenge to the legal sufficiency of education, but was nonetheless a legal challenge in a closely allied context. A parent of two children attending maintained schools in the area applied to the High Court for a declaration that the LEA was prohibited by section 61(1) of the Education Act 1944 from charging such fees. Section 61(1)[40] provided that no fees should be charged

> in respect of admission to any school maintained by a local education authority . . . or *in respect of the education provided* in any such school.[41]

While this appeared to be an absolute prohibition on charging fees, it was by no means conclusive, as it was open to the LEA to argue that instrumental music tuition was *not* part of *the education provided*, but was, rather, an optional extra and thus not caught by the prohibition in section 61(1). The critical issue for the court was thus the definition of 'education'. Mr Justice Forbes had no difficulty in finding that instrumental music tuition should indeed be regarded as falling within the legal definition of education:

> I have no doubt at all that practical tuition in playing an instrument is not only educative and part of education but is certainly something which an education authority is entitled to include in the curriculum if it wishes. I have no doubt that there are many education authorities who, in their particular situations, will do so. If it is possible for a pupil to get an A level as a performing musician, or an O level, that is a qualification towards which a school curriculum might well aim. For this purpose there seems no logical reason for distinguishing between an O level in physics and one in piano playing. I find no difficulty in coming to the conclusion that instrumental music tuition is capable of forming part of the curriculum of any school provided and maintained by local education authorities.[42]

Given that instrumental music tuition was thus unequivocally held to be a part of the education provided in the LEA's schools, it clearly could not be subject to the imposition of fees. On the other hand, the judge went on to hold that *whether to include instrumental music tuition within the curriculum* in its schools was itself a matter within the discretion of the LEA, subject always to the requirement that it must act within the legal bounds of reasonableness. This was because section 23 of the 1944 Act left the substantive content of the secular curriculum to LEAs for determination, subject to schools' articles of government.[43] Thus, an LEA might perhaps stray into the realms of unreasonableness by deciding to exclude music altogether from its curriculum; but to exclude instrumental tuition might be lawful. If, however, it did decide to provide it, then it fell clearly within the ambit of the word 'education' in section 61 and must therefore be provided free of charge.

Although from the point of view of the legality of charging fees for aspects of educational provision this case has now been overtaken by the Education Reform Act, it remains of considerable significance as an emphatic reminder that, subject now to the requirements of the national curriculum, LEAs (and governors) retain extensive discretion as to the substance of educational provision, and this may well serve to compound the difficulties faced by parents seeking to establish *legal insufficiency of education* based on the consequences of expenditure cuts.

THE MECHANISMS OF CHALLENGE

In the last section we looked at aspects of the legal basis upon which a challenge to sufficiency of education could be brought. We turn now to the legal mechanisms that could be used – first through complaint to the Secretary of State, and second through recourse to the courts.

Complaint to the Secretary of State

Aggrieved individuals might well seek to complain to the Secretary of State as to educational insufficiency,[44] arguing either that the LEA is acting in an unreasonable manner or is failing to meet its statutory duty under section 8 of the 1944 Act. The Secretary of State has a general power to issue directions to an LEA on the basis of his satisfaction that it is acting unreasonably, by virtue of section 68 of the 1944 Act; and he may issue a default order in the event of his satisfaction that an LEA is failing to comply with a statutory duty, by virtue of section 99 of the 1944 Act. Recourse to these mechanisms of challenge has, however, very rarely been successful in any context,[45] let alone in one as nebulous as the legal sufficiency of education where one would expect it to be extremely difficult to establish unreasonableness or default of statutory duty.

A parental action group in Northamptonshire, and the South West Association of the Confederation for the Advancement of State Education in Surrey, made complaints to the Secretary of State under sections 68 and 99 as far back as 1981 – at a time when LEAs were under severe centrally-imposed financial constraints, but these complaints were rejected outright by the Secretary of State with highly inadequate explanation of his reasoning.[46] In answer to the Northamptonshire complaint, the Secretary of State stated that he could intervene only in the event of a 'clear breach',[47] and there then followed a bland statement that:

> On the basis of the information provided in the complaint and in the authority's observations, the Secretary of State concludes that . . . the curriculum offered and the equipment employed in support of the curriculum, is not such as to lead him to be satisfied that the authority are in breach of their duty under section 8 of the Education Act 1944.[48]

The Secretary of State's response to the Surrey complaint was no more satisfactory, in terms either of his actual finding or of the explanation of his reasoning: in his decision letter he noted that the 1944 Act had laid down the standard of legal sufficiency in general terms, and that its interpretation involved 'a substantial element of judgment'.[49] He then stated that the process of interpretation involved the consideration of 'general factors including current educational practice in England', and he concluded – again in the form of a bland statement without reference to the detailed substance of the complaint – that he was not satisfied that the Surrey LEA was in breach of its statutory duty.[50]

The refusal of the Secretary of State to intervene in these cases comes as no surprise, not only for the obvious political reason that it was the central government that had instigated the expenditure constraints in the first place and was thus hardly likely to take an adverse view of economy measures at local level, but also because of the belief held by the DES that its power of intervention under sections 68 and 99 is an extremely restricted one – that they are *measures of last resort*. In evidence to the Select Committee on Education, Science and the Arts, when it was conducting an investigation into the secondary school curriculum and examinations, a Deputy Secretary in the DES expressed the view that the Secretary of State would have to be satisfied that there had been a 'clear breach' of statutory duty before intervening under section 99.[51] As an instance of a 'clear breach', he gave a comprehensive school which, as a matter of policy, offered no science and no modern languages for any of its pupils. (This would, of course, now constitute a clear breach of the LEA's obligations under the national curriculum, let alone section 8 of the 1944 Act.) He suggested, further, that the Secretary of State would have to take into account not only the provision of education in one particular school, but also provision in the LEA as a whole: thus, an LEA which decided not to offer any modern languages in a particular comprehensive school in an urban area where there were other schools in the area where such languages *were* taught (and which pupils who so wished could presumably attend), would be less likely to be in breach of section 8 than an LEA which 'systematically as a matter of policy' refused to offer any modern language in a rural secondary school serving a wide area.[52] The Secretary of State would, furthermore, take into account whether the LEA was *striving against adverse circumstances* to make the best provision possible – '*whether the school was trying*'.[53] And he took the view that it was most improbable that government economic policy imposing financial constraints on LEAs would ever force an authority into 'a position of possible illegality'.[54]

This restrictive view of the Secretary of State's power of intervention under section 99 accords, furthermore, with the interpretation by the Court of Appeal and the House of Lords in the *Tameside* case in 1976 in the context of section 68 intervention on the ground of the Secretary of State's satisfaction as to 'unreasonable' conduct by the LEA.[55] Lord Denning there emphasised that

> No-one can properly be labelled as being unreasonable unless he is not only wrong but unreasonably wrong, so wrong that no reasonable person could sensibly take that view.[56]

This is a classic statement of the extremely narrow legal test of unreasonableness which involves total loss of reason or rationality on the part of the authority whose actions are impugned – in this case the LEA whose educational provision is alleged to be legally insufficient – and clearly demonstrates how difficult it would be for the Secretary of State to issue an order to an LEA under section 68 (or 99 in relation to breach of duty). The Select Committee, however, took a very different view, adopting a far less restrictive definition of the Secretary of State's power of intervention:

> It appears to be the Department's view that sections 68 and 99 are dangerously punitive measures, difficult to enforce in the courts, and that they are measures of absolute last resort. We do not take that view. We see, rather, these sections of the 1944 Act as being part of the means by which the Secretary of State may discharge his duty 'to promote the education of the people' in the words of section 1 of the Act. We also believe that these provisions in the Act were designed, precisely, to avoid the necessity of parents taking their problems to the courts. This is both because litigation is inherently vexatious and expensive, but also because many of the issues that might arise could be of a specialist or technical character, and it would be better if the first source of redress were to be someone who might be expected to have specialist advice readily available.[57]

The narrow interpretation adopted by the DES (and by the courts in the *Tameside* case) implies that the curriculum of a school would have to be at 'a point near collapse'[58] before the Secretary of State could intervene. Accordingly the Select Committee recommended that these sections of the 1944 Act be amended to give the Secretary of State power to intervene in circumstances where a 'nationally agreed guaranteed provision' appeared to be at risk,[59] a recommendation which in a sense implied the establishment of at least an embryonic form of statutorily based national curriculum. This, however, the government at that time roundly rejected, along with any idea of establishing an exhaustive set of circumstances in which an LEA might be in breach of its duty under section 8, each case involving 'a substantial element of judgment'[60] and depending not only upon its own facts but upon general factors, including 'the spectrum of current education practice in England'.[61]

The government's position on the establishment of an agreed curriculum has, of course, radically altered, as we have seen in the previous chapter, and it is now possible to lodge complaints through the LEA's complaints machinery as to non-compliance with the national curriculum – and thereafter to complain to the Secretary of State under section 68 or 99. The likelihood, however, of successfully complaining to the Secretary of State under section 68 or 99 on the ground of legal insufficiency of education brought about through expenditure constraints remains nonetheless remote in the extreme. Aggrieved parents may have for this reason, after having failed to obtain satisfaction through complaint to the Secretary of State, to seek redress through challenge in the courts.

Challenge in the courts

Parents have on a limited number of occasions sought redress in the courts for alleged breach of section 8 of the 1944 Act, though on each occasion the challenge has been rebuffed, for reasons either of procedure or substance. Perhaps the leading case in this context arose out of the 1979 'winter of discontent' when there was extensive industrial disruption, including action by the National Union of Public Employees and the General and Municipal Workers' Union, whose members included school caretakers and ancillary staff: *Meade* v. *Haringey London Borough Council.*[62] Education officers in Haringey were informed by the unions that, as from a given date, strike action would be taken by all school caretakers (who were responsible for opening schools) and ancillary staff in the area. The education officers, in response to this information, instructed all headteachers in the area not to attempt to open the schools and to advise parents not to send their children to school. Children were thus excluded from school and provided with no education by the authority. The LEA issued a statement to the effect that it was sympathetic to the cause of those taking strike action, but that they were seeking to lessen the impact of the strike through negotiating concessions from the unions. Parents in the area complained to the Secretary of State under section 99 of the 1944 Act that the LEA was in default of its statutory duty under section 8 to make schools available, but the Secretary of State, Mrs Shirley Williams, refused to issue a default order on the basis of her satisfaction that the LEA was not in breach of its duty. One parent, Dr Meade, then issued a writ against the LEA seeking an injunction requiring the LEA to perform its duty under section 8 by reopening the schools, and a declaration that the LEA was in breach of section 8 and that the schools had been unlawfully closed. By the time of the hearing of the case at first instance, the industrial action had been reduced to one day per week; and by the time it reached the Court of Appeal the action had been called off completely. But the Court nonetheless went ahead with the proceedings in view of the importance of the points of principle at stake.

At first instance, Mr Justice Goulding found for the LEA on the procedural ground that the existence of a statutory remedy through complaint to the Secretary of State under section 99 ousted the jurisdiction of the court to intervene in a case, such as this, where the alleged failure on the part of the LEA was one of 'non-feasance' (failing to carry out action such as opening the schools in the face of a statutory requirement to do so), rather than one of 'mal-feasance' (positively acting in an unlawful manner in the face of a statutory prohibition). The judge went on to hold, furthermore, that in any event the injunction ought not to be granted as the court would have been quite unable to enforce it. The plaintiff appealed to the Court of Appeal, where the LEA argued that it had not been in breach of section 8 on the basis that it had been justified in closing the schools as any other action would have exacerbated the industrial dispute.

The Court of Appeal took the view that the LEA would have been acting unlawfully and *ultra vires* in these circumstances if the action taken by it had been without just cause or excuse: thus, if the LEA had decided to close the schools simply as a token of sympathy with the unions on the basis of considerations which were not relevant to the educational field, then this would have been *ultra vires* and a *positive misuse* (mal-feasance, not mere non-feasance) of the authority's powers for an unlawful purpose. Failure by the LEA here would thus *not* have been a simple failure but positive *ultra vires* action:

> We have a situation where educational facilities exist and are being used by all concerned when *the authority take a decision positively to stop production* as it were. Teachers who are in receipt of their salaries and under a duty to teach are discouraged from doing so. *This is positive conduct bringing the system to a halt.*[63]

If, on the other hand, the LEA had genuinely taken the view that, in order most effectively to perform its duty of making the schools available it was most prudent, in order to avoid exacerbating the industrial dispute, to close the schools for a time, or if it otherwise had compelling and reasonable grounds for closing the schools, it would not have been in breach of duty. As stated by Lord Justice Eveleigh:

> It could be that the local education authority took the view (and it is this they contend) that in order to perform their duties under s. 8 of the 1944 Act it was better to close the schools and not to antagonise employees whose co-operation would be important in the future and also for basic maintenance even during the strike. I can follow this argument. The Act imposes

> a general duty to make education available. It may well be that in order to achieve this end it will be necessary in a state of emergency to close the schools for a while. Provided the grounds which they genuinely have for their action can be regarded as such a state of emergency, in other words, as just and reasonable excuse for the closure, the authority would not be in breach of duty. The local education authority are entrusted with the duty of running the schools, and if what they do is genuinely directed to that end and is a legitimate choice of the various options they would not be in breach of duty.[64]

The Court of Appeal also held that the existence of a statutory remedy of complaint to the Secretary of State did *not* exclude the jurisdiction of the court where the aggrieved parent had suffered damage through action on the part of the LEA which was *ultra vires* or an act of mal-feasance.[65] In view of the Court's categorisation of any improper closure in sympathy with strike action in these circumstances as *ultra vires* or mal-feasance, it is clear that the Court was prepared to assert jurisdiction. However, the Court of Appeal was not able to express any concluded view as to whether, *on the particular facts of this case*, the LEA had acted for improper purposes and thus *ultra vires*: this was a matter of evidence for the trial judge, but the Court of Appeal took the view that a *prima facie* case of breach of duty based on *ultra vires* action and mal-feasance had been made out.[66] The majority in the Court of Appeal,[67] however, endorsed the view of Mr Justice Goulding at first instance that the injunction sought by the parent should be refused on the basis that it would have been difficult to enforce; Lord Denning, on the other hand, took the view that, if the strike had still been in progress, the injunction should have been granted.

The inconclusive nature of the actual decision of the Court of Appeal was attributable to the fact that the strike had already ended. The case is, however, extremely important as authority for the view that the courts may in an appropriate case be prepared to entertain an action by an aggrieved parent for enforcement of section 8, and that they are unlikely to be deflected by the existence of a remedy under section 99. Two critical difficulties for an aggrieved parent in these circumstances nonetheless remain: these are, firstly, to establish that the LEA is acting without just cause or excuse and thus *ultra vires*; and secondly, to establish that there is an appropriate remedy the court can offer. The first may be a well-nigh insurmountable hurdle in the case of an authority which is striving its hardest against severe externally imposed financial constraints to make the most effective provision of education possible, even though that provision may fall far short of the ideal. Even an LEA striving its hardest may from time to time properly judge it most prudent to close schools down and send children home.

The second difficulty is well illustrated in the most recent legal challenge in this context, which arose in the London Borough of Tower Hamlets over a crisis in the provision of primary education for some 400 to 500 children living mainly in the Stepney area of the borough: *R.* v. *Inner London Education Authority, ex parte Ali and Murshid*.[68] This case is of considerable importance as Lord Justice Woolf set about a fundamental re-examination of the nature of the duty created by section 8 and of the remedies which could possibly flow from a breach of the section by an LEA, particularly in the light of the existence of the statutory remedy under section 99. The decision in *Meade* v. *Haringey London Borough Council* had *opened the door* for a legal challenge based on alleged breach of section 8, but had left largely unresolved the exact circumstances in which a court would be prepared to intervene and the remedies that would be appropriate. A further consideration of the issues was thus of the first importance.

This application for judicial review was brought by a Mr Ali, the father of one of the children sent home, and a Mr Murshid, director of a local charity supporting the interests of the Bangladeshi community in Stepney. The application followed the rejection on 20 June 1989 by the Secretary of State of the applicants' complaint under section 99 of the 1944 Act. They had complained that some 400 to 500 primary school children had been denied school places for varying periods, in some cases for a year or more, despite the fact that the LEA (at that time the ILEA, but due to be succeeded by Tower Hamlets Borough Council from 1 April 1990) had been aware of the problem of a shortage of school places from as far back as 1982. The Secretary of State in his decision had asserted merely that he was

> of the view that ILEA is now taking reasonable steps to improve the situation in Tower Hamlets. Accordingly the Secretary of State has concluded that there are no grounds for him to issue a direction to ILEA under section 99 of the 1944 Act.[69]

By the time when the application was heard by the court, Mr Ali's son had in fact obtained a suitable school place: the only remedy therefore sought by Mr Ali was damages based on ILEA's alleged breach of statutory duty under section 8 of the 1944 Act; Mr Murshid, however, sought more extensive relief from the court under which the LEA would have been required to meet its obligations under the Act. The nature of the remedies sought, however, gave rise to preliminary questions of law relating to the court's jurisdiction and power to grant remedies which had to be addressed before consideration of the actual substance of the applications: first, the court had to consider the nature of the duty created by section 8, and, in particular, whether it should be interpreted as creating obligations which could be enforced by the court at the instance of individuals; secondly, whether a breach of section 8 might give rise to an obligation to pay damages to a parent, for instance through having to pay for alternative education or through loss of wages through having to stop work in order to look after a child at home; thirdly, the court had to consider the true effect of the statutory remedy under section 99, in particular whether its effect was to oust the jurisdiction of the court; and fourthly, on the assumption that the jurisdiction of the court was *not* excluded by section 99, how the court should exercise its discretion as to the nature of the remedy to be granted, if any.

The first issue related to the true legal interpretation of the duty created under section 8: the applicants argued that it was an absolute duty and that the relevant criteria of sufficiency, feasibility, expedience and desirability were properly to be determined objectively, if necessary by the court's application of its objective standard to these criteria. The ILEA, on the other hand, viewed the duty as by no means absolute and as properly importing the application by the LEA of its own subjective judgment as to the criteria of sufficiency, feasibility, expedience and desirability. Lord Justice Woolf clearly favoured the latter interpretation rather than the former, taking the view that the duty had been expressed 'in very broad and general terms', and describing it as in the nature of a 'target duty' involving 'a degree of elasticity' in its fulfilment.[70] Lord Justice Woolf continued:

> While there are a number of standards which are required to be achieved by the local education authority, the setting of those standards is, in the first instance, for the local education authority alone to determine as long as those standards are not outside the tolerance provided by the section. There are going to be situations, some of which can and others which cannot

> reasonably be anticipated, where the education provided falls below the statutory standard and the standards which the local education authority would set for itself. It is undoubtedly the position that within the area for which ILEA is responsible at the present time, the statutory standards and the standards that it would set for itself are not being met, but this does not mean that ILEA are necessarily in breach of their duty under section 8. The question is whether ILEA has taken the steps which the statute requires to remedy the situation which exists.[71]

It would be wrong to infer from this, however, that the nature and scope of the steps required to meet the duty are wholly subjective, but rather that there is a degree of tolerance and elasticity in them, and that it is for the LEA *in the first instance* to assess what is required. That tolerance and elasticity could however, in certain circumstances become overstretched, thereby justifying intervention by the Secretary of State and then, if need be, by the court. But nonetheless Lord Justice Woolf was clear that the proper interpretation of section 8 was that it created a 'target' rather than an 'absolute' duty, expressed in general terms and as to whose fulfilment there would be an element of flexibility.

The second preliminary issue related expressly to the remedy of damages sought by Mr Ali: the court had no hesitation in rejecting this claim on the basis that, although it is possible to obtain damages in judicial review proceedings, this is so only if the court is satisfied that the applicant would have been entitled to damages had he brought an ordinary private action against the LEA,[72] and a breach of statutory duty under section 8 would not have given rise to any such award of damages at the suit of an individual as 'the duty imposed by section 8 is intended to enure for the public in general and not intended to give the individual litigant a cause of action'.[73] Lord Justice Woolf declined to follow the view which had been expressed obiter by Lord Denning in *Meade* v. *Haringey London Borough Council* that damages could be awarded for breach of section 8: he would accept that damages could be awarded for personal injury incurred by a pupil as a result of a school having fallen into disrepair, but not in the circumstances of Mr Ali in the instant case.

The third issue was whether the default powers in sections 68 and 99 ousted the jurisdiction of the court to intervene in an appropriate case. Lord Justice Woolf was clear that the court's jurisdiction was *not* thereby ousted, although the existence of the default powers might serve to limit the type of remedy the court could offer. It will be recalled that the majority in the Court of Appeal in *Meade* v. *Haringey London Borough Council*[74] had taken the view that the jurisdiction of the court was not ousted where the LEA had acted *ultra vires* or by way of a positive act of mal-feasance; Lord Denning had gone further, claiming that the court could intervene even in a case of mere non-feasance. Lord Justice Woolf in *ex parte Ali and Murshid* took the view that this involved the drawing of exceptionally difficult and unreliable distinctions between *positive action* which was prohibited by statute, and *inaction* in the face of a statutory duty,[75] and that it was essentially more satisfactory to address the issue from the point of view of what type of remedy the court might be able to award where a 'target duty' in general terms was coupled, as here, with a default power vested in a Minister or another specified body. Lord Justice Woolf agreed that it would be inappropriate in such a case to grant a remedy such as an order of mandamus, which directed the authority to act in any particular manner. In such a case, where an order of mandamus is sought, the court ought to decline the relief on the basis that the Minister's default power offers a more satisfactory remedy, as an order from the court requiring action on the part of the authority could only be in very general terms and would be extremely difficult to enforce.[76] This view would not, however, necessarily apply where the relief sought was an injunction to *prevent* an authority from acting in a particular way, or a declaration seeking to clarify the nature of an authority's legal obligations. It may well be appropriate for the court to award a declaration in a case of inactivity by an LEA, even though it would not be prepared to issue an order of mandamus. As Lord Justice Woolf explained:

> The reason for the inactivity could, for example, be because the public body concerned is under a misapprehension as to the relevant law. A declaration clarifying the legal position could be of considerable value in establishing what the obligations of the public body are.
>
> On an application for judicial review the existence of a default power certainly does not exclude the jurisdiction of the court and may not, even where (as here) the breach of duty can be described as nonfeasance, deprive the Court of the ability to provide a remedy. The default power will, however, still be highly relevant as to whether or not the court should grant relief as a matter of discretion.[77]

Lord Justice Woolf was thus certainly not prepared to accept any argument on the part of ILEA that the court's jurisdiction to appraise the legality of the authority's action or inaction under section 8 was ousted by the existence of the statutory remedies under sections 68 and 99, even though it may well be only in rare circumstances that the court could or should in practice grant a remedy. Damages, as sought by Mr Ali for interference with his son's education would not be available under judicial review as they could not, in Lord Justice Woolf's opinion, have been obtained in an ordinary action, given that section 8 essentially creates duties towards the public at large; an order of mandamus commanding certain action on the part of the authority would be inappropriate as it could only be expressed in general terms and would be well-nigh impossible to enforce. Other forms of relief – notably an injunction to prevent action by the authority or a declaration – may, however, still be appropriate, subject to the court's discretion.

The question of the exercise of its discretion was the final preliminary issue before the court. The court took the view that there would be no prospect of its exercising its discretion in favour of the applicants in the circumstances of the present case: firstly, the authority against whom any order would have to be made, the ILEA, was about to go out of existence on 1 April 1990, less than two months from the date of the hearing, and thus any order would be of only very limited effect in terms of its duration. Even apart from this practical consideration, the only appropriate remedy here would have been a declaration, yet this would have added nothing in the present circumstances as it could have done no more than act as an authoritative legal declaration of the LEA's legal obligations, about which the LEA *was already in no doubt* and which it already *fully acknowledged*. Lord Justice Woolf concluded that no constructive benefit was therefore to be gained from any intervention by the court, and therefore it should exercise its discretion at this stage on the basis of its consideration of these preliminary legal issues not to intervene, rather than go on to consider the substantive issue as to whether ILEA was in fact in breach of its obligations:

> In this case it is clear that a declaration would not assist. *To declare that the public body should perform its duty does not add to or clarify the public body's obligations where, as here, that body accepts obligations*. At this stage it is possible to say that there are not in this case any specific steps which will be able to be identified

which it can be said that the public body is not taking which it should take. The only purpose of continuing the proceedings would be to ascertain whether or not the authority was culpable in reaching the present unsatisfactory situation. Inquests of that sort are not the purpose of judicial review.

In coming to this conclusion, *I derive support from the decision of the Secretary of State not to intervene. He is usually in a better position than the courts to assess whether intervention would be constructive and, while not bound in any way by his decision, the courts will have regard to his decision in deciding how to exercise their discretion.*[78]

CONCLUSIONS

It is abundantly clear from Lord Justice Woolf's conclusions in *ex parte Ali and Murshid* that the courts feel extremely uncomfortable when faced with legal challenges based on the concept of legal sufficiency of educational provision, a concept which necessarily involves consideration of a wide range of substantive educational factors as to which it is fully to be expected that there would be a fairly wide margin of legitimate difference of opinion. They are, on the other hand, at all times anxious to assert a residual jurisdiction to intervene, even though the probability of circumstances arising where they would in fact intervene is extremely low. They asserted their jurisdiction by emphasising that, while the duty under section 8 is not an absolute one but is, rather, a 'target duty' incorporating a measure of elasticity and tolerance, and while it is for the LEA concerned in the first instance to determine what steps are required to be taken by way of fulfilment of that duty, the LEA remains subject to the oversight in this matter of the Secretary of State with his power of intervention under sections 68 and 99, and, ultimately, subject to the oversight of the courts. They also asserted their jurisdiction by refusing to accept ouster of their jurisdiction by the existence of statutory default order procedures. The courts could enter the proceedings either at the request of the Secretary of State, seeking an order to enforce any directions he had already issued under section 68 or 99 (and here a mandatory order from the court might be appropriate),[79] or, as in the cases considered above, at the request of aggrieved parents or other closely interested parties following the Minister's refusal to intervene.

As we have seen, however, no Secretary of State is likely ever to issue statutory directions to an LEA to enforce its duties under section 8 in the context of expenditure constraints which themselves are likely to have originated in central government policy; and the courts are most unlikely to be able to offer any practical remedy to aggrieved parents in the latter category of case. The only type of remedy against an LEA which in these circumstances is likely to be of real value – mandatory relief – the courts tend to feel incapable of formulating in sufficiently precise terms and incapable of enforcing; and other remedies would be of only very marginal benefit to individual applicants in such circumstances. The evidence from the law points to the depressing conclusion that the legal sufficiency of education is an area which, although one of potent political conflict, is one where legal remedies before the courts in England and Wales are an extremely remote prospect. Yet this is so despite the reality that conditions in some LEAs and in some schools have deteriorated to such an extent as to attract extensive and repeated criticism from HMI; and despite the reality of several hundreds of children being sent home from school in inner London as there are no school places available for them or no teachers available to teach them. These children may truly be regarded as being denied their 'right to education' within the meaning of the first sentence of Article 2 of the First Protocol to the European Convention, and it is to be hoped that a challenge in this context before the European Commission and Court of Human Rights will ultimately be brought, though it would involve the marshalling of considerable resources in terms of evidence, finance, energy and perseverance.

In the meantime, it is in the political rather than the legal arena that the whole question of the funding of education will be fought. In the short term, it may be noted that the Labour Party at its 1990 party conference elevated the funding of education to the forefront of political debate as one of its primary commitments for the forthcoming general election, and that the government has responded by finding at least some extra resources for education through Revenue Support Grant for local authorities during 1991–1992: the then Secretary of State, Mr John MacGregor, announced at the end of October 1990 that the government intended to allow for local authority spending of some £17,485 million on schools and colleges in England during 1991–1992, an increase of 16 per cent on the previous year. Mr MacGregor commented that this marked the fact that

> Education is a top priority for this government. We have launched a radical reform programme to lever up standards. The total funding of almost £17.5 billion announced today is over £2,400 million higher than education's share of the 1990–91 settlement. That is further proof of our commitment to secure the ever increasing standards in education that our reforms are designed to bring about.[80]

These increases may lead to some short-term alleviation of the crisis in funding, but there is little doubt that the impact of expenditure constraints over the past decade and more is such that it would require the repeated injection of a considerably higher proportion of overall public expenditure into the education sector to remedy the acute problem of insufficiency of provision that has now developed.

Even if a higher proportion of overall public expenditure were to be directed towards the education service, there would, however, remain a major problem for our poorest schools and our poorest communities which has been substantially exacerbated by the government's educational reforms: as we saw in chapter 2 in the context of choice of school and open enrolment, the government has been determined to subject schools as far as possible to the rigours of market forces, and to this end it has prevented LEAs from imposing pupil intake quotas below the maximum physical capacity of schools. This was formerly done by LEAs largely to protect their most vulnerable schools with the most dramatically falling pupil numbers. Through linking open enrolment with the funding of schools on the basis primarily of the number of registered pupils in attendance, it is clear that the weakest schools will be *increasingly starved of resources* at the very time when they should, arguably, have been having extra resources pumped into them by virtue of a policy of positive discrimination in order to lever up standards. Put in terms of individual and collective interests, the open enrolment policy serves greatly to benefit the interests of those pupils and parents who are able to afford to live in the more socially favoured communities where schools are full and thus well-funded, but on the other hand serves greatly to damage the collective interests of the poorer communities and poorer schools with dwindling rolls and where members of the community have no realistic prospect of being able to move or send their children to more favoured schools in other areas on the basis of geographical impracticality and the expense of travel. Serious and urgent political consideration needs to be given not only to the proportion of overall public expenditure directed towards education, but also to the damaging impact of the policy of subjecting schools to the rigours of market forces on significant sectors of the community.

5

FALLING ROLLS AND THE REORGANISATION OF SCHOOLS

INTRODUCTION

Since the early 1970s we have witnessed a marked decline in the school population, and this has brought with it profound consequences for the organisation and structure of schools. Problems have taken the form of agonising decisions as to whether, and if so, to what extent and at what pace, to take surplus school places out of use; whether particular schools should be reduced in size, or amalgamated, or closed down altogether; whether schools which are retained should be rationalised by merger of sixth form provision, by provision of sixth form colleges or tertiary colleges; whether staff capacity should be reduced or redeployed, with potentially damaging effects upon the curriculum; whether, on the other hand, surplus places should be retained through maintenance of pupil capacity at or near existing levels in order to bring about an improvement in staff–pupil ratios, and to provide a residue of capacity to cater for an upturn in the birth rate and a subsequent rise in pupil numbers. These are merely some of the choices which have been faced by educational administrators in the light of falling rolls: there are many others.

The structural choices made by government – at both central and local authority level – in the context of falling school rolls are among the most crucial and controversial in the whole sphere of the provision of education, and their consequences are necessarily long-term. The very suggestion that schools might be closed or amalgamated, or deprived of their sixth forms – suggestions that have been put forward in many instances in differing circumstances in LEAs throughout England and Wales – inevitably awakens deep-rooted vested interests among school governors, parents, pupils, teachers whose jobs are at stake, and local communities which often regard schools as an integral part of community existence. One of the greatest fears among parents is often the constriction of parental choice of school that a closure or amalgamation would be likely to bring about, thus raising an awkward dilemma in many cases for a Conservative Secretary of State committed at the same time to reducing the number of surplus places and to enhancing parental choice. And it is obvious that a school is an essential element in a community's life: this has often been seen most acutely in the case of village schools, but it is often just as true of urban communities.

The individual interests at stake have, however, often to yield to the collective interest in cost-effective planning for an efficient structure of schooling in an area to the general educational advantage of pupils as a whole – an elementary dilemma faced in the provision of public services. The reorganisation of schools as a result of falling rolls provides an excellent case study of government seeking to strike what it sees as the appropriate balance between individual and collective interests, with the central department frequently seeking to strike a different balance from that preferred by LEAs.

This chapter will seek to explore some of the legal issues arising in the context of school reorganisation in the face of falling rolls. The following chapter will explore the further dimension added to reorganisation proposals by the possibility of one or more schools opting out of LEA control in favour of grant-maintained status under the Education Reform Act 1988, and the impact any such possibility would be likely to have on the LEA's plans for reorganisation of the schools remaining under LEA control.

STATISTICAL BACKGROUND TO FALLING ROLLS

The impact of a declining birth rate was first felt in primary schools in the early 1970s, and this reached the secondary schools sector in the late 1970s. The effects of falling rolls have not, of course, been uniform across the country: there has been a marked movement of population away from the inner cities, whose schools have suffered a disproportionate decline in pupil numbers, while those in more environmentally favoured suburban areas have in many cases been oversubscribed; village schools have continued to decline as it has been found frequently impossible to sustain a properly balanced curriculum without incurring disproportionate staffing costs; and there has been a general trend in population movement towards the southern part of England.

Across the country as a whole, however, it is clear that the decline started in the primary sector in the early 1970s and filtered through to the secondary sector in the late 1970s; but that an upturn in the birth rate has led to increasing pupil numbers in primary schools since 1986 which will filter through to the secondary sector in the early 1990s. In England, the DES has reported primary pupil numbers as having peaked at about 4.9 millions in the early 1970s, reaching a low point of some 3.6 millions in 1985. The figure has been growing since 1986 and is expected to reach some 3.9 millions by 2000. In the secondary sector, numbers have declined in England from some 3.9 millions in 1979 and are expected to reach a low point of some 2.8 millions in 1991, but then to rise each year to about 3.1 millions by 2000.[1]

The rate of school closures reached a peak in England in 1983 when the Secretary of State approved closure proposals for 295 schools (225 primary and 70 secondary schools). This figure has since declined each year: in 1987 closure proposals were approved for 131 schools (88 primary and 43 secondary schools).[2]

DEVELOPMENT OF CENTRAL GOVERNMENT POLICY: GOVERNMENT BY CIRCULAR

It is evident that the government was bound to take *some* defined stance in the face of the impending fall in pupil numbers, if only by way of an express statement that it would leave it to each LEA to determine how best to reorganise its school stock in the light of its own circumstances – maximum local autonomy. In the event, however, both Labour and Conservative governments have used the structural changes necessitated by falling rolls as an opportunity to exert central control, by the promulgation of departmental circulars exhorting LEAs to take action, and by interventionist use of the central department's statutory powers of control over the reorganisation of schools.[3]

The view of the then Labour government as to closures was expressed in a Departmental Circular issued in June 1977,[4] exhorting LEAs to 'make the most realistic assessment possible of future school population trends'[5] in their areas and to 'examine systematically'[6] the educational opportunities provided in their schools and to consider how their school premises might best be used in the light of the projected fall in pupil numbers. Warnings were sounded as to the educational disadvantages of maintaining schools with dwindling numbers, and the attractions of restructuring were spelled out:

curricular restrictions and disproportionate and wasteful allocation of scarce resources were particularly stressed, as were the advantages, if schools or classrooms were closed, in the shape of fuel and maintenance savings.[7] The Circular went on to stress that local circumstances – particularly geographical, social, denominational – might lead to the retention of schools which it would otherwise be right to close, but concluded that:

> Where it can be shown that closure will not lead to a reduction in the quality of educational provision, that full consideration has been given to any social or other problems that may arise, that there will be significant financial savings, and that the problems appear to be outweighed by the educational and financial benefits, *the general policy of the Secretary of State will be to approve proposals to cease to maintain under-used schools.*[8]

Following the change of government in 1979, this broadly receptive attitude of the central department towards LEA proposals for contraction continued for a time. But the central department's attitude was made far more explicit, positive and interventionist in June 1981 by the issue of a further Circular[9] spelling out the need for 'much faster progress'[10] towards removing surplus places. This Circular set out what the government saw as the educational and financial advantages of increasing the speed at which surplus places were being removed. It envisaged the removal by 1986 of some 1.3 million school places in England and Wales 'to the long-term benefit of the education service',[11] a figure which, it stated, would allow for three out of every five surplus places to be *retained* as provision for an eventual upturn in births and for an element of flexibility in differing local circumstances.[12] The Circular emphasised the problems of small primary schools with large classes and mixed age groupings,[13] and small village schools which have to be provided with disproportionately generous staffing and other resources;[14] in the case of middle and secondary schools there was a minimum size below which educational disadvantages would occur unless the LEA provided disproportionate extra resources at the expense of other schools;[15] it was stressed that the range of curricular provision in comprehensive schools tended to be unduly restricted where there was a three- to four-form intake or less;[16] such schools faced a dilemma between excluding some subjects and devoting a disproportionate amount of the time of a few specialist teachers to a minority of pupils; staffing shortages could cause some subjects, including English and mathematics, to be taught by teachers lacking specialist training;[17] and small sixth forms presented further problems in terms of the disproportionate use of resources.[18] The possible savings that could be made would vary according to local circumstances, but the Circular estimated that every 100,000 surplus places withdrawn would on average yield savings approaching £10 million – *excluding* savings on teachers' salaries.[19]

The Circular went on, in interventionist terms reminiscent of the then Labour government's 'request' to LEAs to submit plans for comprehensive reorganisation in 1965,[20] to ask for evidence of positive action on the part of LEAs:

> The Secretary of State considers that there is scope nationally for faster progress, not least in relation to surplus temporary places whose removal does not involve the effort and upheaval of school closures; and that *the limitation of resources and the needs of the education service now make much faster progress essential.* It needs to be brought home to parents and schools that, within the prospective overall financial constraints, keeping surplus places in use is necessarily at the expense of standards of provision in education. To make faster progress requires action by the Secretary of State and action, including a considerable administrative effort, by local education authorities in consultation with voluntary bodies, schools and teachers.[21]

The Circular added positive impetus to these words by stressing that the Secretary of State would carry out his statutory functions in scrutinising LEA proposals for closures, amalgamations and reductions in the size of schools in such a way as to facilitate the removal of surplus places where justified on the merits,[22] and that he would do so expeditiously.[23] As an initial positive step, however, the Circular required each LEA to conduct a thorough review of its existing school stock and to inform the DES by the end of 1981 of the LEA's proposals, including if possible the anticipated number of places to be taken out of use in each year from 1981 to 1986.[24] As a financial incentive, it was stated, first, that in determining the level of each LEA's capital expenditure on education, the Secretary of State intended to take into account the fact that removing surplus places would often involve extra building work in order to expand or improve schools which would receive pupils from closed schools,[25] and secondly, that capital receipts from the sale of county school buildings could be used to finance capital work over and above an authority's prescribed capital allocation.[26] These financial incentives were, further, coupled with an obscure statement to the effect that the Secretary of State intended to take the information received from LEAs into account when considering his plans for educational expenditure in future years.[27]

Circular 2/81 thus left no doubt as to the central government's preferred policy of responding to falling pupil numbers by a deliberate and planned contraction – which would be bound in many cases to mean hard-fought closures and amalgamations. And it was made clear that it would not hesitate to give effect to this policy through financial pressure on LEAs and through the exercise by the Secretary of State of his statutory powers of approval of school reorganisation plans.[28]

In addition to the exertion of pressure upon LEAs to take surplus places out of use through circulars 10/77 and 2/81, the government has used the opportunity presented by the need for reorganisation to exert its influence over the very *form and substance* of reorganisation proposals drawn up by LEAs with a view to furthering some of its own preferences as to educational policy and in conflict with the wishes of some LEAs. This is seen most clearly in DES Circular 4/82[29] concerning the government's anxiety that reorganisation proposals should not involve the loss of successful sixth form provision and of all single-sex provision in an area. Circular 4/82 carefully stresses the importance of diversity of provision,[30] but then goes on to emphasise the need for LEAs in drawing up their reorganisation plans to

> bear prominently in mind the need to retain what is best and has proved its worth within the existing system of secondary education.[31]

Proposals which involved the loss of successful sixth form provision – for example, by the decapitation of a number of secondary schools for children aged 11 to 18 and the provision of a centralised sixth form college – would come up against a presumption of rejection, expressed in the circular in these terms:

> The Secretary of State will not normally approve proposals which have as their consequence the closure or significant change of character of schools which, by a sustained record of success in the provision they make for sixth form education, have already proved their worth under existing arrangements

> and in his judgment can continue to do so, except where he is satisfied that the prima facie case for their retention is displaced by other compelling educational considerations.[32]

Central governmental justification for this was clearly in terms of the maintenance of high standards – particularly academic standards – and the preservation of educational provision of proven worth. Many LEAs nonetheless had been reacting to falling rolls in secondary schools (which often most acutely affect sixth form provision) by drawing up rationalisation proposals which would have involved the centralisation of sixth form teaching in either sixth form or tertiary colleges, and the provision of secondary schools catering for children from 11 to 16 rather than 11 to 18 years. It was particularly in large urban authorities such as Manchester, Birmingham and Sheffield where such proposals were seen to offer an attractive solution to acute problems of making satisfactory sixth form provision. Proposals for centralised sixth form provision submitted by Manchester's Labour-controlled City Council in 1981 were rejected by the then Secretary of State, Sir Keith Joseph, on the basis of the damage that would have been done to three particular 11 to 18 age range secondary schools with successful sixth forms.[33] The local reaction to the Secretary of State's decision was one of relief on the part of supporters of the three schools concerned, but on the part of others was one of concern as to the impact the decision would have on schools as a whole. It was feared in particular that the three particular schools with their successful sixth forms would develop into selective schools in all but name. Schools which had proved able to develop and maintain successful sixth forms had found themselves able to do so by virtue of high parental demand for places: as a broad generalisation, they were popular, successful schools serving the most socially favoured catchment areas. The effect of the government's policy would be to afford such schools special protection in the process of rationalisation of schools in the area as a whole, at the risk – in the view of opponents of the government's policy – of jeopardising the overall pattern of educational provision in the area concerned. This presents a classic example of individual and collective interests in conflict, the individual interests being represented by the parents of children at the three schools granted protection.

The significance of the rejection of the Manchester proposals in 1981, followed by the Government's policy statement on sixth forms in Circular 4/82, is as a manifestation of central government dominance and of constriction of the discretion of LEAs in formulating reorganisation proposals. Not only has the DES seen fit to exert pressure on LEAs to take surplus places out of use, in many cases where individual authorities might have wished to pursue either different policies or a similar policy but at a slower pace, but it has been ready to use reorganisation as a vehicle for deeper direct involvement in the internal restructuring of schools in individual LEAs in pursuit of educational goals which are anathema to many authorities. Although many LEAs with proposals involving sixth form or tertiary colleges saw fit to adjust their plans in the light of the Manchester dispute and Circular 4/82, many proposals including sixth form or tertiary colleges have in practice been approved on their merits by the Secretary of State, though in some cases not without a considerable struggle. Such struggles are, furthermore, still seen today, as exemplified clearly by the reorganisation dispute in the City of Bath discussed in the following chapter in the context of schools opting out in favour of grant-maintained status.[34]

A full consolidation, expansion and updating of the central department's policy stance on school closures has now been provided in DES Circular 3/87, *Providing for Quality: the Pattern of Organisation to Age 19*, and this now supersedes the earlier Circulars already mentioned (Circulars 5/77, 2/81 and 4/82).[35] This Circular draws attention particularly to the need of the education service to address two inter-related issues: first, the need to respond to both the immediate and long-term effects of sharply falling rolls, particularly in the 11 to 19 years age range; and second, the need to make schools as cost-effective as possible.[36] To these principal ends the circular goes on to exhort further and faster progress towards the eradication of surplus places by internal rationalisation within schools and by closures and amalgamations.[37] The Circular spells out the latest version of general considerations that would inform the Secretary of State's approach to school closure proposals submitted for his approval by LEAs. In particular, it emphasises that

> The Secretary of State would not normally be prepared to approve the closure of a school of proven worth unless there was evidence that it could not continue to sustain its established quality and that the alternative proposals would secure at least the same quality and variety of education at lower cost. In all reorganisation schemes he would need to be satisfied that the proposed new arrangements, whether for primary or secondary

> pupils, would provide an appropriate curriculum, sufficiently differentiated so that all pupils could be challenged to the limit of their abilities.[38]

Particular stress is also placed on the need to give full weight to parental preferences for schools of particular types, including grammar schools, denominational schools and single-sex schools; and there is express recognition of the degree of support that rural schools may command in local communities.[39]

The Circular emphasises the government's view of the economic argument in favour of contraction, referring in particular to the disproportionately high unit costs incurred by small schools generally and by schools of any size with a substantial proportion of surplus places. The government concludes that

> The extra expenditure thus incurred is often found at the expense of other schools in the area, to the detriment of value for money in the latter, and is hard to justify unless geographic considerations require it.[40]

Accordingly this Circular exhorts LEAs to proceed towards the removal by 1991 of half the surplus capacity in primary schools and three out of every five surplus secondary school places, and emphasises that the removal of these places is implicitly assumed in the government's expenditure plans for education as set out in the annual Public Expenditure White Paper. Progress in this direction will be an integral part of the normal annual discussions with the local authority associations on local authority expenditure.[41] Although it is, of course, for each LEA to take the initiative in submitting reorganisation proposals for its area, it is clear from this that the government is in a strong position to exert financial pressure on LEAs unwilling to fall into line with the government's strategy for dealing with falling rolls.

REORGANISATION PROPOSALS: THE PROCEDURAL REQUIREMENTS

As would be expected, LEAs (and voluntary school governors) are not permitted to effect significant changes in the structure of their schools without complying with the requirements of statutory provisions and with certain non-statutory requirements set out in DES Circulars, some of which have in a series of important legal decisions (discussed below) been given legally binding authority. Certain minor internal structural changes in a school or schools would not, of course, fall under these statutory and other procedures, but any significant structural alterations, such as a change to the age-range for which the school caters, or whether it is single-sex or co-educational, would certainly invoke the statutory process. This would also be invoked where it is proposed to close a school, or to establish a new school, or where it is proposed to amalgamate two or more schools. 'Amalgamation' is not provided for expressly in the statutory provisions, but is analysed instead as the *closure* of two (or more) schools followed by the *establishment* of a new school, often on the former premises of one of the schools just closed.

The statutory machinery for the establishment and closure of schools or their substantial reorganisation is now to be found in sections 12 and 13 of the Education Act 1980: section 12 deals with county schools and section 13 with voluntary schools. Where an LEA wishes to establish[42] or to close down[43] a county school[44] or to make any 'significant change in its character' or 'significant enlargement' of its premises,[45] it must first publish its proposals for so doing in accordance with section 12(1) and regulations issued by the Secretary of State[46] and submit a copy of its proposals to the Secretary of State. Any ten or more local government electors for the area[47] then have an opportunity within two months to submit objections to the LEA. The LEA must within one month from the closing date for objections submit all objections received (other than any that have been withdrawn in writing) to the Secretary of State, together with its observations on them. In the event of no objections being received,[48] the LEA is free to go ahead without the sanction of the Secretary of State unless the Secretary of State exercises his 'call in' power, under which he may give notice to the LEA within two months from submission to him of the proposals that his approval will be required.[49] But where objections are received, or where the Secretary of State chooses to call the proposals in, central approval is required, and the Minister may then approve or reject the proposals outright, or approve them subject to modifications.[50] Once proposals have been approved by the Secretary of State, or the LEA has, in a case where central approval is not needed, formally determined to implement its proposals,[51] the LEA becomes duty bound to carry them out, though the LEA may request a modification by the Secretary of State.[52]

It is apparent that these statutory provisions are very skeletal in nature, and that they offer individuals seeking to object to reorganisation proposals only the most perfunctory right to submit objections through the LEA to the Secretary of State. The gestation period of a complex set of LEA reorganisation proposals may well run to several years, involving the drawing up by officers of the LEA of a succession of reports for the education committee (or one or more of its sub-committees) on alternative strategies for reorganisation; there may well be lengthy and acrimonious debate in successive meetings of the education committee and of the plenary LEA itself over the issues. Yet it may seem astonishing that there is, with one exception in the context of opting out in favour of grant-maintained status introduced by the Education Reform Act 1988,[53] no *statutory* requirement for an LEA to *consult* any of the interested parties – parents, school governors, teachers, community groups and others – at any point during this possibly lengthy process of drawing up formal proposals for publication and submission to the Secretary of State. The requirement to consult was relegated instead to the level of an administrative exhortation from the Secretary of State to LEAs formerly contained in DES Circular 2/80[54] and Administrative Memorandum 4/84.[55] These have now been superseded by Circular 3/87, which contains the current administrative exhortation from the Secretary of State over the need to consult, revised in the light of litigation considered below:[56]

> The Secretary of State has made clear in previous guidance the importance he attaches to the adequacy of consultation on the part of all promoters. This policy has received judicial backing from recent High Court decisions which hold that parents have a legitimate expectation that they will be consulted on proposals affecting reorganisation of their children's school. The Secretary of State expects appropriate consultation to have taken place with parents, teaching and other staff, governors and other interested parties at the formative stage of the proposals with sufficient information and time available to permit intelligent consideration of and response to the issues involved; such consultation should normally have taken place within the 12 months immediately prior to publication.[57]

As will be seen below, the Secretary of State's exhortations over the need to consult have been an important element in legal challenges to reorganisation proposals formulated by LEAs, but it is worth noting that no attempt was made in the statutory machinery to build in a *statutory duty to consult*: its absence may indeed be symptomatic of a wider disregard for the rights of interested parties opposed to schemes of reorganisation.

Throughout these formative stages in the gestation of reorganisation proposals, interested parties have, then, a complete lack of any statutory involvement in the process. It is not, indeed, until the fully formulated proposals are formally published by the LEA and submitted to the Secretary of State under section 12(1) that the *statutory* process begins to operate. Interested parties have a statutory right to submit objections to the LEA within two months of publication, and the LEA must then transmit those objections (unless withdrawn) to the Secretary of State *along with its observations on them*. There is *no* statutory right for objectors to read the LEA's observations and to submit any counter-observations, nor to see or submit observations on objections submitted by fellow objectors; there is *no* statutory right for objectors to be heard in person by the ministers and officials in the DES considering the matter. Nothing in the nature of a public local inquiry procedure exists, as, for example, in the context of planning disputes. The impression, on the contrary, is of a closed dialogue between LEA and DES officials, out of which some seven or eight months later[58] will emerge a rather perfunctory decision letter under the hand of a DES official. This closed dialogue may well give objectors the impression that these procedures fall some way short of generally accepted standards of due process, the proposers of the scheme (the LEA) engaging in private communications with the 'judge' (the DES) behind the backs of the objectors. From the executive point of view, however, it would be emphasised that the issues here are fundamentally administrative and policy-based and that any analogy with impartial judicial processes is essentially flawed.

It would be unfair and unbalanced from this rather bleak picture of what is undoubtedly a highly executive-orientated procedure to conclude that objections submitted by interested parties are dealt with improperly or cavalierly. DES Circular 3/87 emphatically stresses the importance attached by the Secretary of State to objections, though this must be subject to limitations:

> The government is committed to giving the fullest possible effect to parental preferences for particular schools. This commitment does not however extend to circumstances where to meet it would prejudice the provision of efficient education or the efficient use of resources. A large volume of *expressed*

> *parental commitment* to a particular school will be a consideration (sometimes a very telling one) which the Secretary of State takes into account in deciding proposals, but it will not of itself be conclusive if the educational and financial arguments point the other way.[59]

It is assumed that this clear statement of policy is taken seriously and that systematic, sensitive and comprehensive consideration is indeed given to objections: what is being criticised is, rather, the excessively skeletal terms of the statutory framework enshrined in sections 12 and 13 of the 1980 Act and the very limited procedural *rights* that they afford. The indications are, indeed, that the Secretary of State does reject LEA reorganisation proposals on a wide variety of grounds and that interested parties are by no means always disappointed with the outcome of their objections.[60]

LEGAL CHALLENGE TO PROPOSALS FOR REORGANISATION

From the early 1980s to the present, disputes over school closures and amalgamations have been a leading issue on the local political agenda, and sophisticated pressure group campaigns in respect of particular schools or groups of schools have been organised, in some instances with conspicuous success. It comes as no surprise that some of these campaigns have gone further than local political pressure, organised participation at local consultative meetings arranged by the LEA and the drawing up and submission of voluminous objections under sections 12 or 13 of the 1980 Act: a significant minority of campaigns have been taken as far as the courts on a variety of grounds, challenging in the main the administrative steps taken by LEAs in the drawing up of their proposals. The grounds on which these legal challenges have been brought will now be explored.

Challenge on the ground of failure to consult interested parties while the proposals were at a formative stage

The leading legal challenge on the ground of defective consultation was brought in 1985 by a group of parents of school children in the London Borough of Brent: *R.* v. *Brent London Borough Council, ex parte Gunning*.[61] The proposals under challenge had been published by the LEA on 20 July 1984 under section 12 of the Education Act 1980, and the parents applied to the High Court for judicial review by way of an order of certiorari to quash the LEA's decision to make the proposals and a declaration that the publication of the proposals was *ultra vires*, void and of no effect and that the proposals were thus not lawfully before the Secretary of State. The applicants in *ex parte Gunning* argued that the period allowed by the LEA for consultation on the final proposals had been too short and that the final consultative document had been wholly inadequate.[62] The proposals had had a lengthy gestation period, going back to before 1980: following several rounds of consultations at that time, the LEA in July 1983 had accepted a recommendation to tackle the falling rolls problem in Brent by reducing the number of pupils to be admitted into each form rather than by closing schools.[63] In December 1983, however, there was a change in the delicate political balance of Brent Council, and the new chairman of the education committee asked the Director of Education to prepare a fresh report on educational provision in the area, in the light both of increasing pressure from central government to restrict expenditure and 'fresh information'[64] about the cost of maintaining the existing school stock. The Director presented his report to the education committee on 2 May 1984. Mr Justice Hodgson found that this report largely ignored the first factor underlying the chairman's request for a further report – central government pressure – and that the only 'fresh information' related to high projected maintenance expenditure at two named schools. The report contained no information about the many other schools in the area.[65] The report invited the education committee to consider, among other options, closing down the two named schools. The education committee at its meeting on 2 May was, however, unprepared to go ahead with firm recommendations for submission to the full LEA. Instead, it requested the Director, after having had consultations with a teachers' panel, to prepare yet another report which could then be released for general consultation. The Director's response was a brief additional report. On 10 May the full LEA met: it had before it both of the Director's reports and the minutes of the education committee's meeting of 2 May. The LEA resolved to go ahead with public consultations on the basis of some eight proposals – some for specific closures and amalgamations, others of a general policy nature.[66]

The consultation document to be used for this purpose was then drawn up by the Director. On the facts, Mr Justice Hodgson had no hesitation in concluding that this final consultation document was 'sparse of information and reasoning'.[67] Reference was made in it to fresh information about the cost of maintaining existing school stock, yet the document contained no details of what that information was.[68] The judge concluded:

> In my judgment that document, on the most favourable criteria to the local authority, was wholly inadequate, and it is clear from the evidence that, at the public meetings, no real attempt was made to flesh it out. On the question of cost it was, in my judgment, positively misleading.... It is clear from the evidence that the manifest inadequacy of this document was deeply resented by the parents, a resentment which was vociferously and publicly expressed.[69]

Moreover, the timetable proposed for the consultation process was extremely short: the consultation document was not received by most parents (delivered by their children) until 4 or 5 June 1984, yet the public meetings were scheduled for and took place on 7 June; and written responses were required to be submitted to the Director by 15 June. The judge found this timetable for consultation to be 'wholly inadequate' and 'woefully deficient'.[70]

The Director duly compiled a report setting out his conclusions in the light of comments made during the consultation process, and these were considered by the education committee on 5 July. It was at this point that friction between the education committee (with its co-opted members) and the full LEA became evident: the education committee refused to submit a formal report to the LEA recommending any particular proposals for closures and amalgamations. Instead, it passed motions expressing concern as to the perfunctory nature of the consultation process and recommending the LEA to instigate further investigations into alternative methods of tackling the problem of falling rolls before undertaking any closures or amalgamations.[71] The LEA then met on 12 July: it threw out the education committee's recommendations and resolved instead to publish and submit a package of proposals to the Secretary of State for approval – proposals which involved a number of proposals for closures and amalgamations and which were *materially different* from the earlier proposals on which the highly perfunctory consultations condemned by the judge had taken place.[72]

On the facts it was clear to the judge that the process of consultation adopted in Brent in 1984 had been seriously inadequate: not only were the Director's final consultation document and the timetable inadequate, but the final proposals submitted to the Secretary of State had never as such been put out for consultation. Although they were clearly able to establish defective consultation as a matter of fact, the applicants nonetheless faced a legal obstacle in that the legislation – as explained above – contains *no statutory obligation* on the part of the LEA to consult. LEAs had merely been *exhorted* by the Secretary of State in Circular 2/80[73] and Administrative Memorandum 4/84[74] to carry out consultations while their proposals were at a formative stage. In the absence of any *statutory* duty to consult, the applicants were forced to rely on the common law, under which the courts have in recent years developed a doctrine known as *legitimate expectation* applicable to relations between government and individual citizens affected by governmental decision-making. Where in the course of a decision-making process a past practice (for example, of consultation) has been consistently adopted by government officials, a legitimate expectation, recognised by and enforceable through the courts, may be created in the minds of individuals affected by these decisions.[75] Such legitimate expectation could be strengthened by other factors, including the strength of the individual's interest in the type of decisions being taken, and by administrative pronouncements in the form, for instance, of departmental circulars exhorting LEAs to act in a particular way.

The applicants in *ex parte Gunning* argued that they had a legitimate expectation that the LEA would consult them fully and effectively when the proposals were being formulated. Mr Justice Hodgson had no difficulty in holding that they did indeed have such an expectation:

> The parents had no statutory right to be consulted, but that they had a legitimate expectation that they would be consulted seems to me to be beyond question. The interest of parents in the educational arrangements in the area in which they live is self-evident. It is explicitly recognised in the legislation (see, for example, section 6 of the Education Act 1980). The legislation places clear duties upon parents, backed by draconian criminal sanctions. Local education authorities habitually do consult on these matters. In 1980 and 1983 this local authority itself had had comprehensive consultations which had led to the decision in 1983 to retain all school sites. Local education authorities are

> exhorted by the Secretary of State to consult, and the results of the consultations are something which he takes into account. On any test of legitimate expectation, it seems to me that these parents qualify.[76]

Thus, in the absence of any statutory requirement as to consultation, the court was prepared in the light of (a) past practice in Brent, (b) widespread practice in other LEAs, (c) parents' inherent interest in and statutory responsibilities for the education of their children and (d) explicit administrative exhortations to LEAs over consultation from the Secretary of State, to construct at common law a legally recognisable legitimate expectation that they would be properly consulted, thus giving them the required standing to bring an application for judicial review.

Although *ex parte Gunning* and other applications for judicial review on similar lines[77] have thus clearly established a legitimate expectation on the part of interested parties in this context, the exact *content* of that expectation is left unclear as it is dependent in large part on the precise meaning attached to 'consultation', and whether the legitimate expectation will be regarded by the court as having been met will depend very much on the court's interpretation of the exact chain of events in the instant case.

In *ex parte Gunning*, Mr Justice Hodgson stated that, for consultation to meet the required legal standard, it ought to be

> upon proposals of some specificity into which those consulted can get their teeth, whether the proposals be framed in general policy terms or in terms of specific options.[78]

What these words might mean in practice is unclear, but some more specific guidance was offered by counsel acting on behalf of the parents in *ex parte Gunning*, Mr Stephen Sedley, QC, in his submissions to the court. This has come to be known as the 'Sedley formula' for adequate consultations, and was cited with approval by Mr Justice Hodgson in his judgment. The Sedley formula provides four essential criteria for proper consultations:

1. consultations must take place while the proposals are still at a 'formative stage';
2. the proposer must give sufficient reasons for any proposal to permit 'intelligent consideration and response';
3. 'adequate time' must be given for such consideration and response; and

4 the product of consultation must be 'conscientiously taken into account' in finalising any statutory proposals.[79]

The first criterion – that the proposals be still at a *formative stage* when the consultation takes place – is in practice the most difficult to interpret. In another application for judicial review on this ground, *Nichol* v. *Gateshead Metropolitan Borough Council*,[80] the main basis for the parents' attack on the consultation process was that the LEA had consulted parents not on each one of six separate possible *patterns* for school organisation in the area[81] which had been set out in a report by the Director of Education, but rather on only *one* of those patterns, *the LEA having already made a clear decision of policy in favour of that pattern*. The preferred pattern was one of secondary schools for pupils aged 11 to 16 years, with tertiary college provision for all older children. The LEA had formed the view that it was quite proper for them to take the initial policy decision in favour of that one pattern of provision, to 'have an overall view' and to 'take the lead' in going out to consultation on that single pattern without permitting parents to submit views on the alternatives. The LEA had been persuaded of this by what it saw as the sheer impracticality of doing otherwise: it would not have been a realistic method of consultation, in the LEA's view, had they presented *alternative* patterns.

Mr Justice McCowan held at first instance[82] that the LEA's view was in clear breach of the principle that consultation be at a *formative* stage in the planning process. The LEA had at the point of consultation become all but committed in principle to one pattern: where critical decisions of policy involving considerable groundwork have been taken beforehand, it would be extremely hard on the strength of adverse comments received during consultation to unravel the process and start again. This, the judge concluded, 'illustrates the mischief of consultation at the stage adopted by this council'.[83]

Gateshead Council, however, successfully appealed against Mr Justice McCowan's decision to the Court of Appeal:[84] Lord Justice O'Connor, giving the leading judgment, took the view that to require consultation over each pattern of organisation would be 'in effect requiring a referendum, and that is not what consultation means'.[85] It was perfectly proper for the LEA to have taken an initial policy decision in favour of one pattern, provided that it had proceeded to genuine consultations as to the detailed proposals within that pattern.

Challenge on the ground of failure by the LEA to consider a report from its education committee

The second major ground of legal challenge over the drawing up of proposals by LEAs has been based on a technical failure in some cases to comply with a statutory procedural requirement. This may appear at first sight improbable, as sections 12 and 13 of the Education Act 1980 are almost entirely silent as to the procedures involved in drawing up proposals (although detailed formalities for the *publication* of proposals are laid down by Statutory Instrument).[86] A fruitful means of challenge has, however, been found in the Education Act 1944, under which LEAs are bound to

> consider a report from an education committee of the authority before exercising any of their functions with respect to education: provided that an authority may dispense with such a report if, in their opinion, the matter is urgent.[87]

The rationale behind this provision lies in the expertise of the members of education committees, whose function it is to advise the full LEA, whose members would not necessarily have the requisite level of educational expertise. The 1944 Act requires that education committees comprise at least a majority of LEA members, but beyond this there is a wide power of co-option. Such co-option is generally necessary in order to secure compliance with the requirement that:

> Every education committee of a local education authority shall include persons of experience in education and persons acquainted with the educational conditions prevailing in the area for which the committee acts.[88]

It is not at all clear what is meant by 'experience in education', though the courts have indicated that this should be given a broad construction.[89] It seems, however, that the essential purpose of the requirement that the LEA should 'consider a report' from its education committee before exercising a 'function with respect to education' is that it should first have the benefit of expert guidance on the issue in hand. Education committees were thus intended to have a significant part to play in the decision-making process, and their reports would have to be taken seriously. It is worth noting that the LEA must 'consider' the committee's report, not merely 'receive' it, although, of course, it may well decide after due consideration to *reject* it. This process should not be seen, then, as a mere token formality, and, indeed, it could give rise to tension between the education committee and the LEA, notably in the case of a 'hung' LEA with strong co-opted voices on the education committee. It is, on the contrary, regarded by the courts as a mandatory legal requirement of some substance.

The leading legal authority in this context is the Court of Appeal decision in *R.* v. *Kirklees Metropolitan Borough Council, ex parte Molloy*:[90] the LEA resolved to close a school by adopting the minutes of a meeting of its education committee which in turn had confirmed the minutes of a meeting of its schools sub-committee which contained a bare resolution to authorise publication of a statutory notice to close the school. The schools sub-committee had had before it a report by the Director of Education containing comments on the outcome of consultation but which contained *no evaluation or recommendation*. The Court of Appeal, affirming the decision of Mr Justice Mann at first instance, held that *a bare recommendation* from an education committee did not constitute a 'report' within the meaning of the Act: the LEA had had before it from the education committee a mere recommendation in the terms of an earlier sub-committee's resolution. Lord Justice Nicholls, giving the leading judgment of the Court of Appeal, stressed the importance of the presence on the education committee of persons of 'experience in education' and persons acquainted with local educational conditions,[91] and went on to attempt a definition of a 'report' for these purposes:

> In my judgment, what is envisaged by a report in this context is an appraisal by the education committee of the matter under consideration, including their comments or views on the way ahead. How full and detailed the appraisal needs to be for the document to be fairly and reasonably described as a report from the education committee on a particular topic will depend on the particular educational function which the council are exercising, the complexity and novelty of the situation, the difficulty of the problem, the gravity of the consequences and all the other circumstances of the case. But where, as here, the committee are making a specific recommendation to the council, it seems to me that, in general, for the document placed before the council to constitute the required report, it must at least include some explanation of the principal reason or reasons

> why the committee are making that recommendation. A bare recommendation will not suffice. Particularly where a matter is known to be controversial the council need to know why the education committee are making their recommendation, so that the members of the council can consider the committee's recommendation intelligently . . . . How detailed the statement of the reasoning will need to be will, again, depend on the circumstances. But, in the ordinary way, the statement of the education committee's reasons for their conclusion will involve of necessity some comment on the principal factors which led the committee to their conclusion.[92]

The existence of some form of cogent reasoning or evaluation of the issues would thus appear to be essential. Five further points should, however, be noted. Firstly, the education committee need not present an *independent* report of its own: it may quite validly *adopt* – either expressly or by implication – a report submitted by one of its officers.[93] Secondly, there would be no objection to presenting as a 'report' a composite set of documents, including the minutes of one or more meetings, provided that there can be rationally derived from them a coherent, reasoned evaluation of the issues. Thirdly, the committee presenting the report need not unanimously support it, though it would clearly be desirable for the reasons for any dissenting voices to be expressed. Fourthly, it is not crucial that the report should contain any positive *recommendation*: an education committee faced with a wide disparity of conflicting views may not be able to formulate any positive recommendations, but it should still be possible to present a valid 'report' in the form of an evaluation of the issues.[94] And fifthly, only limited reliance can be placed upon the power contained in paragraph 7 for an LEA to *dispense* with a report 'if, in their opinion, the matter is urgent':[95] this must be done by a clear, collective consideration of the urgency of the matter.

Other applications for judicial review have been based (wholly or in part) on this ground of challenge. Thus, in *ex parte Gunning*,[96] the parents claimed that the LEA had made its decision that consultations should take place on reorganisation proposals (a 'function with respect to education') without having first received a formal report from the education committee on the matter: what the LEA had had before it when deciding to go out to consultation was two reports from the Director of Education, together with the minutes of a previous education committee meeting which contained a resolution requiring the Director to prepare a further report.[97] The LEA submitted that these documents, taken together, did constitute a 'report' from the education committee on which the LEA could act. Mr Justice Hodgson, however, firmly rejected this submission: the LEA, he found, had clearly decided *not* to report at that stage, but rather to commission further research by the Director as an interim step. No coherent 'report' had come from the education committee.[98]

A contrasting decision is that of the Court of Appeal in *Nichol* v. *Gateshead Metropolitan Council*:[99] in 1982, the Director of Education had prepared a report for the Education Committee on educational provision in the Gateshead area forecasting a fall of some 25 per cent in the secondary school population there by 1991. The education committee decided in principle that reorganisation would be necessary, and requested the Director to present a second report setting out in detail the various available options. This the Director did, setting out his conclusion that the balance of advantage lay in favour of one of the several options (option (b)), involving reorganisation on the basis of 11–16 age range secondary schools with centralised tertiary college provision for 16–19-year-olds. At a meeting on 9 January 1983, the education committee passed a resolution that option (b) be adopted in principle, and requesting the Director to prepare yet another and more detailed report on this one option. The wording of the resolution was taken directly from the Director's second report outlining the several options, and the resolution referred directly to that report. The LEA itself then met on 3 February and confirmed the education committee's resolution that option (b) be adopted in principle and that the Director prepare a further report on option (b), but adding a further resolution that there be a further round of consultations on the basis of that further report.

The essential question was whether, in passing that resolution on 3 February, the LEA had truly considered a report from its education committee, given that the committee's submission had been merely in the form of a bland resolution favouring adoption of option (b). The Court of Appeal held that the education committee had indeed submitted what could properly be construed as a 'report' within the meaning of the Act in the sense that it had effectively *incorporated* the reasoning contained in the Director's second report. That second report had been circulated to all members of the education committee and to all members of the full LEA; some 17 of the 19 LEA members who had been present at the earlier education committee were also present at the LEA meeting of 3 February; and the explicit reference in the education committee's resolution to option (b) as the preferred option clearly referred the LEA back to the Director's report. As Lord Justice Nicholls concluded,

> It seems to me that the committee are telling the council that they have considered the report which is itself before the council and that their view is that the reorganisation of secondary education should go forward on the basis of option (b) for the reasons given in the report which makes it the preferred option. In my judgment the council received far more than a bare recommendation from the education committee and the requirements of paragraph 7 were satisfied.[100]

Lord Justice Nicholls' broad statement of principle in *ex parte Molloy* as to the circumstances in which an LEA may properly be regarded as having considered a report is by no means easy to apply: *ex parte Gunning*, *Nichol* v. *Gateshead* and *ex parte Molloy* depend for their outcome very much on their own particular facts. Mr Justice Hirst in another application on this ground commented that:

> What is required by way of report in any given case must depend on the precise circumstances and cannot be governed in advance by any formula.[101]

Nichol v. *Gateshead* indicates that the courts may take a comparatively flexible approach to what constitutes a report, but nonetheless LEAs would be well advised to ensure that deliberate and clear steps are taken at each stage in the formulation of the reorganisation proposals to ensure that a proper report from the education committee is duly considered, and that that consideration is clearly minuted, if challenge on this ground is to be avoided.

Challenge on the ground of sexual discrimination

An intriguing line of challenge based on inequality of provision of educational facilities as between the sexes has been developed by some groups of parents and been given substantial endorsement by the courts. The possibility of challenge on this ground may give rise to considerable disquiet among LEAs faced with great difficulties in seeking to effect a balanced reorganisation of schools in the light of falling rolls.[102] It is now clear, furthermore, that LEAs when drawing up plans for reorganisation must take into account in avoiding sex discrimination not only places available in schools maintained by themselves but also those in any grant-maintained (and perhaps private) schools in the area.[103]

One such challenge arose in Bristol, where the LEA, Avon County Council, had sought to overcome the problem of falling rolls by reorganisation proposals which would have included the closure of Merrywood Boys' School, the only *single-sex* comprehensive school for boys in the City of Bristol: *R.* v. *Secretary of State for Education and Science, ex parte Keating*.[104] The LEA had, however, proposed to retain two single-sex comprehensives for girls, partly in the light of pressure from the city's large Muslim population, who for religious reasons prefer their daughters to be educated separately from boys. The proposals, which were due to come into effect in September 1986, were duly approved by the Secretary of State in January 1985.

The parents originally sought judicial review of the *Secretary of State's* decision on the ground that it was in breach of the Sex Discrimination Act 1975. At an early stage in the hearing, the Secretary of State conceded that he had made his decision without taking the possible impact of the 1975 Act into account, and that he had thus failed to have regard in exercising his discretion to a relevant consideration. He did not, however, make any concession as to the possible impact of the 1975 Act on the reorganisation question as a matter of law. The Secretary of State's narrow concession was, however, enough for his decision to be quashed by the court. This did not, however, put an end to the matter, as the LEA's proposals were still alive and the Secretary of State could still go ahead and approve them afresh, but this time having regard to the provisions of the Act. It was thus vital that the court should give its ruling on the impact of the Sex Discrimination Act on the reorganisation proposals, and therefore the court permitted the parents to amend their application for judicial review by directing their challenge towards the *LEA's* proposal to close Merrywood Boys' School.

It was submitted by counsel for the parents that the LEA, in carrying out its function under section 8 of the Education Act 1944 of securing 'that there shall be available for their area sufficient schools', had failed to comply in particular with section 23 of the Sex Discrimination Act 1975. This provides that:

> It is unlawful for a local education authority, in carrying out . . . its functions under the Education Acts . . . to do any act which constitutes sex discrimination.

What is meant by 'sex discrimination' is indicated in section 1(1) of the 1975 Act: it arises wherever in the provision of education or educational facilities a boy (or a girl) is treated on the grounds of his (or her) sex '*less favourably*' than a member of the opposite sex. By adoption of a policy involving closure of the only single-sex boys' school, while maintaining single-sex education for girls, the LEA was treating boys 'less favourably' than girls.[105] The LEA contended, on the other hand, that it had, under section 8 of the 1944 Act, a wide discretion as to the nature and scope of the educational provision it chose to make, so long as it remained squarely within the concept of 'sufficiency' of schools: so long as there was 'sufficient' provision for both sexes, the fact that schools might be *different in character* as between boys and girls was legally insignificant. The LEA also challenged whether adoption of its policy could be said to constitute 'less favourable' treatment of boys: *different* treatment is not necessarily the same thing as *less favourable* treatment; and to deprive boys of an option (of single-sex education) which was left open to girls did not necessarily constitute less favourable treatment, in the absence of some identifiable *detriment*.[106]

Mr Justice Taylor concluded in *ex parte Keating* that the LEA's proposals did indeed amount to unlawful discrimination. His approach was to ask whether the loss of the option available to the girls of single-sex education, but unavailable to boys, would be a loss which a reasonable boy, or his reasonable parents, would regard as constituting less favourable treatment. Alternatively, one could ask whether a reasonable boy or parent would consider the option to have either single-sex or co-educational schooling to be *an option of value*. The judge concluded that it could indeed be reasonably regarded as the loss of an option of value and thus as less favourable treatment.[107]

Despite this conclusion as to unlawful action on the part of the LEA, it would still have been open to the judge to refuse in his discretion to intervene, on the ground that to do so would have caused enormous administrative inconvenience and delay for the authority, which was seeking in good faith to rationalise its schools in difficult circumstances. Mr Justice Taylor expressed sympathy for the LEA faced with these difficulties, but concluded on balance that to refuse a remedy here would be unacceptably to whittle down the effect of the Sex Discrimination Act, or even to ignore it.[108]

A second challenge on similar grounds arose in Birmingham, not over the closure of one particular school but over existing unequal provision of *selective* single-sex schools for boys and girls: *Equal*

Opportunities Commission v. *Birmingham City Council*.[109] Birmingham City Council's attempts to rationalise its secondary schools in the face of falling rolls had been bedevilled by changing policies according to the philosophy of the political party in power. The Labour group when in power had sought to eliminate all selective provision as part of the overall rationalisation, but eight selective voluntary aided schools had managed to continue in existence through a policy of resistance and through changes in political control. Of those eight remaining selective single-sex schools, by the mid-1980s five provided for some 390 boys at the entry age of 11 years, and three for some 210 girls at age 11.[110] A consequence of this was that girls with a test mark near the borderline had a substantially smaller chance of obtaining a grammar school education in Birmingham than boys with comparable marks. In these circumstances the Equal Opportunities Commission brought an application for judicial review against the City Council seeking a declaration that the Council's arrangements were unlawful under section 23 of the Sex Discrimination Act 1975, read in conjunction with section 8 of the Education Act 1944.[111] The Commission also sought an order requiring the LEA to consider without delay how this unlawful provision could be removed. The House of Lords, affirming the decisions of the judge at first instance and the majority in the Court of Appeal, held that there had indeed been unlawful discrimination on the part of the Council:

> It is enough that, by denying the girls the same opportunity as the boys, the council is depriving them of a choice which . . . is valued by them, or at least by their parents, and which (even though others may take a different view) is a choice obviously valued, on reasonable grounds, by many others.[112]

It was also held that the intention or motive of the LEA was irrelevant in considering whether it was acting unlawfully.[113]

The House of Lords was clearly of the view that it was time for Birmingham to institute positive steps towards the elimination of this considerable disparity of available selective places for boys and girls, even though LEAs must in a context such as this face formidable practical difficulties. These practical problems of securing equality of provision of educational facilities could indeed extend well beyond the admission of pupils to include numerous other aspects of provision, including the size of classes, the quality of school buildings, pupil–teacher ratios and much more,[114] and it is entirely possible that there will be further litigation in one or more of these contexts.

Challenge on the ground of failure to have proper regard to parental wishes

Although this would at first sight seem to be the most obvious, practical and fruitful ground of challenge, it is in law the most difficult to establish. Section 76 of the Education Act 1944 provides that:

> In the exercise and performance of all powers and duties conferred and imposed on them . . . the Secretary of State and local education authorities shall have regard to the general principle that, so far as is compatible with the provision of efficient instruction and training and the avoidance of unreasonable public expenditure, pupils are to be educated in accordance with the wishes of their parents.

As we have seen, parents have sought unsuccessfully to rely on this section in a number of different circumstances, notably in the context of parental choice of school (see chapter 2 for discussion).[115] The consistent view of the courts in litigation over choice of school has been that this section does no more than lay down a *general principle* which must be borne in mind; that it is quite proper to make exceptions from this general principle; that there may well be other matters to which regard should also be had; and that in any event the provisos contained within the section itself – concerning efficient education and financial considerations – are themselves of potentially very wide application.

Given this weight of legal authority, it came as some surprise that a group of parents in Strathclyde sought to challenge a decision by Strathclyde Regional Council taken in April 1988 to close down a school and amalgamate it with another school in the area through a petition for judicial review in the Court of Session relying on section 28(1) of the Education (Scotland) Act 1980, which is in virtually identical terms to section 76 of the 1944 Act quoted above. Although this book is primarily concerned with the law of education in England and Wales, it is instructive to look at this Scottish litigation as the legal principles on this point are identical.

The parents in this Scottish case, *Harvey* v. *Strathclyde Regional Council*,[116] adduced evidence to the satisfaction of the judge of first instance, Lord Dervaird (the Lord Ordinary in the Outer House of the Court of Session), to the effect that the overwhelming majority of the parents in the area were against the LEA's proposals. This led the Lord Ordinary to conclude as a matter of law that, in the absence of countervailing evidence put forward by the LEA as to the provisos referred to in section 28(1) (adverse educational impact or excessive cost), the *onus* fell on the LEA to demonstrate that they *had* had regard to the general principle of compliance with parental wishes. A *prima facie* inference of failure to have due regard to the general principle had thus been raised. This inference could, of course, be displaced, but the Lord Ordinary held that the LEA had failed to do so. In reaching this conclusion the Lord Ordinary relied particularly on the absence of any reference in the material placed by the LEA before the court to the terms of section 28(1) itself.[117]

The idea that section 28(1) (or section 76 of the 1944 Act) may give rise to any displacement of the normal location of the onus of proof – normally on the *parents* in seeking to establish their case that the LEA had failed to comply with its obligations – was certainly novel. Not surprisingly the LEA appealed to the Scottish Court of Appeal, the Inner House of the Court of Session, where three judges of the First Division found unanimously for the LEA. They held that the Lord Ordinary's approach had been entirely wrong and that there was no basis for the view that the existence of a divergence between parental wishes and an administrative decision by the LEA might give rise to a rebuttable presumption that the LEA had failed to have proper regard to the general principle.

On final appeal by the parents to the House of Lords, the First Division's decision was upheld, and any suggestion of a shifting burden of proof was rejected. Lord Keith expressed the view that section 28(1) (or section 76) could be the foundation for challenge in the courts only in a narrow range of circumstances:

> In order to succeed in securing judicial review the applicant must show either that the respondents paid no regard at all to the general principle embodied in section 28(1), or that they paid to it a degree of regard lesser than any reasonable education authority would have paid.[118]

Total disregard of parental wishes or utter unreasonableness or irrationality would indeed be extremely hard to establish: this may well be seen substantially to undermine the value of the section in any really significant sense. It is a provision with very little practical value to parents. Lord Keith concluded that the mere fact that the LEA's proposals for closure were in conflict with the wish of the majority of the parents to keep the school open 'goes no distance at all to establish the applicant's case'.[119] And he emphasised that it raised no presumption whatsoever regarding the extent to which the LEA had had regard to the general principle in the section.

CONCLUSIONS

The nature of the issues at stake here is such that it was perhaps inevitable that considerable conflict would arise. The decisions that are being taken here by LEAs and by central government involve consideration of relative political, social and educational priorities, and it is clear in the context of falling rolls that there is in each area a collective interest in achieving through rationalisation the best possible educational provision for all. This inevitably involves the striking of a sensitive and difficult balance between collective and individual interests, and we have seen that it may well be that the central government and LEAs may wish to strike that balance rather differently. While in no sense losing sight of the collective interest, however, it is entirely proper to give full recognition to the interests of individuals affected by reorganisation schemes to have a realistic opportunity to submit their views on the proposals *while they are at a formative stage*, and to insist that all statutory procedural safeguards are properly complied with. The courts, particularly through the application in this context of the doctrine of legitimate expectation, have considerably strengthened the position of individuals opposed to reorganisation plans, and it is clear that there is now a greater awareness among LEAs of the requirement of effective consultation. It remains incredible, however, that the statutory requirements for the submission of objections following the formal publication of reorganisation proposals under section 12 provide such negligible protection of individual interests. It is hard to draw any other conclusion than that they never were intended as any more than a purely formal gesture towards the individual interest, and that this position will remain for the foreseeable future. The legal challenges on the ground of sex discrimination rightly emphasise the importance of ensuring equality of educational provision as between the sexes. The courts have demonstrated their willingness to intervene here even, perhaps surprisingly, where to do so would be likely to cause considerable difficulties for the LEA in restructuring their educational provision in such a way as to ensure compliance. The attempt, finally, to rely on the very limited statutory protection in the Education Acts of parental wishes was doomed to failure from the outset, given the very guarded phraseology of section 76 of the 1944 Act (and its Scottish equivalent) and the restrictive manner in which it has been interpreted over the years.

6

GRANT-MAINTAINED SCHOOLS – A FURTHER DIMENSION TO REORGANISATION

INTRODUCTION

The previous chapter discussed some of the many problems faced by LEAs seeking to put forward well coordinated, socially and educationally viable and cost-effective plans for reorganisation of their schools in the light of falling rolls. A major further dimension to the issues has, however, been added by the creation under the Education Reform Act 1988 of a new category of maintained schools – known as grant-maintained schools – independent of LEA control and funded directly by central government grants. Grant-maintained status is dealt with in a separate chapter for the sake of clarity, but must nonetheless be recognised as inextricably connected with reorganisation plans as a whole, as any proposal by the governors of an existing LEA-maintained school to opt out will, if successful, inevitably have significant consequences for the organisation and structure of the LEA schools that remain. This presents yet another classic example of the realisation of the individual interests of some (the proponents of grant-maintained status) potentially jeopardising the collective interests of the remainder of the community. The impact of one or more schools opting-out is likely, furthermore, to be particularly acute if it occurs at the very time when the LEA is in the process of a wider process of structural reorganisation. Experience of applications for grant-maintained status hitherto has been that the probability of this coincidence of events is high: the majority of opting-out proposals have hitherto come from schools which have been under some form of structural threat – for instance, closure, amalgamation or loss of sixth form provision – under an LEA's wider plans for reorganisation. The impossibility of disentangling opting-out proposals from reorganisation as a whole is clearly illustrated by the

City of Bath reorganisation dispute which reached the Court of Appeal in *R.* v. *Secretary of State for Education and Science, ex parte Avon County Council*,[1] and will be discussed later in this chapter. It is, however, necessary first to explore the rationale for the introduction by the government of this new category of school, heralded by the Secretary of State as 'the jewel in the crown of parent power',[2] and to consider a number of the most significant differentiating features of grant-maintained schools and of the process of acquisition of grant-maintained status.[3]

RATIONALE FOR GRANT-MAINTAINED SCHOOLS

The government's major justification for the creation of this new category of school as spelled out in its 1987 consultation paper[4] has been largely in terms of the promotion of the autonomy of schools from the strictures of LEA control and, in some cases, allegedly unwelcome curricular pressure (though the evidence for the latter was extremely slight); the opportunity of governors to run their schools as individual institutions with their own identifiable ethos and spirit; the responsiveness of schools to parental wishes and thus the enhancement of accountability on the part of the direct providers of educational services (teachers) through the school's governors to the consumers (parents) leading to greater efficiency, cost-effectiveness and rising standards; and the enhancement of parental choice of school through increasing the diversity of provision of schools within the maintained sector and hence expanding the scope for the operation of market forces in this context. It is, however, worthy of note that there is a major overlap between some of these justifications – notably autonomy, parental involvement and accountability – and those given for the provisions of the Education Reform Act concerning open enrolment and delegated financial management. This would appear to raise an implicit assumption that the new policies of open enrolment and delegated management would not go far enough to achieve these goals: hence the need for a new category of school free even from the residual powers of control and influence remaining to LEAs following implementation of the 1988 Act. There may well, however, have been a more fundamental underlying purpose behind the government's opting-out proposals, namely the determination further to erode local authority functions in respect of education through the destruction of the LEA monopoly over the provision of maintained schools, this being consistent with the government's approach to central–local relations over a wide spectrum of governmental functions. The extent of this erosion will depend largely upon the scale of opting out: Mrs Thatcher has, indeed, spoken when Prime Minister of her vision of opting out on a substantial scale, drawing an analogy with the sale of council houses, and has hinted at legislative change to introduce some form of incentive in the shape of poll tax reductions as an inducement to parents to vote in favour of opting-out. Her then Secretary of State for Education and Science, Mr Kenneth Baker, had a more limited vision of opting out. The early indications are, indeed, that Mr Baker's vision was the more accurate, the majority of proposals hitherto having come predictably from schools threatened with unwelcome closure, amalgamation or other structural proposals. There may, however, be many waiting in the wings, content to observe the initial fortunes of the early grant-maintained schools or awaiting the outcome of the forthcoming general election before themselves taking positive steps towards opting out.

THE CHARACTER OF GRANT-MAINTAINED SCHOOLS

In many fundamental respects, grant-maintained schools will operate on a similar basis to their LEA-maintained counterparts. They will be obliged to meet the requirements of the national curriculum,[5] be subject to the same limitations on charging for 'extras' as LEA-maintained schools,[6] and be subject to inspection by HMI. Very importantly, they will not immediately on attaining grant-maintained status be permitted to make any significant changes in their basic educational character: thus, a school's character as comprehensive, grammar or secondary modern, or as single-sex or co-educational, and the age-range of the pupils for which it provides, will remain unchanged, unless formal statutory proposals for change of character are put forward under section 89 by the governors. Any such proposals would require the approval of the Secretary of State, and he originally stated that he would not normally approve such changes within the first five years after acquisition of grant-maintained status.[7] This was to allay the fears of many critics that grant-maintained status would often be merely the first step towards the reintroduction of selective admissions; but in the longer term such fears could well be justified, and the Secretary of State has recently announced the lifting of the five year rule.[8] The *religious* character of former voluntary schools will also be preserved, both by an inbuilt majority on the governing body enjoyed by foundation governors (see below), and by a requirement that the school's trustees give their written consent to any proposal for a significant change in its religious character.[9]

Despite these similarities, grant-maintained schools will be radically different from LEA-maintained schools. The principal differentiating features will be: first, the composition and functions of their governing bodies; second, their financial position; and third, their independence from the LEA in which they are located. These three differences are not merely administrative or technical, but are likely to have a profound effect upon the whole ethos of the school. They will now be considered in turn.

Composition and functions of the governing body

The government has stressed that the governors of grant-maintained schools will be expected to assume 'very considerable responsibilities and powers', and that their composition must be such as to enable them to enjoy 'effective executive management' of the school.[10] Each grant-maintained school will be run in accordance with an Instrument of Government[11] made by order of the Secretary of State[12] and providing for the constitution of the governing body. The membership of the governing body[13] must include:

(a) five elected ***parent governors***
(b) one or two elected ***teacher governors***
(c) the ***headteacher ex officio***
(d) in the case of a former county school, a number of appointed ***'first' governors***; or, in the case of a former voluntary school, a number of appointed ***'foundation' governors***.

The 'first' or 'foundation' governors must outnumber the other governors by at least one, and they must include at least two parents among their number.[14] First governors will be appointed by the governing body itself; foundation governors will be appointed by the body entitled to appoint foundation governors of the school in its voluntary status. First governors should be members of the local community 'committed to the good government and continuing viability of the school',[15] and must include members of the local business community.[16] Foundation governors of former voluntary schools will have the special responsibility of ensuring, so far as practicable, the preservation and development of the established character of the school at the time when it became grant-maintained, and compliance with any trust deed relating to it.[17]

Up to two *additional governors* may be appointed by the Secretary of State in the event of a failure on the part of the governing body in his view adequately to carry out its responsibilities.[18] If this should happen, extra first or foundation governors may be appointed to match the number of additional governors.[19]

Elected (parent or teacher) governors will hold office for four years, subject to re-election;[20] appointed (first or foundation) governors will normally hold office for between five and seven years, subject to re-appointment,[21] reflecting the need for a longer-term commitment to the school.

The school will be run in accordance with Articles of Government made by order of the Secretary of State.[22] The Articles must among many other matters require in particular that the governors agree their admissions policy and arrangements with the Secretary of State and establish appeals committees to deal with parental disputes over the admission and expulsion of pupils; that they adhere to the requirements of the national curriculum and establish procedures for dealing with complaints in this context; and that they prepare an annual report to parents and hold an annual parents' meeting. The governors will thus take over responsibility for the admission of pupils and for establishing and publishing details of their admissions criteria and arrangements, though these must be consistent with the school's previous character. An admissions limit will be set and stated as an integral part of the approved proposals for acquisition of grant-maintained status, and this will normally be at the level of the school's actual physical capacity,[23] and the governors will be expected to admit children up to this limit, subject to parental demand and, in the case of selective schools, the children's ability and aptitude. Grant-maintained schools will thus be brought within the principle of the open enrolment provisions applicable to LEA-maintained schools.[24]

A further significant responsibility will be for staffing: staff will generally transfer on incorporation to the employment of the governing body, and the governors will assume all the rights, powers, duties and liabilities of an employer.[25] Existing staff at the school will be required to transfer to the employment of the governing body unless they resign or obtain redeployment. It is true that governors of LEA-maintained schools will under delegated management likewise assume extensive staffing responsibilities,[26] but staff at county and voluntary controlled schools will remain the employees of the LEA. With the transfer of employment from the LEA to the governing body in the case of grant-maintained schools, teachers' conditions of employment will remain largely as before, and the School Teachers' Pay and Conditions Documents[27] will be applied to grant-maintained schools. But the transfer will have profound significance for governing bodies assuming the status of employers: they will become potential defendants in actions for negligence brought by parents on the basis of employers' vicarious liability for the negligent actions or omissions of their employees in the course of employment; they will be potential defendants in actions brought by former employees for unfair dismissal under the employment protection legislation; and they will be responsible for the health and safety of staff and pupils under the health and safety legislation.

In addition to their new responsibilities as employers, governors will assume further responsibilities through having transferred to and vested in them from the date of incorporation of the new grant-maintained school all land or property used or held (otherwise than on trust) by the LEA for the purposes of the school immediately before the incorporation date.[28] Where, in the case of a former county school, land or other property was formerly held by the LEA as trustees, this will transfer to and be vested in the first governors of the new grant maintained school as trustees.[29] In the case of a former voluntary school, any property held on trust will remain with the former trustees. Disputes over property rights and liabilities will be determined where possible by a new statutory body known as the Education Assets Board.[30] The governors will hold property previously held by the LEA for the lifetime of the school in its grant-maintained status: in the event of the eventual discontinuance of the school, any such property will normally revert to the LEA. While proposals for the acquisition of grant-maintained status are under consideration, restrictions will be imposed on the capacity of the LEA to appoint, dismiss or redeploy staff[31] or to dispose of property.[32]

Financial position

The underlying principles adopted by the government on the financing of grant-maintained schools are (a) that there should be parity of funding with LEA-maintained schools, and (b) that local ratepayers should be unaffected by the school's change of status.[33] The annual maintenance grant which the governors of grant-maintained schools will receive directly from the DES[34] will be calculated on the basis of the amount that would have been paid to the school concerned under its formula-based scheme of local financial management under sections 33 to 43, which will take the number of registered pupils at the school as the central determining factor.[35] The annual maintenance grants will be calculated in accordance with regulations made by the Secretary of State,[36] and the amount paid will be recouped by the DES from the LEA concerned.[37]

This apparently simple financial provision will in reality be complicated by several factors, including the need to take account of services provided centrally by the LEA, and services formerly provided by the LEA but for which grant-maintained schools may now make alternative provision. LEAs will retain certain responsibilities for the welfare of pupils at grant-maintained schools, including the enforcement of school attendance and provision of free school transport, and no diversion of funds in respect of these services from the LEA to the governors will be made; but in the case of certain other services provided centrally by the LEA for LEA-maintained schools, the governors of grant-maintained schools will assume responsibility, and a share of the LEA's budget will be diverted to the governors to reflect the cost of this provision. Such services will include school meals, the administration of pay, tax and superannuation of the school's employees, educational advisory services and school cleaning. The governors (and, very importantly, the headteacher) will indeed assume a weighty responsibility here in the context of negotiating contracts with suppliers.

Provision will also be made for the payment to grant-maintained schools by the DES of 'special purpose grants'[38] and capital grants.[39] The phraseology of the Act here is vague, and casts considerable doubt on the scope and purpose of special purpose grants, but the government has indicated[40] that these grants will be used to parallel existing grants paid to LEAs for in-service training through the Local Education Authority Training Grants Scheme and through the Education Support Grants Scheme. Grants of 100 per cent for approved capital projects will be paid by the DES on the basis of bids submitted by governing bodies, allocated out of total resources available nationally for capital projects at all maintained schools.[41]

The fundamental principle of parity of financial resources has been strongly emphasised by the government throughout the debate over grant-maintained schools: concern has, however, been expressed as to the potential scope of special purpose grants and as to the possibility of more favoured treatment of grant-maintained schools in consideration of bids for capital project grants.[42] And pronouncements by the Secretary of State before the 1990 Conservative Party Conference in a letter to Conservative constituency associations referred explicitly to cash benefits to schools which opted out,[43] leading to calls by the Opposition for an investigation by the Public Accounts Committee into the funding of grant-maintained schools.[44] A further factor which may seriously undermine the principle of parity of resources is the likelihood that grant-maintained schools with strongly committed and well-organised parent bodies will attract significantly greater voluntary contributions than their LEA-maintained counterparts.

Independence from LEA control

It is the prospect of independence from LEA control, freedom of choice and the ability of the governors and parents to mark *their* school with *their* favoured individuality and ethos which has been at the heart of the government's promotion of grant-maintained status. Individual involvement by parent and business community governors in the organisation and running of schools has been an underlying theme in central government education policy since 1979. The government sought to strengthen parental choice of school in the Education Act 1980;[45] it gave parent and business community representatives enhanced representation on school governing bodies in the Education (No. 2) Act 1986;[46] and it strengthened the curricular planning role of governors also in the 1986 Act.[47] The Education Reform Act 1988 now continues this trend, notably through the delegation of financial management and staffing decisions to the governors of secondary and larger primary schools.[48] The creation of grant-maintained schools independent of LEA control and enjoying substantial decision-making autonomy may be simply a further development in the same trend as the earlier developments mentioned. The government has heralded grant-maintained status as its response to parental demand for greater responsibility in running schools and as the provision of

> a new and powerful dimension to the ability of parents to exercise choice within the publicly provided sector of education. The greater diversity of provision which will result should enhance the prospect of improving education standards in all schools. Parents and local communities would have new

> opportunities to secure the development of their schools in ways appropriate to the needs of their children and in accordance with their wishes, within the legal framework of a national curriculum.[49]

In one sense the promotion of a category of schools whose governing bodies would enjoy independence from the LEA may be perceived as merely a further manifestation of the encouragement of members of the public to be responsible and involved citizens – a general social trend which underlies a good deal of current government policy. Furthermore, governors and headteachers may well be eager to be free from certain LEA bureaucratic procedures, and may welcome the prospect of greater discretion in the allocation of scarce resources, particularly over staffing decisions, though they will have to live with the reality of a greatly increased administrative burden in carrying out their responsibilities. In another sense, however, the promotion of grant-maintained status may be seen as a deeply political measure further eroding the power and responsibilities of LEAs and centralising power in the hands of the Secretary of State. In this second and more disturbing sense, the creation of grant-maintained schools must be seen in the context of other critical provisions of the 1988 Act – notably those concerning the national curriculum and the delegation of financial and staffing management – as a broadly based attack by central on local government.

THE ACQUISITION OF GRANT-MAINTAINED STATUS

It was readily predictable that proposals by schools to opt out of LEA control would give rise to bitter disputes at local level, with LEAs themselves eager to retain control over the maintained schools in their area, and LEAs, governors, teachers, parents and others concerned over the potential divisiveness of the presence of a grant-maintained school in their midst. The government on the other hand, eager to promote opting-out, has provided funds for the Grant-Maintained Schools Trust which is charged with advising and assisting governors considering a change of status. The procedural protections afforded by the Act to parents and others opposed to opting out were among the most controversial and hard-fought during the Education Reform Bill's passage through Parliament, prompting a significant government defeat in the House of Lords over the procedural requirements for parental ballots. And the procedural requirements rapidly became a source of legal challenges in the courts, with notable disputes in both Birmingham and Bath (discussed below), and will almost certainly continue as a fertile source of applications for judicial review.

The possibility of acquiring grant-maintained status is open to all county and voluntary secondary schools and to primary schools with over 300 pupils,[50] unless proposals for the closure of the school have *already been approved* by the Secretary of State under section 12 or 13 of the 1980 Act. In its eagerness to promote grant-maintained status, the government has now stated its intention to extend eligibility to *all* primary schools. The process may be initiated either by the governors themselves of their own motion, or by means of a parental resolution mandating the governors to act. If the initiative is taken by the governors, they must pass a formal resolution at a governors' meeting to hold a ballot of parents, and this must then be confirmed by a second resolution within a specified period.[51] Between these two resolutions, the governors are required to hold consultations with their LEA (and the school's Trustees if it is a voluntary school), and must consider any views expressed by the LEA (or Trustees) before voting on the second resolution.[52] In order to *mandate* the governors to hold a parental ballot, parents must present a written request signed by a number of parents of registered pupils at the school equal to at least 20 per cent of the number of registered pupils.[53] In the event of either a dual resolution in favour of a ballot or a parental mandate, the governors become bound to hold a secret postal ballot of parents either within three months of the second governors' resolution or two months and 28 days following receipt of the mandate,[54] the actual arrangements for the election being organised by the Electoral Reform Society as the body 'prescribed'[55] for this purpose by the Secretary of State.[56] The Secretary of State has, however, assumed a power to issue guidelines which must be 'taken into account' by governing bodies in determining ballot arrangements.[57]

Eligible to vote in the secret postal ballot will be every person known to the governing body to be a parent of a registered pupil at the school and named in the school's Admissions Register.[58] Governors are under a duty to include in the Admissions Register the name and address of every known parent of a registered pupil.[59] Governors may well face problems in the identification of parents: they are under a duty to take reasonable steps to identify parents,[60] and they are also charged with the determination of disputes in this context.[61] 'Parents' would include guardians and every person with actual custody of the child;[62] a child's natural parents would normally qualify, even where divorced, as would a step-parent and perhaps other relatives.[63]

The governing body must ensure that the Electoral Reform Society take reasonably practicable steps to secure that each eligible voter receives

> such information about the procedure for and consequences of acquisition of grant-maintained status for a school as may reasonably be expected to enable him to form a proper judgment.[64]

This information must include a general explanation as to the procedure for acquisition of grant-maintained status; the constitution and powers of the governing body of such schools; and the conduct and funding of such schools.[65] It is also necessary to inform eligible voters of the identity of as many of the proposed governors of the school as possible;[66] and of the proposed date of incorporation of the grant-maintained school.[67] Governors must also make this information available to staff working at the school.[68]

It should be emphasised that this is the *formal* information *statutorily required* to be sent by the Electoral Reform Society to eligible voters. The reality is that there is almost certain to be a good deal of campaigning at local level by several interested parties – the governors, the LEA, local political party organisations, unions, individual councillors and perhaps others. This is merely noted in passing in DES Circular 10/88:

> Interested parties will be free to make their own views known to parents and others as they think fit, but such expressions of opinion will not form part of the factual material included with ballot papers.[69]

That parents may be subjected to vigorous campaigning by interested parties was vividly illustrated in Birmingham in the Small Heath School dispute (discussed below), where there was evidence of much confused and misleading information being issued by different parties. The Government has sought to lay down guidelines for the conduct of such campaigns,[70] but the campaigning for and against opting-out proposals in the period leading up to the parental ballot is likely to remain intense and often bitter.

In the Parliamentary discussions of the Education Reform Bill, a great deal of debate focused on the majority of parents voting in favour of grant-maintained status that should be required. As originally drafted, the Bill provided merely for a simple majority of *parents actually voting* in the ballot rather than of those *eligible to vote*. The fear was widely expressed that the absence of any threshold requirement would be a form of 'activists' charter'[71] and would enable a small minority of activist parents to induce a fundamental and irreversible change in the character of the school. It was sought during the Standing Committee stage in the House of Commons to introduce an amendment requiring that at least 40 per cent of eligible voters support opting out, but the government successfully resisted this proposal.[72] In the Lords the government was, however, defeated: the Bishop of London led a revolt against the government and successfully introduced an amendment requiring *a majority of eligible voters*.[73] When the Bill returned to the House of Commons, however, for consideration of the amendments made by the Lords, the government used its majority to push through a compromise measure which is the final formulation incorporated now in sections 61(8) and 62(1) of the Act: a simple majority of those parents *who actually vote* is all that is required, but in the event of fewer than 50 per cent of eligible parents voting, a second ballot must be held within 14 days. The result of the second ballot is determined by a simple majority of those actually voting, irrespective of the percentage of parents this represents. The thinking behind this requirement of a second ballot is that, in the event of a low turnout, there will be greater time and a further opportunity to mobilise opinion in favour of or against the proposal to opt out.

If the ballot result is in favour of opting out, the governors are then duty bound within six months to publish formal statutory proposals for submission to the Secretary of State under section 62, and there are detailed provisions in section 63 as to where the proposals are to be published. The proposals must contain an extensive range of information, but in particular they must describe the existing character of the school and state the number of pupils for whom accommodation can be provided;[74] they must also explain the composition of the governing body.[75] Very importantly, they must spell out the proposed arrangements for the admission of pupils,[76] and, in particular,

> specify the number of pupils intended to be admitted to the

school in each relevant age group in the first school year beginning on or after the proposed date of implementation of the proposals.[77]

The Secretary of State in considering the proposals will thus have a clear picture of both the number of pupils who can be accommodated, and the number intended to be admitted. In view of the open enrolment provisions in sections 26–32 of the Act, it is clear that grant-maintained schools will be under pressure to set the intended admissions number at maximum accommodation capacity, and be expected by virtue of their admissions arrangements to admit up to that number.

Objections may be lodged with the Secretary of State within two months of the publication of the proposals,[78] and the Secretary of State may then approve the proposals, approve them with modifications, or reject them.[79] This process is closely analogous to the procedures for proposals for school closures and amalgamations or significant changes in their character under sections 12 and 13 of the Education Act 1980. It is noteworthy that there is no statutory right to any form of hearing by objectors, nor to any form of public local inquiry. The consideration of the proposals and objections by the Secretary of State is very much an internal, closed governmental process.

The Act acknowledges the probability that there will in many cases be an interaction between proposals (perhaps covering several schools in an area) by an LEA under section 12 of the 1980 Act for rationalisation by way of closures and amalgamations, and proposals by the governors of individual schools for opting out. Governors may well view opting out as a means of forestalling an unwelcome closure or other structural proposal by the LEA. The Act imposes an important new statutory duty on LEAs, before formulating proposals under section 12 of the 1980 Act, to consult the governors of any school concerned which might be eligible for grant-maintained status. The idea here is that governors should be forewarned and should have the opportunity to consider carefully the prospect of acquisition of grant-maintained status and initiate the process promptly in order to avoid the possibility of section 12 proposals being approved by the Secretary of State before statutory proposals for opting-out have been published by the governors under section 62. Where dual proposals are published – by the LEA for rationalisation under section 12 and by the governors for grant-maintained status under section 62 – the Act provides that the Secretary of State shall consider both sets of proposals together, but shall not determine the proposals under section 12 until he has made his determination in respect of the proposal for grant-maintained status.[80] If the Secretary of State *approves* the proposal to opt out, he will automatically reject the proposal under section 12 in respect of that school.[81] This is, however, almost bound to have a significant effect on his consideration of rationalisation proposals in respect of any other school involved in the LEA's section 12 proposals, which are likely to be a composite package of proposals: as in the Bath City case discussed below, it is likely to lead to their rejection, or at the least, he is likely to have to use his powers of modification of proposals under section 12 in this context.

LEGAL CHALLENGE TO THE ACQUISITION OF GRANT-MAINTAINED STATUS

At the time of writing,[82] four major legal challenges have been brought in the context of the acquisition of grant-maintained status – one against the governors of the school concerned; one against the decision of the Secretary of State to approve opting-out proposals; and two concerning the position of the governors of voluntary schools. These important decisions will now be considered.

The Birmingham Small Heath case

The first litigation arose out of the bitter struggle in Birmingham over the proposal by the governors of Small Heath School that a ballot of parents should be held, and involved parallel applications for judicial review by Birmingham City Council (the LEA), anxious to retain the school within its control, and by a group of parents opposed to opting out.[83]

This litigation raised a wide range of problematic legal issues over opting out, including the conduct of the governors and the headteacher in the debate over the future of the school, raising the statutory requirement that, where political questions are brought to the attention of pupils at school, they must be offered a 'balanced presentation of opposing views';[84] the propriety of governors who were also teachers or other employees of the LEA taking part in formal deliberations of the governing body, or voting on the issues, on account of their possible financial interest in the future of the school; the extent of the governors' statutory obligation to consult the LEA following their initial resolution that a ballot on grant-maintained status be held; and the circumstances in which a court might in its discretion refuse to grant a remedy striking an administrative decision or act down, despite having found that the public authority under challenge has acted illegally in some respect.

Small Heath School was (before becoming grant-maintained) a co-educational comprehensive county secondary school for pupils aged 11 to 16 years. It thus had no sixth form. Its catchment area was 'one of the poorest parts of Birmingham's inner ring',[85] and some 80 to 90 per cent of its pupils were Muslim, coming mainly from Pakistan or Bangladesh. There was evidence that no more than about 60 per cent of the parents understood English, and that at least 16 different languages were spoken among the parents, and with a variety of dialects among those sixteen languages. The school faced many problems, but its social and ethnic mix undoubtedly served to give it a strong element of cohesion and identity, and it was generally perceived as successful both in educational terms and as a significant community resource. This perception gave focus to strong feelings among a group of parents that the school should remain as a community resource under LEA control rather than opt out. Other parents, strongly supported by the headteacher, however, argued that the school could be more responsive to community needs if its governors enjoyed full managerial control as a grant-maintained school independent of the LEA.

The composition of the governing body of the school had been revised with effect from 1 September 1988 by virtue of section 3 of the Education (No. 2) Act 1986. There were 16 members, comprising four LEA nominees, the headteacher, four elected parents' representatives, two elected teachers' representatives, and five co-opted members. One of the elected parent governors happened to be a non-teaching staff employee at the school. The governing body met on 9 November 1988 to explore the merits of grant-maintained status. The governors formally resolved at this meeting[86] by a majority of 13 votes to 2 that a ballot of parents on the issue should be held. Those present and voting in favour of this resolution included the headteacher, the two teacher representatives and the 'employee parent' governor.

Certain consultations and communications – which will be examined in more detail below – then took place between the governors and the LEA. Then, as required by the Act,[87] a second governors' meeting was held on 14 December 1988 for further consideration of the issues: the governors voted on this occasion by 10 votes to 3 in favour of holding a parental ballot. On this occasion too, the headteacher, the two teacher representatives and the 'employee parent' representative were present, although the two teacher representatives abstained from voting.

On 13 January 1989 the ballot papers were sent to parents under section 61, and the ballot closed on 3 February, the parents voting by 435 to 338 in favour of seeking grant-maintained status. Formal proposals for the change were then published by the governors on 1 March;[88] and on 14 June the Secretary of State gave his approval to the proposals[89] which were scheduled to come into effect on 1 September 1989.

The main grounds of challenge on the part of the LEA were that the governors had not adequately consulted the LEA between the two governors' resolutions, as required by section 60(3); and that the four governors who were employed at the school – the headteacher, the two teacher-governors and the 'employee parent' governor had improperly taken part in the deliberations of the governing body and, in some cases, voted on the resolution, despite having a disqualifying pecuniary interest in the outcome. The parent applicants based their additional challenge on the grounds that the information issued to parents before the ballot[90] had been inadequate, especially as it had been distributed only in English, despite the multi-lingual character of the parent body; that the headteacher and certain other governors had acted improperly by themselves actively campaigning on the issue of grant-maintained status; and that the dissemination of certain information and documents by the headteacher to parents through the intermediary of pupils fell foul of the statutory curricular requirement that political issues be presented to pupils in a balanced manner. These major grounds of challenge will now be examined in turn.

Consultation

The LEA's first challenge was based on their contention that they had been inadequately consulted[91] by the governors as to their decision to hold a ballot between the governors' two formal resolutions. 'Consultation' is not defined in the section, but the LEA contended that it must at least involve clear identification of the governors' 'proposals' for the school in the event of its becoming grant-maintained, and that proper consultation at this stage was of critical importance to the LEA given the short period of time available between the two resolutions.[92] The LEA contended that the consultation process had been defective in that the governors' plans had failed to make clear, in particular, the governors' proposals in respect of pupils with special educational needs and the proposed use of recreational and library facilities at the school which had hitherto been available for use by the general public. The governors, on the other hand, argued that they were not obliged at this early stage to produce fully formulated 'proposals' for consultation, and that on the facts they had in any event carried out sufficient consultations with the LEA. Various communications had in fact passed between the headteacher and the Acting Chief Education Officer, and meetings had taken place between LEA officials and governors at which officials had set out what they saw as the disadvantages of opting-out 'in clear and forceful terms'.[93] The Acting Chief Education Officer and another officer had attended the governors' meeting of 14 December at which the second formal resolution was passed and at which there was an extensive discussion of the issues.

Lord Justice Woolf in The Divisional Court was clearly of the view that the LEA's submissions as to inadequate consultation were without substance: the governors could not be expected at this stage to have formulated their plans on all points in highly specific terms; adequate efforts had been made to communicate the substance of the proposals to the LEA, and sufficient opportunities had been afforded to the LEA to communicate their views to the governing body. The judge clearly regarded it as significant that no complaint about the process of consultation had been made by the LEA while the process was continuing: Birmingham City Council as a large LEA with legal advisers and experienced education officers on its staff could readily have been expected to have requested further information if they had felt it necessary, yet this had not been done. In a sense, they had by their silence waived any right to demand further information. The judge concluded that:

> If governors, as here, are prepared to discuss the matter fully with the local education authority and its officers and to make sufficient time available for this purpose, to provide any information which is reasonably required and to give careful consideration to the views expressed, the governors will certainly . . . have fulfilled their legal obligations with regard to consultation.[94]

The LEA thus clearly failed to satisfy the court at first instance as to this ground of challenge, and indeed the point was not pursued when the case reached the Court of Appeal.

The pecuniary-interest issue

The second major ground of challenge by the LEA was that the headteacher, the two teacher governors and the 'parent employee' governor had improperly taken part in the governors' deliberations as they had had a direct pecuniary interest in the outcome, contrary to paragraph 2 of Schedule 2 of the Education (School Government) Regulations 1987.[95] The LEA relied principally on the earlier decision of the Court of Appeal in *Bostock* v. *Kay*[96] in which it had upheld the decision of Mr Justice Jowitt at first instance declaring that teacher governors were disqualified from taking part in a governors' meeting on the issue of whether a school should become a City Technology College. In order for the regulations to have the effect of disqualifying the employee-governors, it would have to be shown that the change to grant-maintained status was sufficiently probable and that the consequences which might flow from that change for the employee-governors were sufficiently radical. The courts have traditionally taken a stringent approach to provisions of this kind disqualifying parties from participating on account of financial interest, placing considerable emphasis on the need to prevent conflicts between private interests and public duties.

In *Bostock* v. *Kay*, the Court of Appeal, in holding that the employee-governors were disqualified, had been influenced by the possibility that teachers employed at a City Technology College might earn more money than their counterparts in LEA-maintained schools, and by the prospect that, if not offered a position by the governors of the newly created City Technology College, they might be made redundant. It had been argued by the governors that these possibilities were too remote to be operative as disqualifying factors, but the Court of Appeal disagreed, endorsing the opinion of Mr Justice Jowitt at first instance that

> Any teacher invited to vote on these proposals would understandably be tempted at the very least to ask how it would affect him financially.[97]

In the Small Heath case, Lord Justice Woolf, although aware that the change to grant-maintained status was less radical than that to City Technology College status, nonetheless felt bound to follow the decision in *Bostock* v. *Kay* and thus upheld the LEA's contention that the employee-governors were disqualified. He went on, however, to express concern over this consequence of the 1987 Regulations, given that it is widely recognised that the headteacher and other teacher representatives on the governing body ought to have a particularly important contribution to make to these very important deliberations about a school's future.

When the governors challenged this finding on appeal, however, the Court of Appeal declined to follow its earlier decision in *Bostock* v. *Kay*, on the basis that there were significant differences between City Technology Colleges and grant-maintained schools. Lord Justice Glidewell (who, coincidentally, had also delivered the leading Court of Appeal judgment in *Bostock* v. *Kay*) emphasised that:

> The only necessary changes when a county school becomes a grant-maintained school are that the cost of the school's financial support is transferred from the local education authority to the Secretary of State, and that the governors gain a greater measure of autonomy. The school itself need not alter at all. If a voluntary, or county, school becomes a CTC the change is much more fundamental. The old school ceases to exist, and a completely new institution takes its place, albeit in the same building. The staff of the old school may well be, but need not be, engaged by the governors of the CTC and may be made redundant. The curriculum taught at the CTC may well differ from that taught at the former school, as may the age-range of the pupils. Moreover, in *Bostock's* case there was evidence that teachers at a CTC would probably work longer hours than they did at the former school, and thus earn more.[98]

The parental challenges

The governors' decision to seek to hold a ballot was challenged also by a group of parents of children at Small Heath School on grounds relating essentially to the content of the information which had been issued to parents concerning grant-maintained status and the manner in which it had been disseminated. Much of the press publicity concerning Small Heath focused on these aspects of the dispute, and in the litigation they raised issues of fundamental importance to the manner in which ballots are held. Central to this aspect of the dispute was the ethnic and linguistic diversity of the parents of children at Small Heath.

Under section 61, the governing body are required, having passed the second resolution in favour of holding a ballot, to 'secure that all necessary arrangements for the ballot are made by such body as may be prescribed'.[99] To this end, they must 'secure that the prescribed body take such steps as are reasonably practicable' to secure that all parents eligible to vote receive specified information concerning the nature and procedures for acquisition of grant-maintained status as well as specified information relating to the school concerned.[100] The body which has been 'prescribed' for those purposes by the Secretary of State is the Electoral Reform Society.

The section is silent as to the precise form this information should take, and in particular, whether it should be conveyed in any language other than English. The Secretary of State has, however, issued statutory guidance to governors under section 61(6),[101] which governors are required to 'take into account'. This requires an element of conscious consideration, but it does not mean that it must be slavishly followed. This guidance indicated that the Electoral Reform Society would issue eligible parents with, among other information, a factsheet concerning grant-maintained status. It indicated that it would be for the governors to decide whether to supply any of this information in languages other than English, and that the Electoral Reform Society would for this purpose hold stocks of their factsheets in Bengali, Chinese, Greek, Gujerati, Hindi, Punjabi, Turkish and Urdu. The headteacher of Small Heath School, acting on behalf of the governors as a whole, requested the Electoral Reform Society to send out the information in English, Urdu and Bengali, but the Society found this impracticable as their packing and despatching machinery did not have the required mechanical facility to do this. As a compromise measure, the factsheets were sent out only in English, but translated copies were made available on parental request. The availability of translations was made known to parents through the intermediary of the children (by 'pupil post', as it was called). The parents submitted that the governors had failed in their obligation under section 61(3) to secure that the Electoral Reform Society should 'take such steps as are reasonably practicable' to bring the required information to the parents' attention. Lord Justice Woolf concluded that the general presumption was that, where an English statute requires information to be provided, it need be provided only in English. On the facts of this case, given the multiplicity of languages spoken by the parents, it could not reasonably have been expected that the information should be provided in each language spoken. While it would have been desirable for the material to have been provided in the three languages requested by the headteacher, failure to do so did not constitute a breach of section 61(3). By taking the practical steps of ensuring the availability of translations where requested, and making this facility known to parents through 'pupil post', the governors had satisfied the statutory requirements.

The parents went on, however, to challenge certain actions of some of the governors, and in particular of the headteacher, by 'entering the ring in an improper manner and campaigning in favour of the change in status',[102] thereby bringing about a state of confusion in the minds of some of the parents. The governors' response was that the very reason why they had 'entered the ring' was to counter misconceptions as to the school's future which had arisen as a result of a large amount of inaccurate information having been issued by several other parties to the dispute. To this end, certain of the governors distributed leaflets to parents through 'pupil post' setting out their viewpoint in favour of the change to grant-maintained status, and giving notice of public meetings to discuss the issues. Lord Justice Woolf concluded that there was no legal requirement preventing the governors from taking such steps to counteract inaccuracies and confusions which were then circulating:

> Faced as Mr Knight [the headteacher] and the governors were with a situation where Christian parents were being told the school would become a Muslim school, where Muslim parents were being told the school would become a Christian school, parents were being told that they would have to pay school fees and pupils would lose the right to free meals and would not be able to use leisure facilities, and all teachers would leave the school and the school would become a conservative government school, the course which was adopted by the governors was perfectly understandable and not objectionable.[103]

A final basis for challenge in this context related specifically to the conduct of the headteacher and the two teacher governors in distributing the leaflet through the intermediary of the pupils and explaining the contents of the document to the pupils for them in turn to convey to their parents. This, it was submitted, was in breach of section 45 of the Education (No. 2) Act 1986, a statutory curricular requirement that in maintained schools political issues be presented in a balanced manner. This is believed to be the first legal challenge based on this important curricular requirement, though it is regrettable that it was relegated to the level of a subsidiary challenge in this way.[104] Section 45 imposes a duty on the LEA, the governing body and the headteacher to

> take such steps as are reasonably practicable to secure that where political issues are brought to the attention of pupils while they are . . . at the school . . . they are offered a balanced presentation of opposing views.

The children, it was contended, had been brought into the political conflict: in particular, the views expressed in the document communicated through 'pupil post' had been exclusively in favour of grant-maintained status and had thus clearly failed to offer a 'balanced presentation of opposing views', and the headteacher had additionally expressed his views orally to the children. This could be regarded as an unusual context for section 45 to be invoked, the section being primarily intended to operate as an element of constraint on the substantive content of the school curriculum, but the dissemination of material concerning the future status of the school could nonetheless be construed as falling within the ambit of the section. Lord Justice Woolf concluded, however, that, even on the assumption that a proposed change in the school's status was an issue to which section 45 applied, there had on the evidence been no breach: a 'perfectly objective' approach had been adopted in the oral statements to the pupils, and no fault could be found with the written document, given the context of the perceived need to take steps to counter the various misconceptions as to grant-maintained status circulating at the time among the parents.

The outcome of the challenges: discretion to refuse a remedy

As has been seen, the only ground of challenge to the governors' actions which met with any success was that brought by the LEA based on the employee-governors' pecuniary interest in the school's change of status: Lord Justice Woolf felt bound to follow the earlier Court of Appeal decision in *Bostock* v. *Kay*. On appeal by the governors on this point, however, the Court of Appeal distinguished *Bostock* v. *Kay* by reference to material differences between grant-maintained schools and City Technology Colleges, thereby exonerating the employee-governors from any impropriety. The LEA's short-lived victory in the Divisional Court on the pecuniary-interest point was, however, purely academic because, although Lord

Justice Woolf held the governors' resolution to have been technically flawed, he nonetheless declined in his discretion to grant the LEA a remedy quashing the decision to hold a ballot. This raises a point of wide significance for potential applicants for judicial review – that the remedies available on an application for judicial review are discretionary in nature, and a court may well hold in favour of applicants in terms of the substance of their challenge, yet nonetheless decline to grant them a remedy by virtue of the exercise of its discretion. In the exercise of this discretion the court is likely to have regard to a wide range of factors and in particular to the possibly conflicting public interests involved: the public interest in adherence to the letter of procedural requirements, the avoidance of any question of financial self-interest, bias or other impropriety in the taking of decisions, and the importance of maintaining public confidence in the decisions of the governing body, may have to be weighed against the public interest in achieving an administratively workable scheme for the future of the school and the avoidance of educational disruption; and, in weighing these considerations the court may have regard to the nature, extent and practical consequences of the irregularity complained of.[105]

In exercising his discretion to deny a remedy in the present case, Lord Justice Woolf emphasised four particular considerations: first, although the LEA's challenge was directed expressly at the second governors' resolution, any relief with respect to that resolution would be of no value unless the subsequent ballot was also quashed, and the fact that certain of the employee-governors had voted in the second resolution had had no effect whatsoever on the outcome of the ballot (in which parents had voted by 435 to 338 in favour of opting-out). Secondly, although the employee-governors should not have taken part in the deliberations of the formal governors' meeting nor voted for or against the resolution, it was perfectly proper for them to make their views known in advance to their fellow governors (and others), and the other governors would have been bound to have been aware of the headteacher's views; and even if the disqualified governors had not voted in the resolution, the second resolution in favour of holding a ballot would still have been passed, albeit with a reduced majority. Thirdly, even though LEA representatives had been present at both of the governors' formal meetings, no objection had been raised on behalf of the LEA to the presence or participation of the employee-governors. And fourthly, it was necessary to weigh the administrative inconvenience which would be caused by quashing the resolution (and the subsequent ballot) against the policy consideration of requiring strict compliance with the regulations. In seeking to strike this balance, Lord Justice Woolf concluded:

> While recognising that the policy considerations will normally outweigh any administrative inconvenience, the courts – particularly in the education field, where children can be affected adversely – are entitled to take into account the consequences of their decision. The result of quashing the ballot would be to prevent the decision of the majority of the parents in favour of a change in the status of the school being implemented in time for the next academic year as is now planned. This will result in the school teachers and the governors and the children being plunged once more into strife and uncertainty.[106]

As is so often the case, it is almost impossible to disentangle the educational, social and political from the more technically legal considerations in this dispute. The social and political dimension was what attracted most of the press coverage: it is normal for opponents of a particular school opting out to point to the potentially divisive, separatist and elitist impact the change of status would have on the provision of education in the area as a whole. Where that school is one which draws a high proportion of its children from one or more ethnic minority groups, predictions of separatism and divisiveness are still made, though they take on a further social dimension, raising fundamental arguments about multi-cultural education in our society. A majority of the governors and of those parents who voted in the Small Heath ballot expressed the view, doubtless for many different reasons, that their children's educational future and their community would genuinely be better served by the attainment of grant-maintained status for their school. The LEA and a group of parents opposed to opting-out challenged this by alleging deficiencies in the technical procedures laid down in the Education Reform Act 1988 and in Regulations. As is normal in the judicial review process, what was truly a challenge on social, political and educational grounds was transformed into a challenge on grounds of technical legality. Procedural defects such as failure to consult properly, pecuniary interest and inadequate dissemination of information are, indeed, often fruitful mechanisms of challenge in the courts, and educational disputes have in recent years frequently been the context of such challenges. But parents and others opposed to opting out will be able to derive little comfort from the restrictive interpretation given in this case in the Court of Appeal to governors' pecuniary interests, an interpretation which appears to attach a higher value to practical convenience than to procedural propriety; nor from the apparent judicial endorsement of what could be viewed as seriously inadequate efforts to distribute the factsheets in languages other than English, and of the involvement of the pupils themselves in transmitting information through them from a section of the governors to parents. Indeed, many would say that the involvement of pupils in any way in this context is highly undesirable even if not illegal. This emphasises the improbability of any successful legal challenge based on the very general phraseology of section 45 of the Education (No. 2) Act 1986. And this case serves as a solemn reminder to all those contemplating judicial review proceedings that technical victory on a point of law may well give way to the judicial weighing of wider policy considerations.

City of Bath case – Beechen Cliff School

The second major challenge to have reached the Courts at the time of writing is the challenge brought by Avon County Council against the Education Secretary concerning the latter's approval of proposals by the governors of Beechen Cliff School in Bath for grant-maintained status, and his simultaneous rejection of a composite set of reorganisation proposals by the LEA for reorganisation of secondary education in Bath in response to the pressures of falling rolls: *R.* v. *Secretary of State for Education and Science, ex parte Avon County Council.*[107] Significantly, this was the first judicial consideration of section 73 of the Education Reform Act 1988, a most important provision dealing with the interaction between proposals by an LEA (or governors of a voluntary school) for reorganisation under section 12 of the 1980 Act, and proposals under section 62 of the 1988 Act by the governors of one of the schools affected by the LEA's (or governors') proposals to opt out rather than face the consequences of reorganisation. Given that the majority of opting-out proposals have arisen in this context, this first judicial consideration of section 73 was bound to have great significance for other LEAs and governing bodies in a similar relationship – a relationship of considerable stress and perhaps antagonism. The stakes in such a case are high: the governing body is desperate to defend its school from reorganisation, perhaps involving amalgamation or closure; the LEA, taking a wider view of educational provision in its area as a whole, is anxious that its coordinated plans for school provision in the area should not be thrown into disarray by the removal from its proposals of a significant element, a removal which would almost certainly have profound consequences for the other schools in the area. This was just the relationship between the governors of Beechen Cliff School in Bath and Avon County Council.

Avon County Council had, over a period of years and after extensive consultations, drawn up a composite package of reorganisation proposals for the City of Bath, and these were submitted to the Secretary of State under section 12 of the 1980 Act on 22 February 1989.[108] In essence, these proposals involved reducing the number of secondary schools serving Bath City from six to five by the closure of Beechen Cliff Boys School; creating a new sixth form college on the Beechen Cliff site to make centralised provision for sixth form education in the city; and 'decapitating' the remaining five secondary schools of their sixth forms, thus limiting their age range to 11 to 16 years. The governors of Beechen Cliff School were, however, adamant that their school should retain its identity as a secondary school serving the full 11 to 18 years age group, and passed resolutions[109] under section 60 of the 1988 Act in favour of holding a ballot on opting out. In February 1989 a majority of the parents voted in favour of seeking grant-maintained status, and formal proposals to this end were then drawn up by the governors and submitted to the Secretary of State under section 62 on 17 April 1989.

The submission of opting-out proposals by the governors thus activated the provisions of section 73: this provides that, where an application for grant-maintained status is published before an LEA's section 12 proposals have been decided, the Secretary of State must consider both sets of proposals together on their merits, but must make his determination of the grant-maintained status proposal first. If he approves the grant-maintained status application, he will automatically reject the section 12 proposal in respect of *that* school, but he must then go on to consider the effect of that decision on the remaining section 12 proposals.[110] It may be that these remaining proposals will be bound to be rejected in the sense that they cannot stand on their own, the newly approved grant-maintained school having been severed from their midst, in which case the LEA will have to undertake a complete reappraisal of its proposals. There may, however, possibly be room for a *modified* approval by the Secretary of

State of the LEA's remaining proposals, though this may in practice be unlikely as the severance of an entire school from a scheme of proposals is likely to be too radical a change to permit modified approval of the proposals that remain. The Secretary of State in such a case would be in danger of purporting to approve by modification proposals which had never truly been submitted to him under section 12, and this itself would be susceptible to judicial review by those opposed to the modified scheme.[111]

The Secretary of State on 16 August 1989 issued his determinations of both the LEA's and the governors' proposals, and in doing so displayed a most regrettable lack of respect for the interested parties through a virtually total absence of reasoning. His decision letters stated merely that:

> In reaching his decision, the Minister concluded that the merits of the application by the governors of Beechen Cliff School for grant maintained status outweighed those of the authority's proposal.[112]

Avon County Council were dismayed by the consequences of this decision for their wider proposals on which they had held extensive consultations and which had emerged only after a gestation period going back to the early 1980s, and brought an application for judicial review of the Minister's determination in the High Court. The Minister's reasons, which had been so conspicuously absent from the initial decision letters, were spelled out in an affidavit put before Mr Justice Hutchinson, and the judge found in favour of the LEA on the central grounds that the Minister had misconstrued section 73 by giving the application for grant-maintained status *priority* over the section 12 reorganisation proposals, when they should properly have been weighed against one another equally in the balance together; and that the Minister had evinced a failure to give proper consideration to the *wider consequences* for the remaining schools in Bath of his decision in favour of grant-maintained status for Beechen Cliff School.

The LEA's victory in the High Court was, however, short-lived: the Secretary of State did not appeal against the decision of the Court, but instead took his own decision back for reconsideration in the light of the High Court's findings. On 30 March 1990 he made *identical determinations*, accepting the proposal for grant-maintained status for Beechen Cliff and rejecting the Avon proposals in the round, but on this occasion he scrupulously spelled out his reasoning at considerable length and in terms which were far less readily amenable to judicial challenge. He made it explicitly clear that he had adopted a three-stage procedure, as required by section 73(4)(b), namely consideration of the merits and demerits of the grant-maintained status application, followed by those of the section 12 reorganisation proposals, followed by a consideration of both sets of proposals together.

The Minister took the view that the grant-maintained status proposal was sound in that Beechen Cliff was clearly a viable, well-established and popular school of proven worth with a strong sixth form and with every expectation of retaining its existing strong demand for places. The LEA's proposals, on the other hand, although achieving a reduction in surplus capacity, addressing the problem of small sixth forms, keeping capital costs to a minimum and creating more co-educational places in accordance with parental wishes expressed during the consultation process, would nonetheless bring about what the Minister saw as major disadvantages: they involved the closure of Beechen Cliff, one of the stronger and more popular schools in the city; by removing all 11 to 18 provision, they also involved closure of another well-established sixth form of proven worth; they failed to make the most effective possible reduction in surplus capacity; and, above all, through centralisation of all sixth form provision in one sixth form college, they eliminated ***competition between institutions*** and ***parental choice*** at sixth form level. Both competition and parental choice are, of course, fundamental to the government's philosophy of education and underlie much of the Education Reform Act 1988.

The Minister went on in his decision letter to put forward what he saw as three feasible alternative approaches for consideration by the LEA, each of which might co-exist with Beechen Cliff as a grant-maintained school:[113]

(1) closure of one school to provide premises for a sixth form college; closure of the sixth forms of either three or four of the remaining schools, and providing either one or two 11 to 18 years schools co-existing with the college (to provide choice and competition at sixth form level);
(2) closure of two schools, one providing premises for a sixth form college; closure of the sixth forms of either two or three of the remaining schools and providing one or two 11 to 18 years schools co-existing with the college;

(3) closure of two schools and leaving the remainder as 11 to 18 years schools with no centralised sixth form college provision.

The Minister then concluded, balancing the grant-maintained school proposal against the LEA's reorganisation proposals, that it would be preferable to accept the governors' proposals to opt out given the established strength and viability of Beechen Cliff, and that the LEA's proposals were seriously flawed and ought to be reconsidered in the light of the alternative options he had outlined, each of which he considered to be feasible and to avoid the serious flaws in the LEA's scheme. He did not feel that the necessary reconsideration and resubmission of fresh LEA proposals ought to delay implementation of the new reorganisation scheme by more than one year; nor that his determination would 'inhibit to an unacceptable extent'[114] the options available to Avon; nor that any fresh problems in terms of providing an equal balance between single-sex and co-educational provision available to male and female pupils as required by the Sex Discrimination Act 1975 would be irresoluble by the LEA. For all of these reasons he followed his earlier determinations and accepted the grant-maintained status proposal by the governors of Beechen Cliff and rejected the LEA's proposals in the round.

Again Avon County Council sought to challenge the Secretary of State's determination: this application for judicial review was heard by the Court of Appeal even though technically it was not an *appeal* against the earlier judgment of Mr Justice Hutchinson but a first instance challenge to the Minister's fresh determinations.[115]

The three major grounds of challenge were that the Minister had unlawfully treated the grant-maintained school application as 'paramount', that he had been mistaken in regarding his three alternative solutions as feasible options, and that he had failed to give proper consideration to the difficulties which would be faced by the LEA as a result of their obligations under the Sex Discrimination Act 1975.

The 'paramountcy' argument was very similar to the unlawful priority argument which had been accepted by Mr Justice Hutchinson in the earlier challenge: the Court of Appeal, however, adopted a radically different view of the LEA's submission, emphasising that the legislation in this context expressly leaves the determination of the issues to the discretion of the Minister and that it would not be unlawful for him to adopt policy preferences, provided always that they were not applied inflexibly without taking account of all relevant considerations according to law. As stressed by Lord Justice Ralph Gibson:

> The Acts of 1980 and 1988 . . . empower the Minister to approve or to reject the proposals. They provide no test to be applied. They do not, for example, require the Minister to approve that set of proposals which will, in probability, most nearly accord with the wishes of the majority of parents and schoolteachers . . . . The task given to the Minister, however, by the section is to consider both sets of proposals together. The process is not one of fact-finding in the ordinary sense but of *judgment and evaluation*. It includes judgment of the future course of events by reference to the existing facts, to the accumulated knowledge and experience available to the Minister in his Department, to his policy for securing the objects of the legislation, and to his assessment of the prospects for success of that policy in achieving those objects.[116]

It will readily be appreciated that it is extremely difficult to challenge a decision based, as here, on a Minister's *judgment and evaluation* of competing criteria in relation to which he is entitled to adopt policy preferences and have regard to his own and his department's experience and his own underlying educational philosophy. The three judges in the Court of Appeal unanimously rejected this challenge based on 'paramountcy', emphasising that it could succeed only if it were shown that the Minister could not rationally have made these determinations on the basis of having adopted an irrational policy of priority or paramountcy. The evidence was merely that he had applied policy preferences to which he was properly entitled in the light of his judgment and evaluation of the issues.

The court came to a similar conclusion in respect of the challenge to the feasibility of the three alternative solutions propounded by the Minister in his decision letter. Lord Justice Ralph Gibson again pitched the requirement for any successful legal challenge here very high:

> For it to be shown that the Minister in this regard misdirected himself by supposing there to be feasible options, it would, in my judgment, have to be demonstrated that, on the material before him, he could not reasonably hold the view that such options existed.[117]

The Court of Appeal held that the Minister had, indeed, spelled out his three alternative proposals in his decision letter and, though the LEA or others might well assert that other proposals were educationally preferable for various reasons, this went no distance towards an assertion of illegality as required for a successful legal challenge which involved the taking of a decision which no rational person in the Minister's position could take. Indeed, one assertion by the LEA – that the Beechen Cliff site was the only site that the Minister could rationally entertain as the site for the sixth form college was, in the Court of Appeal's view, fatally flawed as the LEA itself had proposed another of the schools in the group – Culverhay – as a possible site for the sixth form college as recently as February 1988.[118]

The third main ground of challenge was based on sections 23 and 25 of the Sex Discrimination Act 1975. The assertion was not that the Secretary of State was acting in a discriminatory fashion or had misdirected himself as to the meaning of the provisions in any way, but that he had failed, in considering the proposals submitted by the governors of Beechen Cliff and Avon County Council, to give proper consideration to the difficulties which would be faced by the LEA in complying with *its* obligations under the Sex Discrimination Act to refrain from sexually discriminatory behaviour. This challenge was based on the decisions in *R.* v. *Secretary of State for Education and Science, ex parte Keating*[119] and *Equal Opportunities Commission* v. *Birmingham City Council*[120] discussed in the previous chapter, and recognised the obligation on the part of the LEA to make available an equal number of places for male and female pupils in single-sex schools or in selective schools (though no obligation to provide *any* single-sex or *any* selective schools). The Avon proposals had sought to strike a legally acceptable balance, taking into account parental demand for an increase in the number of available co-educational places, through Beechen Cliff ceasing to exist as an 11 to 18 years school for boys and the establishment of a co-educational sixth form college on its premises. Beechen Cliff being permitted, however, to opt out and continue to exist as a school for boys only would plainly have upset the balance of available single-sex places in the area, given that in striking this balance an LEA must take account both of schools provided directly by it and of grant-maintained (and perhaps also private) schools in its area. This is indeed likely to be a serious consequence of any single-sex school being permitted to opt out in the face of a balanced scheme of LEA proposals for reorganisation: the LEA is likely to have to reconsider its obligations under the Sex Discrimination Act and to ensure that its revised proposals remain balanced in terms of the availability of single-sex places. As Lord Justice Ralph Gibson commented:

> I see force in the submissions [of Avon County Council] because, on Beechen Cliff achieving grant-maintained status, although it will thereafter be maintained by the Minister and not by Avon as local education authority, the places for boys in that single-sex school will continue to be available at public expense. It seems at least arguable to me that it would not be open to Avon, without breach of the Sex Discrimination Act, to decide to cease to provide to an equal extent single-sex places for girls so as to deprive any girls of the option of attending a single-sex school.[121]

Although conceding that the LEA had raised a relevant and probably intractable problem which *they* would have to face, the Court of Appeal rejected the challenge *in relation to the determination by the Secretary of State*, as he had on the facts plainly had regard to the sex discrimination question and had taken the view that it would not be impossible for the LEA on reconsideration to come up with fresh proposals consonant with its obligations under the Sex Discrimination Act.

The Court of Appeal was thus clearly not prepared to accept Avon's three main challenges on grounds of paramountcy, irrationality or sex discrimination.[122] Indeed, the Court described the litigation as fundamentally misconceived in the sense of seeking to challenge under the guise of an application for judicial review what was in essence a disagreement as to educational policy. As Lord Justice Ralph Gibson commented:

> It is, I think, misconceived in so far as it asks the court to intervene in what is, when analysed, a dispute as to educational policy between Avon and the Minister. Avon, including the officials and members who have worked on the task of re-organising secondary education in the city of Bath, and the teachers and parents who have also worked in the processes of consultation which have been carried out for that purpose, believe that the proposals put forward are the best available for the children of Bath; and they believe, it seems, that it was wrong and unreasonable on the part of the Minister not to approve them and, instead, to approve grant-maintained status for Beechen Cliff School. The Minister, however, was acting

> under powers given by Parliament in the Act of 1988. If he was acting lawfully within those powers, there is no purpose in seeking to demonstrate that the proposals put forward by Avon are, in the view of those putting them forward, superior for the purposes of advancing the quality of secondary education for the children of Bath. Parliament did not entrust the making of that judgment to the court but to the Minister who is answerable in respect of his decisions to Parliament.[123]

This classic expression of judicial restraint reflects how difficult it may be to challenge a decision of the Secretary of State on grounds of *substance* where a statute has vested the decision-making power in him in the widest discretionary terms. It would take a very extreme form of unreasonableness in the shape of a decision no rational Minister could entertain, or clearly taking irrelevant considerations into account, or the omission of some clearly relevant factor, before a challenge on grounds of substance would be likely to succeed, in the absence of evidence of bad faith or a Minister acting for an improper purpose. *Procedural* challenge is usually more productive, but very hard to level at a Minister making a determination such as this, where the statute lays down virtually *no* procedural formalities for the Minister to follow. Procedural challenge *might* be successful if levelled by opponents of opting out at school governors who *are* under the Act constrained by a multitude of statutory procedural requirements, in the context of passing the initial resolutions, holding the parental ballot and drawing up their formal proposals for submission, but the *Avon* case shows how difficult it is to challenge a determination by the Secretary of State sheltered as he is by extremely generous discretionary power.

Particular considerations relating to governors, especially of voluntary schools

As we have seen, there is by no means always a coincidence of interests between school governors and their LEA in the case of county schools: in the case of voluntary schools, there may be an even greater divergence of interests as the governors may assume a more significant role in connection with proposals for the discontinuance of the school, and the school's owners or trustees – usually Church authorities – may well wish to oppose or significantly influence proposals favoured by the governors. These particular considerations relating to the governors of voluntary schools were well illustrated by two disputes arising in London – one concerning the proposed reorganisation of the Haberdashers' Aske's Hatcham Boys' and Girls' Schools (both voluntary controlled schools); the other concerning proposals by the Roman Catholic Church authorities for the reorganisation of Roman Catholic secondary education in the Westminster Diocese and the attempts by the governors of Cardinal Vaughan School (a voluntary aided school) to escape the proposed reorganisation by seeking grant-maintained status.

In the Haberdashers' Aske's Schools dispute – *Brunyate* v. *ILEA*[124] – the schools were owned by a charity of which the Haberdashers' Company were the trustees (the foundation), and they were governed by a joint governing body comprising 21 governors, of whom seven were appointed by the foundation, two were teachers, two were parents, and the remaining 10 were appointed by the ILEA. The ILEA governors were appointed for terms of four years and were, by convention, appointed in proportion to the representation of the main political parties on the ILEA itself. There were eight Labour and two Conservative ILEA-appointed governors at the time of the dispute.

The governing body decided in May 1988 to institute a process of consultation with interested parties as to the future of the schools in the light of the impending demise of the ILEA under the Education Reform Act 1988 and the possibility under that Act that the schools might cease to operate as voluntary controlled schools under the new LEA (in their case, Lewisham London Borough Council) and become instead either grant-maintained schools or City Technology Colleges.[125] The ILEA was strongly opposed to any such change of character, and wrote to all 10 ILEA-appointed governors seeking to elicit from them undertakings that they would support the ILEA's policy that the schools should retain their existing status. The two Conservative ILEA-appointed governors refused to give any such undertakings, and on 17 January 1989 the ILEA resolved that they should be removed from the governing body under section 21(1) of the Education Act 1944, which gives the appointing authority an apparently unfettered power to remove the governors of a voluntary school.[126]

In the application for judicial review, which was brought by the two governors who had been removed, the essential question was whether the LEA's power of removal of an LEA-appointed governor of a voluntary school could be exercised solely for the purpose of od rev (Or other members)

securing implementation by the governing body of the LEA's policy in relation to the school's affairs. At first instance, the Divisional Court held that the LEA could indeed lawfully act in this way as it was entitled to have a policy in relation to the affairs of a voluntary school and to remove any governors it had appointed who were thwarting that policy.[127] On appeal, however, by the governors to the Court of Appeal and then by the ILEA to the House of Lords,[128] a much more restrictive view was taken of an LEA's power of removal of voluntary school governors.[129] Great emphasis was placed on the view that LEAs and voluntary school governing bodies were 'entirely distinct and independent entities each having their own separate statutory duties and powers'.[130] It was stressed that

> Just as the governing bodies of voluntary schools are independent of local education authorities, so also, it is accepted, individual governors, so long as they hold office as such, have both the right and the duty to exercise the function of their office independently in accordance with their own judgment. It follows implicitly . . . that the power of removal cannot be exercised in a way that would amount to a *usurpation* of the governors' independent role.[131]

The independent function being exercised by the governors in this case was their power under section 14 of the Education Act 1944 to initiate the process leading to the discontinuance of their schools – a necessary precursor to the establishment of a new grant-maintained school or City Technology College on the premises.[132] This separate statutory function was vested in the governors, and in carrying it out the LEA-appointed governors acted independently and in no sense as *delegates* of their appointing LEA. Thus, for the LEA to attempt to remove its appointees on the governing body for failing to comply with its policy preferences was a clear usurpation of the governors' independent function.

(2) A similar dispute arose over the reorganisation of Roman Catholic secondary education in London: *R* v. *Trustee of Roman Catholic Diocese of Westminster, ex parte Mars*[133] and *R.* v. *Trustee of Roman Catholic Diocese of Westminster, ex parte Andrews*.[134] Here, the dispute lay between the governors of one of the voluntary aided schools concerned – the Cardinal Vaughan Memorial School for boys – and the school's trustees, the Westminster Roman Catholic Diocese trustee, a company limited by guarantee with Cardinal Basil Hume, the Archbishop of Westminster, as President of the company's board

of directors. The trustee company was in a position analogous to the LEA in the other disputes considered above, having a wider concern with the provision of education in the area, while the governors' primary concern was with the interests of their own particular school.

The trustee company was anxious to bring about a wide-ranging reorganisation, in the light of falling rolls, involving eight Roman Catholic secondary schools within the central area of the diocese. Two of these schools would be closed altogether; the remaining six schools would have their sixth forms removed; and sixth form provision would be centralised in a single newly established sixth form college. The Cardinal Vaughan School would have its age range reduced from 11 to 18 years to 11 to 16 years. These proposals were approved by the ILEA but were opposed by the Cardinal Vaughan School governors by a narrow majority, by an overwhelming majority of the parents, and unanimously by the headteacher and the staff. In view of the divergence of opinion among the members of the governing body, the President of the trustee company, Cardinal Hume, on 19 June 1987 wrote to two of the school's foundation governors (appointed by the trustee company) who had opposed the diocesan scheme, setting out his view that the reorganisation proposals were in the best interests of Roman Catholic education in the area as a whole and seeking their support. The two governors concerned, however, felt unable to change their minds and, on 7 September 1987, the Cardinal accordingly terminated their appointment as foundation governors and appointed two alternative foundation governors in their place. An application for judicial review was brought to quash the Cardinal's termination of the two foundation governors' appointments on the basis that their dismissals were unreasonable as they had been effected with the sole purpose of imposing the trustees' reorganisation scheme on the governing body which had rejected it, and that the trustees were thereby usurping the governors' independent statutory responsibility for determining the character of the school.

At first instance, Mr Justice Simon Brown agreed that

> the role of the foundation governors is an independent statutory role, not bound to act merely as agents or cyphers for the trustees, but rather to arrive in conscience at their own individual conclusions[135]

but he went on to find that it did not follow from this that they were immune from dismissal by the trustees on the basis of a conflict over policy. While the trustees could not *require* them while in office to follow any particular policy, it was still proper in the event of a policy difference for the trustees to replace them with others of a different conviction, provided that their removal did not fall foul of the generally applicable legal requirement of reasonableness.[136]

Mr Justice Simon Brown's judgment was delivered on 16 December 1987, and at that stage the governors did not seek to appeal against it. But subsequently the Haberdashers' Aske's Hatcham Schools' case came to court in *Brunyate* v. *ILEA*,[137] and the Court of Appeal (by a majority) and the House of Lords (unanimously) held, as we have seen, that, in the case of a voluntary *controlled* school, the governors could *not* be dismissed in closely analogous circumstances. In view of the Court of Appeal and House of Lords decisions in *Brunyate*, the governors in the Cardinal Vaughan dispute were permitted to appeal to the Court of Appeal, despite the fact that they were by then out of time, and the Court of Appeal followed the lead provided by the *Brunyate* case and overturned Mr Justice Simon Brown's earlier decision, holding that no material distinction could be drawn between the relationship between the governors and the trustee in the Cardinal Vaughan School dispute and that between the ILEA and the governors in the *Brunyate* case.[138]

The sequel to the Court of Appeal decision in the Cardinal Vaughan dispute was that the parents of pupils at the school voted overwhelmingly to opt out in favour of grant-maintained status, but formal consideration of the proposal by the Secretary of State could not be given until the trustee company had nominated the initial foundation governors of the school.[139] Cardinal Hume initially refused to nominate the 12 foundation governors required, thereby frustrating any further progress towards acquisition of grant-maintained status for the school, but the issue was finally resolved when the Secretary of State threatened to use his overriding power in section 99 of the 1944 Act to appoint the initial foundation governors on behalf of the trustee company.[140] The school subsequently went ahead with acquisition of grant-maintained status,[141] and the plans for reorganisation of Roman Catholic secondary education in the diocese went ahead without the Cardinal Vaughan School (and the Oratory School, Brompton) as feeder schools for the new sixth form college.[142]

It is evident from these cases that very similar issues of conflicting individual and collective interests are likely to arise in the voluntary sector as in the case of county schools. In the *Brunyate* case, it is clear that the ILEA was anxious to avoid what it considered to be the probable adverse impact on the overall provision of schooling in the area that might come about through the Haberdashers' Aske's Hatcham Schools opting out or becoming independent City Technology Colleges; in the Cardinal Vaughan School dispute, the collective interest was represented by the trustee company seeking to further what it saw as the best interests of Roman Catholic pupils in the area as a whole. The governors' focus in both cases was much more narrowly upon their own respective schools and the interests of their own particular pupils. As in the other disputes considered above, it may be very difficult to strike an appropriate balance between these apparently irreconcilable collective and individual interests, but the resolution of such difficulties is what much of representative democracy is about. One view is that the resolution of these conflicts properly lies under the statutory mechanisms created by the 1988 Act with the Secretary of State through his consideration of opting-out proposals – and objections to those proposals – submitted to him under section 62 (or negotiating an agreement with the proposers of a City Technology College under section 105). In the Haberdashers and Cardinal Vaughan disputes, however, the representatives of the collective interest sought improperly to circumvent the established statutory procedures by exerting pressure on selected governors whom they had appointed and who were unsympathetic to the collective cause. This was the predominant view of the courts, which considered that this was an abuse of the discretion as to removal vested in the appointing bodies[143] in that it usurped the governors' independence of action.

A very different view would, however, be that this interpretation leaves it very unclear just *when* an appointing LEA or trustee would *ever* be able to use its apparently unfettered power of removal – a consideration which applies with equal force to both county and voluntary school governors. One interpretation of these cases is that the power cannot ever be used in the context of differences of *policy* and is confined to instances of improper conduct on the part of governors: if this is correct, it is an extreme judicial narrowing of the unqualified phraseology of the Act. It may be that Mr Justice Simon Brown's view in *ex parte Mars* is to be preferred: the independent authority of appointed governors within their statutory sphere must be respected while they hold office as such, but they may nonetheless be removed by their appointing authority, provided their removal is based on grounds which accord with the legal requirements of reasonableness. This view would be consistent with the widespread practice of LEAs, following local government elections, of removing some existing LEA-appointed governors on the governing bodies of county schools and making fresh appointments in order to adhere to the political party balance on the LEA as a whole: in a recent decision concerning a county school, this practice was endorsed by the Court of Appeal, which took the view that the *Brunyate* case did *not* state that party political considerations could not legitimately operate in relation to the appointment and re-appointment of school governors following elections. The *Brunyate* principle operated not in that widely accepted context but rather where an appointing LEA was seeking to usurp the governors' independence through seeking to exert improper pressure upon them to toe the party line and through removing governors as a measure of party discipline: *R* v. *Warwickshire County Council, ex parte Dill-Russell.*[144]

CONCLUSIONS

As was widely predicted, the schools most likely to seek to opt out at an early stage have tended to be those which have been under unwelcome structural pressure from their maintaining LEA – by being under threat of closure or amalgamation or of losing their academically selective status. The prediction made by Mrs Thatcher – with which Mr Baker was in evident disagreement – that schools would wish to opt out on a massive scale, notably in Labour-controlled LEAs where the authority was overburdening the schools with unnecessary bureaucracy and, in some cases, promoting curricular policies of an extremist nature, has not at this stage been borne out.[145]

Beyond the easy conclusion that opting-out may be attractive to schools under structural threat, it is too early at this stage to predict the scale on which schools will opt out in the future. There may well be many governing bodies which prefer to observe the fortunes of the early grant-maintained schools in their early stages before taking any firm steps. Some governing bodies may prefer to wait until they have had some experience of delegated financial and staffing management as a form of interim measure before considering their positions. Others may prefer to await the outcome of the next general election, given that a Labour government would almost certainly pass early legislation to abolish grant-maintained status, and schools which had opted out may find the terms on which they are brought back within the LEA fold less than favourable.[146]

It is perhaps unfortunate that the majority of the early ballots in favour of opting out have been in the context of forestalling reorganisation: this has tended to give the impression of opting out as a short-term tactical manoeuvre in response to an immediate threat rather than as a genuinely desired fundamental long-term change in the whole ethos of the school. Governors and parents seeking to opt out are indeed assuming a major responsibility by instigating a change which will continue to condition the whole character of the school perhaps for long after they cease to be governors or parents of registered pupils. There is no provision for opting out for an experimental period and then perhaps reverting to LEA control, other than by discontinuance of the grant-maintained school[147] followed by the establishment of a new LEA-maintained school on the premises. The Secretary of State has, furthermore, indicated that he would not anticipate consideration of proposals for discontinuance within the first 10 years.[148]

The main governmental justification for grant-maintained schools has been enhancement of parental choice, diversity of provision, independence and the encouragement of parental involvement in the running of schools. The major danger is, however, the development of a divisive and elitist category of school which could do considerable damage to the provision of education in an area as a collective whole, with grant-maintained schools enjoying considerably greater parental support in cash, kind and spirit than their LEA-maintained counterparts, and the latter offering the statutory minimum provision for the majority of children in the area.

7

EVALUATION AND OUTLOOK

The last ten years have been a period of immense change and immense controversy in the governance of schools, as indeed in many other sectors of state activity. This has, furthermore, taken place against a demographic, economic and social background which has presented enormous problems and which itself has necessarily conditioned much of educational policy-making and administration throughout the period. The fall in the birth rate which led in the late 1970s and the 1980s to dwindling pupil numbers profoundly affected the structure and organisation of schools and led to agonising decisions for most LEAs giving rise to a considerable volume of conflict and many major local disputes as to closures and amalgamations, as well as having a significant impact on parental choice of school and on the curriculum: the availability of surplus places may in some areas have enhanced choice, while at the same time closures and amalgamations have served to inhibit it; and it has frequently been found to be extremely difficult in a cost-effective way to maintain a balanced curriculum, particularly at sixth form level, where pupil numbers have fallen below a given level. It has also been a period of economic difficulty in which education along with other public services has had to compete for the allocation of scarce resources. Expenditure constraints, as we have seen, have had a devastating effect on educational provision in many areas, leaving many schools with deteriorating fabric, unable to provide adequate equipment and books and, above all, with a crisis in the supply of appropriately qualified teachers attributable in large part to government decisions as to salary levels but also to the dispiriting working environment encountered in many areas, most notably perhaps in some inner London boroughs. These problems are, furthermore, being accentuated by the considerable demands now placed upon the teaching profession by the national curriculum in terms of teacher supply, equipment, books and other resources. Furthermore, the impact of these economic constraints is not just educational: educational deprivation cannot be considered in isolation from other forms of social deprivation which seem now to be endemic in many inner cities. The provision of educational services of the standard of excellence which we would all wish to see in deprived inner-city areas presents a problem of considerable magnitude for hard pressed LEAs.

It is against this background of demographic change and economic and social problems that LEAs and schools are now being subjected to the government's overriding policy of imposing on schools the rigours of competitive market forces by virtue of the reforms contained in the Education Reform Act 1988. It is always easy to justify this policy by asserting that it serves to raise standards by making schools more effectively accountable to their consumers. The counter-argument is, however, that parental choice of school is utterly hollow in areas of deprivation where the mass of the population are economically incapable of relocating and considerations of geographical practicality render the possibility of their children attending schools in other areas meaningless. Parental choice then becomes choice only for those who already enjoy relative economic strength, and their flight to the more favoured schools in the more favoured locations in itself significantly accentuates the level of deprivation in the less favoured schools whose falling rolls bring about diminishing resources, thereby still further lowering consumer satisfaction in those schools and hastening the exodus of those pupils who still have the possibility of going elsewhere. This amounts to a progressive cycle of deprivation which is exceptionally damaging to the community interest.

Not only does it accentuate inequality and deprivation, leading towards a dispirited and hopeless educational environment, but there is a strong probability that it will in many cases contribute significantly to the many invidious decisions which must be taken by LEAs as to which schools should be closed down and when. Those decisions are all the more invidious because the most vulnerable schools – usually those located in run-down inner-city areas – are very often seen as serving a highly significant community purpose. This is not in any way to argue that inner-city schools should never be closed: clearly hard decisions of this nature must be taken by virtually every LEA in a time of falling rolls. What is, however, argued, is that these decisions should not be entirely 'market-driven' as now largely tends to be the case through the implementation of the dual policies of open enrolment and formula-funding based on pupil numbers. A balanced and sensitive social policy approach would undoubtedly include consideration of pupil numbers and expressed parental preferences, but would also give great weight to an evaluation of the social cost to the community of any proposed closure. The market forces ideal may appear superficially attractive as offering choice, freedom and direct accountability, but it carries great potential danger for many schools and for many communities, offering only very limited protection for the weak, exacerbating the impact of expenditure constraints upon schools with diminishing pupil numbers, and undermining the capacity of LEAs for rational planning for the long or even the medium term.

It should be obvious from the foregoing chapters that this book has been written at a time of major upheaval in the provision of education, both through the implementation of the reforms contained in the Education Reform Act 1988 and the continuation of reorganisation necessitated by falling rolls. The broad thrust of much of the argument in those chapters has been that those reforms have not only had the effect of destabilising the system, but that they have themselves in many contexts been extremely damaging. What the future holds for the education service is extremely difficult to predict and is in any event substantially dependent upon uncertain political developments. In the event of the Conservative government being returned to office at the general election which must be held not later than the summer of 1992, it would be reasonable to assume that the philosophy of subjecting the education service as far as practicable to the rigours of market forces will continue, with all the uncertainty inherent in that philosophy for LEAs. The open enrolment policy will be applied to its full effect and the more vulnerable schools will become increasingly unviable, thereby quite possibly bringing about closures which would not otherwise have taken place. Those in the vulnerable category that manage to survive are likely to be pushed further towards legal insufficiency of provision by further denial of funding, though any illegality is most unlikely to be checked by the courts, largely for the procedural reasons discussed in chapter 4.

Through this depressing picture may perhaps be discerned a ray of light in the further modification of the national curriculum, evidencing at least some willingness on the part of central government to heed the warnings of the teaching profession as to over-prescription and overcrowding of the curriculum, and to learn some lessons from the turbulent summer of 1991 in the context of the testing of seven-year-olds. That is certainly welcome, but what would be even more welcome would be a reconsideration of the institutional mechanisms for promulgating the Orders prescribing the substantive contents of the programmes of study and testing arrangements, with a particular emphasis on bringing the teaching profession and LEAs formally into that structure on a considerably more substantial basis than is presently the case.

It is also to be expected that there will be further erosion of LEA functions, though how far this will be taken can only at this time be highly speculative. Certainly there will be strong encouragement for schools to opt out of LEA control by increasing the financial incentives and, perhaps, by legislation amending the procedural steps required. Whether the scale on which schools opt out will be greatly increased by these measures, thereby realising Mrs Thatcher's early predictions that most schools would opt out, leaving only a limited residue under LEA control, cannot at the time of writing be judged. What can be said with some confidence, however, is that both the prospect and the actuality of schools opting out will continue seriously to undermine LEA plans for reorganisation.

We have seen the functions of LEAs becoming increasingly residual through the erosion of their powers in two essential directions – upwards to the central department, notably through opting out and the national curriculum, and downwards to school governing bodies, primarily through the delegation of financial and staffing management. This is a process that will undoubtedly continue as more schools opt out, as the national curriculum takes a clearer shape and as delegation is fully implemented. LEAs will be left with a miscellaneous residue of functions involving co-ordination, supervision, inspection and advice, though still with their fundamental statutory duty under section 8 of the 1944 Act to provide 'sufficient' schools. Whether in this residual form they will have the capacity to ensure that sufficiency is very much an open question. What is extremely difficult to predict, and may well prove to be the most politically volatile issue of all in the educational context in the coming years, is whether the government will drive this erosion of LEA functions to its conclusion by deciding that there is no longer any genuine role for LEAs to play in the provision of educational services. The government has, indeed, a notable track record of abolishing sectors of local government: both the Greater London Council and the Metropolitan County Councils were abolished under the Local Government Act 1985, and the ILEA was abolished under the

Education Reform Act 1988. These serve as clear precedents for radical structural change in the future. The prospect that the funding of education should be entirely removed from local government has been an important feature of political debate over the reform of local government taxation and was a central pillar of Mr Michael Heseltine's Conservative Party leadership campaign. An important part of the political prize for the removal of education funding from local government is that it would potentially open the way to considerable reductions in local government taxation, given that education is clearly the most expensive local authority service. The consequences would, however, be far more than merely financial, as they would involve a fundamental shift in the balance between central and local government of truly constitutional dimensions and would cast considerable doubt over the continued existence of LEAs, even as bodies exercising no more than a limited residue of functions. The consequential expansion of the DES in such a situation may well be accompanied by the creation of a range of statutory advisory and functional bodies, whose members would no doubt be appointed by the Secretary of State, largely in the mould of the National Curriculum Council and the School Examinations and Assessment Council, taking over the remaining functions of LEAs. At the time of writing, however, this cannot be other than highly speculative. What is certain, though, is that such developments would create a political storm of major proportions, at the centre of which would be the County Councils, many under Conservative control, fearful for their continued existence and by no means prepared to meet their demise without a prolonged struggle. The potential here for increased centralisation and authoritarianism is, however, awesome.

Finally, in the event of the Conservative government continuing in office, one can assume that education will adopt a prominent position in Mr Major's 'Citizens' Charter'. At the time of writing, White Papers offering a detailed explanation of the government's proposals in this context are awaited, though it is expected that schools will be placed under a legal obligation to publish performance 'league tables', and that there will be a radical reform of HMI, probably involving some form of privatisation.

It is perhaps rather easier to predict what the future may hold in the event of a Labour government coming to power at the forthcoming general election, in that the threat to the very existence of LEAs would be lifted and the continued erosion of their powers would in several particular respects be stemmed. It is true that local authority finance would be subject to fundamental review in the process of finding a replacement for the community charge, but it is most improbable, whatever the outcome of that review, that the funding of education would be wholly removed from local government. It is probable that limitations would be placed upon the delegation of financial and staffing management to governing bodies, thereby ensuring a more considerable role for LEAs to play, and the exodus of schools from LEA control to direct funding from the DES as grant-maintained schools would clearly be stopped: legislation designed to bring grant-maintained schools (and city technology colleges) into the LEA sector would undoubtedly be introduced, though its implementation may well take a considerable time, given the complexity of the initial impact this would be likely to have on the organisation of the provision of schools in the area as a whole. It would be necessary for LEAs to make adjustments to their overall provision of schools in view of the return of the grant-maintained schools to the LEA fold, but for the future the position would be more stable as the LEAs would not have to live under the continual threat of disruption caused by the prospect of one or more schools in their midst opting out. It is also probable that LEA planning would achieve far greater coherence and structure through the repeal of the open enrolment provisions of the Education Reform Act and reinstatement of the capacity of LEAs to impose admissions quotas. This, together with a reconsideration of the formula-funding of schools based on pupil numbers, would go a long way to protect the most vulnerable schools in many communities. Finally, it is certainly to be expected that a Labour government would seek to loosen the over-prescriptive provisions of the national curriculum, though in this context it would seem that the Conservative government has already made a start, and it is unclear at present precisely to what extent the parties remain at odds on this issue.

These policy differences between the major political parties are not marginal matters involving fine distinctions, minor adjustments and fine tuning. On the contrary: they go to the very heart of the relationship between central and local government, questioning the level of authoritarian control we are prepared to tolerate in our society, even to the extent of casting doubt upon the very existence of local government involvement in school education; they also go to the very heart of educational and social policy, raising fundamental questions as to whether these should be driven essentially by market forces or by a broader consideration of social need; and they go to the very heart of the fundamental question as to where the balance ought to be struck between individual and collective interests in our society.

NOTES

1 INTRODUCTION

1 See A. Bainham, *Children, Parents and the State*, London, Sweet & Maxwell, 1988, chs 1 and 7.
2 [1985] 3 All ER 402.
3 See M. D. A. Freeman, *The Rights and Wrongs of Children*, London, Frances Pinter, 1983, especially chs 1 and 2, and J. Eekelaar, 'The Emergence of Children's Rights' (1986) *Oxford Journal of Legal Studies* 161.
4 See I. Kennedy, *Treat Me Right: Essays in Medical Law and Ethics*, Oxford, Clarendon Press, 1988, pp. 111–18.
5 Mill's Essay *On Liberty*, ch. 5, reproduced in full in and quoted from M. Warnock (ed.), *Utilitarianism: John Stuart Mill*, Glasgow, Fontana Press, 1986, pp. 238–9.
6 See M. D. A. Freeman, op. cit., n. 3, especially ch. 2.
7 Ibid., p. 4.
8 J. S. Mill, op. cit., n. 5, pp. 239–40.
9 (1954) 347 US 483.
10 (1896) 163 US 537.
11 Emphasis added.
12 This is now qualified by the open enrolment provisions of the Education Reform Act 1988, discussed in chapter 2.
13 See especially Article 13.
14 See UK *Treaty Series No. 46 (1954)*, Cmd 9221, 1954.
15 Ibid., p. 7.
16 See 'Sect "Has No Right to Veto School TV"', *The Independent*, 21 December 1990.
17 (1982) 4 EHRR 293.
18 Ibid., p. 303.
19 Ibid., p. 305.
20 Ibid.
21 See HL Deb. Vol. 465, cols. 1314–33 (4 July 1985).

2 CHOICE OF SCHOOL

1 See L. Bash, 'Education Goes to Market', ch. 2 of L. Bash and D. Coulby (eds), *The Education Reform Act: Competition and Control*, London, Cassell, 1989.
2 See K. P. Poole, *Education Law*, London, Sweet & Maxwell, 1988, p. 65 for explanation of these categories.
3 See S. M. Poulter, *English Law and Ethnic Minority Customs*, London, Butterworths, 1986, ch. 7, and S. M. Poulter, *Asian Traditions and English Law: a Handbook*, Stoke-on-Trent, Runnymede Trust with Trentham Books, 1990, ch. 11.
4 See Education Reform Act 1988, ss. 6–13.
5 See White Paper, *Educational Reconstruction* Cmd 6458, 1943, paras 27–35.
6 See DES Circular 4/74, *The Organisation of Secondary Education*, 16 April 1974.
7 See chapter 6.
8 See Education Reform Act 1988, s. 20(3)(a), and see wider discussion in chapter 3.
9 See P. McAuslan, 'Administrative Law, Collective Consumption and Judicial Policy' (1983) *Modern Law Review* 1.
10 See *Belgian Linguistics Case (No. 2)* (1968) 1 EHRR 252 at p. 281.
11 Applications Nos. 10228 and 10229/82 v. United Kingdom (1982) 7 EHRR 141.
12 Under s. 7, Education Act 1980, discussed below.
13 (1982) 7 EHRR 141 at p. 143.
14 Ibid., p. 143.
15 Application No. 946/81 v. United Kingdom (1981) 5 EHRR 480.
16 Ibid.
17 Contrast the position in the USA where members of the Amish community successfully challenged the State of Wisconsin's compulsory school attendance laws as being inconsistent with their constitutional right freely to exercise their religion under the First Amendment to the US Constitution: see *State of Wisconsin* v. *Yoder* (1972) 406 US 205, discussed in P. Marson, 'Parental Choice in State Education' (1980) *Journal of Social Welfare Law* 193 at pp. 203–6.
18 See White Paper, *Educational Reconstruction*, Cmd 6458, 1943, paras 43–62.
19 See A. Stillman, 'Legislating for Choice', ch. 6 of M. Flude and M. Hammer (eds), *The Education Reform Act 1988: Its Origins and Implications*, Basingstoke, Falmer Press, 1990, at pp. 89–90.
20 HL Deb. Vol. 353, col. 590 (10 July 1974).
21 See D. Milman, *Educational Conflict and the Law*, London, Croom Helm, 1986, pp. 35–7.
22 But not school governors.
23 See R. Buxton, *Local Government*, 2nd ed., Harmondsworth, Penguin, 1973, p. 213.
24 [1955] 1 QB 408.
25 At p. 424.

26 [1972] 1 Ch. 12.
27 Lord Denning, MR, at pp. 36–7.
28 *Winward* v. *Cheshire CC* (1979) 77 LGR 172.
29 Ibid. at pp. 181–2.
30 Ibid. at p. 182.
31 Parents also sometimes withheld their children from school, thereby forcing their LEA to invoke school attendance order proceedings under s. 37: see *Re DJMS (a Minor)* [1977] 3 All ER 582. But this route to adjudication by the Secretary of State was closed by s. 10, Education Act 1980.
32 See HC Deb., Vol. 948, cols 447–8 (Written Answers) (24 April 1978).
33 *Secretary of State for Education and Science* v. *Tameside Metropolitan Borough Council* [1976] 3 All ER 665.
34 *Per* Lord Denning, MR in the Court of Appeal, at p. 671.
35 See D. Bull, 'School Admissions: a New Appeals Procedure' (1980) *Journal of Social Welfare Law* 209; Paul Meredith, 'Executive Discretion and Choice of Secondary School' (1981) *Public Law* 52; T. Buck, 'School Admission Appeals' (1985) *Journal of Social Welfare Law* 227; J. Tweedie, 'Rights in Social Programmes: the Case of Parental Choice of School' (1986) *Public Law* 407. For an important recent study of practice in Scotland under the Education (Scotland) Act 1981, see M. Adler, A. Petch and J. Tweedie, *Parental Choice and Educational Policy*, Edinburgh, Edinburgh University Press, 1990.
36 Though the Callaghan government's abortive Education Bill 1978 contained provisions on choice of school which were in many respects similar: for a comparison between the 1978 Bill and the 1980 Act, see Paul Meredith, op. cit., n. 35.
37 s. 6(3)(a).
38 s. 6(3)(b).
39 s. 6(3)(c).
40 See Education (School Information) Regls 1981, SI 1981 No. 630, as amended by Amendment Regls 1983, SI 1983 No. 41 and 1988, SI 1988 No. 1023. These are now supplemented and amended by new Regulations as to curricular information issued under s. 22, Education Reform Act 1988, discussed in chapter 3: see Education (School Curriculum and Related Information) Regls 1989, SI 1989 No. 954, as amended by Amendment Regls 1989, SI 1989 No. 1136 and 1990, SI 1990 No. 1109.
41 See SI 1981 No. 630, Schedule 2, para. 15.
42 'Racism and Parental Choice', *The Independent*, 24 April 1990.
43 See 'School "Apartheid" Claims Triggered by MacGregor Ruling', *The Independent*, 23 April 1990.
44 It is understood that judicial review proceedings are pending in the Cleveland dispute: see 'School rights test', *The Independent*, 19 July 1991.
45 s. 26(9).
46 s. 31(2).
47 s. 8(2)(a).
48 These procedures did not, of course, apply where the pupil numbers fell below the relevant point simply through undersubscription rather than

intention on the part of the LEA.

49 Under the statutory procedures laid down in ss. 12 and 13.

50 See A. Bradney, 'The Dewsbury Affair and the Education Reform Act 1988' (1989) *Journal of Education and the Law* 51; see also Kirklees Metropolitan Council, *A Report by the Chief Executive on the Dewsbury Schools Affair 1987-1988*, 1988. For discussion of the Kirklees Report, see 'Dewsbury Schools Row Avoidable, Report Says', *The Independent*, 10 December 1988.

51 See A. Bradney, op. cit., n. 49, at p. 51.

52 See 'Children Refused Entry to School of their Choice', *The Independent*, 3 September 1987; 'Dewsbury Schools Dispute Heads for Lengthy Deadlock', *The Independent*, 14 September 1987; 'No Official Checks on Pupils' Progress at School in Pub', *The Independent*, 7 December 1987; 'Dewsbury's Choice Dilemma', *The Guardian*, 11 September 1987.

53 For discussion of the legal issues, see S. M. Poulter, *English Law and Ethnic Minority Customs*, London, Butterworths, 1986, ch. 7, especially at pp. 195–201.

54 'National Anxiety at Kirklees,' *The Independent*, 10 September 1987 (leading article). See also, 'Culture Clash in the Classroom' (leading article), *The Independent*, 7 September 1987.

55 The application for judicial review is unreported, but see A. Bradney, op. cit., n. 49, at pp. 52–3; 'Parents Win the School of Their Choice', *TES* 15 July 1988; 'Dewsbury Rebels Win Fight Over Schools', *The Independent*, 13 July 1988; 'Who Was on the Side of the Angels?' *The Independent*, 14 July 1988.

56 See A. Bradney, op. cit., n. 49, at p. 53.

57 Under the Education Reform Act 1988, ss. 162–96.

58 (1990) 88 LGR 589.

59 See *TES*, 2 November 1990, p. 7.

60 See now also *R.* v. *Kingston-upon-Thames Borough Council, ex parte Kingwell, The Independent* Law Reports, 4 June 1991; *R.* v. *Bromley London Borough Council, ex parte C, The Independent* Law Reports, 13 June 1991.

61 See Tweedie, op. cit., n. 35; Bull, op. cit., n. 35.

62 Their composition and procedure are laid down in outline in Schedule 2.

63 Schedule 2, Part I, para. 1(4).

64 See Schedule 2, Part II.

65 See ibid., para. 11.

66 Ibid., para. 5.

67 Ibid., para. 6.

68 Ibid., para. 10.

69 Ibid., para. 1(2).

70 Or possibly the absence of a member: see Bull, op. cit., n. 35, p. 217.

71 Schedule 2, para. 8.

72 Which has statutory powers of supervision over these tribunals: s. 7(6) and Schedule 2, para. 10.

73 Council on Tribunals, *Code of Practice as to the Constitution and Procedures*

of Appeal Committees Established Under the Education Act 1980 and the Education Act 1981, February 1985. Annex 1 provides guidance on reaching a decision.

74 Ibid., paras 5 and 7.
75 Ibid., para. 7.
76 Ibid.
77 Ibid., para. 7(h).
78 Ibid., para. 7(i).
79 Ibid., para. 4.
80 See D. Bull, 'Monitoring Education Appeals: Local Ombudsmen Lead the Way' (1985) *Journal of Social Welfare Law* 189.
81 Council on Tribunals, *Annual Report for 1987/88*, 1989, para. 2.31.
82 Council on Tribunals, *Annual Report for 1988/89*, 1990, Appendix C, Part I.
83 Unreported: CO/197/84, 10 May 1984: available on LEXIS. See Paul Meredith, '*R.* v. *South Glamorgan Appeals Committee, ex parte Evans* (1985) *Journal of Social Welfare Law* 162. See now also *R.* v. *Governors of Bishop Challoner Roman Catholic School, ex parte C, The Independent* Law Reports, 1 August 1991.
84 Established in *Associated Provincial Picture Houses Ltd.* v. *Wednesbury Corporation* [1948] 1 KB 223.
85 Annex 1.
86 See Council on Tribunals' *Code of Practice*, op. cit., n. 71, para. 7(g).
87 See DES Circular ll/88, *Admission of Pupils to County and Voluntary Schools*, 20 October 1988; Paul Meredith, 'Educational Reform' (1989) *Modern Law Review* 215 at pp. 221–4.
88 DES, July 1987.
89 Ibid., paras 1–4.
90 ss. 26(4)–(8), 27 (4)–(9) and 28.
91 ss. 28(7) and 32(1).
92 s. 38(3)(a).
93 s. 38(3)(b).
94 See DES Circular 7/88, *Education Reform Act: Local Management of Schools*, 6 September 1988, para. 104(c).
95 Ibid., para. 112.
96 See T. Wragg, 'How Vouchers Could Privatise Schools', *The Independent*, 18 October 1990, p. 19.

3 LEGAL CONTROL OVER THE CONTENTS OF THE SECULAR CURRICULUM

1 See A. Lester and D. Pannick, *Independent Schools and the European Convention on Human Rights: a Joint Opinion*, London, ISIS, 1982.
2 *Educational Reconstruction*, Cmd 6458, 1943, para. 1.
3 The word 'comprehensive' here has its ordinary meaning rather than the technical meaning of 'non-selective'.
4 See Ministry of Education, *Administrative Memorandum No. 25 and Model*

Instrument, Articles of Government and Rules of Management, 26 January 1945.

5 *William Tyndale Junior and Infants School Public Inquiry: a Report to the ILEA by Robin Auld*, QC, ILEA, 1976.

6 For full text and extensive commentary, see *TES*, 22 October 1976; see also T. Devlin and M. Warnock, *What Must We Teach?*, London, Temple Smith, 1977.

7 Cmnd. 6869, 1977.

8 Ibid., para. 2.19.

9 DES Circular 14/77, *Local Education Authority Arrangements for the School Curriculum*, 29 November 1977.

10 See DES, *Local Authority Arrangements for the School Curriculum: Report on the Circular 14/77 Review*, 1979, para. 2.

11 Ibid., para. 13.

12 Ibid., para. 14.

13 DES, 1977.

14 Ibid., para. 2.23.

15 Ibid., paras 4.6 and 4.7; it suggested that older pupils might also be included.

16 See National Union of Teachers, *Partnership in Education: the NUT Commentary on the Taylor Report*, 1978; National Association of Headteachers, *The National Association of Headteachers' Commentary on the Taylor Report, 'A New Partnership for Our Schools'*, 1978.

17 s. 31.

18 See chapter 2.

19 s. 3(5). For the position in respect of aided and special agreement schools, see s. 4.

20 s. 17(1).

21 s. 17(2).

22 For the position regarding aided and special agreement schools, see s. 19.

23 s. 18(1)(a).

24 s. 18(1)(b).

25 s. 18(1)(c).

26 s. 18(2).

27 s. 18(3)(a).

28 s. 18(3)(b).

29 s. 18(3)(a)(i).

30 s. 18(3)(a)(ii).

31 s. 18(5).

32 s. 18(6)(a).

33 s. 18(6)(b).

34 s. 18(6)(c)(ii).

35 s. 18(6)(c)(i). See 'Birth Control Proposal Dilutes Governors' Power', *TES*, 19 August 1988.

36 s. 18(6)(c)(iii).

37 See chapter 1, and see discussion in the section on 'Sex education and ... family values' below in the context of sex education.

38 Speech to National Council of Women in Britain, 3 March 1984: DES Press Notice 32/84.

39 See HL Deb. Vol. 470, cols 1138–51 (5 February 1986).
40 Ibid., col. 1139.
41 Ibid., cols 1141, etc.
42 Ibid., col. 1142.
43 D. C. Ewens, 'Policy, Evidence and Political Education' (1987) *Political Quarterly* 96 at p. 97.
44 See also s. 44 which prohibits the promotion of partisan political views in teaching. For an illustrative case from the US, see *Tinker* v. *Des Moines Independent Community School District* (1969) 393 US 503.
45 DES Circular 7/87, *The Education (No. 2) Act 1986: Further Guidance*, 7 August 1987, Annex II, paras 4–5.
46 See discussion in chapter 6 of *R.* v. *Governors of Small Heath School, ex parte Birmingham City Council* and *R.* v. *Governors of Small Heath School, ex parte Khan*, *The Independent* Law Reports, 30 June 1989 (Divisional Court) and 3 August 1989 (CA), where a subsidiary challenge based on section 45 was rejected.
47 Education Reform Act 1988, s. 23(1)(a)(ii).
48 See generally Philip Meredith, *Sex Education: Political Issues in Britain and Europe*, London, Routledge, 1989.
49 (1976) 1 EHRR 711.
50 Ibid., p. 733.
51 Ibid., p. 730.
52 Ibid.
53 Ibid., p. 731.
54 Ibid.
55 Ibid., pp. 731–2 (emphasis added).
56 The Court also noted the fact that, in Denmark, children could be educated in private schools not subject to the statute, or in the parental home, but the Court's findings were not dependent on the existence of these alternative forms of education.
57 See speech by Mr Christopher Patten, Minister of State for Education and Science, to annual conference of Church of England Diocesan Directors of Education, Croydon, 18 June 1986: *DES News*, No. 151/86.
58 Ibid.
59 *Curriculum Matters* Series, No. 6.
60 Ibid., para. 40.
61 Ibid., para. 45 (emphasis added).
62 Ibid., para. 41.
63 Emphasis added.
64 DES Circular 11/87, 25 September 1987.
65 Ibid., para. 19 (emphasis added).
66 Para. 19.
67 Ibid., para. 22.
68 See ibid., para. 21.
69 A similar measure had been earlier introduced in the House of Lords as a Private Member's Bill by the Earl of Halsbury but received insufficient support: see Local Government Act 1986 (Amendment) Bill 1986.

70 Translated from Danish by Louis MacKay, London, Gay Men's Press, 1983.
71 See 'Baker in Plea on Gay Book', *The Times*, 17 September 1986.
72 London, Gay Men's Press, 1984.
73 See HC Deb., Standing Committee A, cols 1208–12 (8 December 1987).
74 'A Grass-roots Rebellion', *The Times*, 18 December 1986 (leading article).
75 Ibid.
76 Haringey London Borough Council, *Mirrors Round the Walls – Respecting Diversity: First Report of Curriculum Working Party on Lesbian and Gay Issues in Education*, March 1988. See also 'Haringey Schools Should Teach Gay Issues, Report Says', *The Independent*, 31 March 1988.
77 Para. 11.19 (emphasis added).
78 Department of the Environment Circular 12/88, *Local Government Act 1988*, 20 May 1988, para. 20.
79 Op. cit., n. 64.
80 Ibid., para. 25.
81 See *Gillick* v. *West Norfolk and Wisbech Area Health Authority* [1985] 3 All ER 402, and see chapter 1.
82 DES Circular 11/87, para. 23.
83 A challenge to local authorities supporting gay organisations or arts groups producing gay plays is far more probable.
84 *The Secondary School Curriculum and Examinations: Initial Government Observations on the Second Report from the Education, Science and Arts Committee, Session 1981–82*, Cmnd. 8551, May 1982, pp. 11–12 (Emphasis added).
85 Cmnd. 9469, 1985.
86 DES, July 1987.
87 Ibid., para. 4.
88 Ibid., paras 5–6.
89 Ibid., para. 10.
90 Ibid., para. 27.
91 Op. cit., n. 85.
92 The Consultation Document was published in July 1987, and the Education Reform Bill presented to Parliament on 20 November 1987: see Paul Meredith, 'Educational Reform' (1989) *Modern Law Review* 215 at pp. 215–16.
93 The government was forced to use two guillotine motions on the Bill to curb discussion: see ibid., p. 215.
94 There were some significant amendments in the Lords, where the government's majority was far less predictable, notably on religious education.
95 The government anticipated that independent schools would broadly follow, but they are excluded from the duty to comply. Grant-maintained schools are, as their very name implies, 'maintained' schools and are bound by the national curriculum. The government has stated its intention to make compliance with the substance of the national

curriculum a condition of grant for City Technology Colleges. See Consultation Document, *The National Curriculum 5–16*, DES, July 1987, para. 39.

96 s. 1(1).
97 s. 1(2).
98 s. 2(2).
99 s. 3(1).
100 s. 3(2).
101 s. 4(1).
102 s. 4(2).
103 s. 3(3).
104 s. 2(2)(a)–(c).
105 s. 20.
106 s. 14(2).
107 s. 14(3)(a)–(c).
108 s. 14(4).
109 s. 14(2).
110 s. 14(6)(b)(i).
111 s. 20(2).
112 s. 20(3).
113 s. 20(4).
114 s. 20(5).
115 s. 20(6).
116 National Curriculum Council, *Mathematics in the National Curriculum*, December 1988; see *The Independent*, 6 December 1988.
117 National Curriculum Council, *English for Ages 5 to 11*, November 1988; see *The Independent*, 16 November 1988.
118 See 'History Group Set to Defy Ministers over Curriculum', *The Independent*, 18 December 1989; 'History Curriculum "Should Emphasise Need to Learn Facts"', *The Independent*, 19 March 1990; 'Facts and Dates Will Form Core of History Teaching in Schools', *The Independent*, 27 July 1990.
119 See 'Ministers Get Support on Teaching of History', *The Independent*, 28 December 1990.
120 s. 20(3).
121 s. 14(4)(e).
122 ss. 17–19: see section on 'Increasing consumerism' above.
123 s. 22. See Education (School Curriculum and Related Information) Regls. 1989, SI 1989 No. 954. For assessment results relating to individual pupils, which may not be made available to any person other than the pupil's parents, the governing body or the LEA (s. 22(5)), see Education (Individual Pupils' Achievements) (Information) Regls 1990, SI 1990 No. 1381.
124 s. 23. See also DES Circular 1/89, *Education Reform Act 1988: Local Arrangements for the Consideration of Complaints*, 9 January 1989.
125 See Education (National Curriculum) (Attainment Targets and Programmes of Study in Mathematics) Order 1989, SI 1989 No. 308. Equivalent Orders have at time of writing been issued for Science (SI

1989 No. 309), Modern Foreign Languages (SI 1989 No. 825), English (SI 1990 No. 423), Technology (SI 1990 Nos. 424 and 1531), Geography (SI 1991 No. 678) and History (SI 1991 No. 681). See also Education (National Curriculum) (Assessment Arrangements for English, Mathematics and Science) Order 1990, SI 1990 No. 1543.

126 Consultation Document, *The National Curriculum 5–16*, para. 10. See N. Harris, 'The National Curriculum – Framework or Straitjacket?' (1989) *Journal of Education and the Law* 105.

127 DES, *Standards in Education 1988–1989*, 1990.

128 See 'MacGregor to Relax National Curriculum', *The Independent*, 1 August 1990; 'MacGregor Beats a Retreat over Curriculum and Testing', *The Independent*, 2 August 1990; 'MacGregor's Triple Retreat', *The Independent*, 2 August 1990 (leading article).

129 See '"U-turn" on Tests for Seven-year-olds', *The Independent*, 19 October 1990. See also 'Tests Simplified for Pupils Aged 7', *The Independent*, 8 January 1991.

130 See 'Clarke Retreats on National Curriculum', *The Independent*, 5 January 1991.

131 See 'Maths and Science tests to be cut', *The Independent*, 9 May 1991.

132 See 'MacGregor's Triple Retreat', *The Independent*, 2 August 1990 (leading article).

133 See 'Sect "Has No Right to Veto School TV"', *The Independent*, 21 December 1990.

134 It has recently been suggested that section 23 might be used to challenge the setting of Standard Assessment Tasks under the testing arrangements: see 'Parents in England "can challenge school tests"', *The Independent*, 25 April 1991.

4 EXPENDITURE CONSTRAINTS AND THE LEGAL SUFFICIENCY OF EDUCATION

1 For a discussion of the first two published HMI *Effects Reports – Report by HMI on the Effects on the Education Service in England of Local Authority Expenditure Policies – Financial Year 1980–81*, February 1981, and *Report by HMI on the Effects of Local Authority Expenditure Policies on the Education Service in England – 1981*, March 1982 – see Paul Meredith, 'Individual Challenge to Expenditure Cuts in the Provision of Schools' (1982) *Journal of Social Welfare Law* 344. It is not clear at the time of writing in what form, if at all, any such reports will appear in the future, following the government's proposed privatisation of HMI: see 'Schools to get cash to pay inspectors', *The Independent*, 3 July 1991.

2 DES, *Schools in Hackney – Some Issues: a Report by HMI*, 1990.

3 See Second Report of Select Committee on Education, Science and the Arts, 1989–90, *The Supply of Teachers for the 1990s*, HC 208-I.

4 DES, *Standards in Education 1988–89: the Annual Report of HM Senior Chief Inspector of Schools*, January 1990. See now also DES, *Standards in Education 1989–90: the Annual Report of HM Senior Chief Inspector of Schools*, February 1991.

5 DES, *Standards in Education 1988–89*, para. 3.
6 Ibid.
7 Ibid., para. 4.
8 See ibid., paras 5 and 33–45.
9 Ibid., para. 5.
10 Ibid.
11 See ibid., paras 6 and 46–65.
12 Ibid., para. 6.
13 Ibid., para. 11.
14 Ibid., para. 12.
15 Ibid.
16 Ibid., para. 16.
17 Ibid.
18 Ibid., para. 17.
19 Op. cit., n. 2.
20 Ibid., para. 5.
21 Ibid.
22 Ibid., para. 20 (emphasis added).
23 Ibid., para. 21.
24 Ibid., para. 27.
25 Ibid., para. 19.
26 Ibid., paras 28–9.
27 Ibid., para. 35.
28 Ibid.
29 Ibid., para. 39.
30 Ibid., para. 32.
31 See 'What Must Be Done to Recruit Enough Teachers for September', *The Independent*, 19 July 1989; 'Unqualified Staff Forced to Teach Key Subjects', *TES*, 10 November 1989; 'Harassed Heads Plumb Depths of a Staffing Crisis', *TES* 10 November 1989; 'Straw Urges New Study on Staffing in Schools', *The Independent*, 4 January 1990.
32 Op. cit., n. 3.
33 Ibid., para. 5.
34 Ibid., para. 91.
35 Ibid.
36 See 'Pupils Sent Home as Schools Fail to Fill Teaching Posts', *The Independent*, 6 September 1989; 'Another Year But Still No Place to Go', *TES*, 12 January 1990.
37 See chapter 3.
38 ss. 33–51.
39 [1981] 1 WLR 768.
40 See now ss. 106–11, Education Reform Act 1988.
41 Emphasis added.
42 [1981] 1 WLR 768 at p. 773.
43 See chapter 3.
44 After having unsuccessfully complained to their LEA under section 23 of the 1988 Act.
45 See chapter 2 in relation to attempts by parents to invoke s. 68 in order to attain their choice of school.

46 For discussion of the Northamptonshire and Surrey complaints, see Paul Meredith, 'Individual Challenge to Expenditure Cuts in the Provision of Schools', op. cit., n. 1, pp. 347–9.
47 DES Press Notice, 1 May 1981.
48 Ibid. For the local resolution of the Northamptonshire complaint, see *The Guardian*, 21 July 1981; *Where*, No. 171 (September 1981), p. 6.
49 See DES Press Notice, 15 February 1982.
50 Ibid.
51 See Second Report from Select Committee on Education, Science and the Arts, 1981–82, *The Secondary School Curriculum and Examinations*, HC 116–I, para. 9.11.
52 Ibid., para. 9.12.
53 Ibid., para. 9.13 (emphasis added).
54 Ibid., para. 9.14.
55 *Secretary of State for Education and Science* v. *Tameside Metropolitan Borough Council* [1976] 3 All ER 665.
56 Ibid. at p. 671.
57 HC 116–I, para. 9.16.
58 Ibid., para. 9.17.
59 Ibid., para. 9.18.
60 See *The Secondary School Curriculum and Examinations: Initial Government Observations on the Second Report from the Education, Science and Arts Committee, Session 1981–82*, Cmnd 8551, 1982, p. 12.
61 Ibid.
62 [1979] 2 All ER 1016. See also N. Harris, 'Education by Right? Breach of the Duty to Provide "Sufficient" Schools' (1990) *Modern Law Review* 525 at pp. 526 and 528–9; and N. Harris, 'Legal Consequences of Teacher Shortages' (1990) *Journal of Education and the Law* 174.
63 *Per* Lord Justice Eveleigh, at p. 1028.
64 Ibid., p. 1027.
65 Lord Denning went further and took the view that the Court could intervene even where it was an action amounting to non-feasance: ibid., p. 1023.
66 See ibid. at pp. 1033–5, *per* Sir Stanley Rees.
67 Lord Justice Eveleigh and Sir Stanley Rees.
68 *The Independent* Law Reports, 15 February 1990. See N. Harris, op. cit., n. 61.
69 LEXIS transcript.
70 Ibid.
71 Ibid.
72 Supreme Court Act 1981, s. 31(4).
73 LEXIS transcript.
74 Eveleigh L.J. and Sir Stanley Rees.
75 As had been recognised by Sir Stanley Rees in *Meade* v. *Haringey London Borough Council* at p. 1032.
76 Though the court could award a mandatory order at the instigation of the Minister to enforce his directions made under s. 68 or 99.
77 LEXIS transcript.
78 Ibid. (emphasis added).

79 See *Secretary of State for Education and Science* v. *Tameside Metropolitan Borough Council* [1976] 3 All ER 665, where in fact such an order was, however, refused.
80 DES Press Notice 351/90, 31 October 1990. See also DES Press Notice 364/90, 8 November 1990 for further explanation of the expenditure proposals.

5 FALLING ROLLS AND THE REORGANISATION OF SCHOOLS

1 See DES *Annual Report 1985*, 1986, para. 21, and DES Circular 3/87, *Providing for Quality: the Pattern of Organisation to Age 19*, 6 May 1987, paras 14 and 15.
2 See HC Deb. Vol. 131, cols 13–14 (Written Answers) (12 April 1988).
3 Education Act 1980, ss. 12–16.
4 DES Circular 5/77, *Falling Numbers and School Closures*, 13 June 1977.
5 Ibid., para. 3.
6 Ibid.
7 Ibid., para. 4.
8 Ibid., para. 7 (emphasis added).
9 DES Circular 2/81, *Falling Rolls and Surplus Places*, 16 June 1981.
10 Ibid., para. 19
11 Ibid., para. 5.
12 Ibid.
13 Ibid., para. 9.
14 Ibid., para. 10.
15 Ibid., paras 11 and 12.
16 Ibid., para. 12.
17 Ibid.
18 Ibid., para. 13.
19 Ibid., para. 15.
20 See DES Circular 10/65, *The Organisation of Secondary Education*, 12 July 1965.
21 DES Circular 2/81, para. 19 (emphasis added).
22 Ibid., para. 22.
23 Ibid.
24 Ibid., paras 25–9 and Annex.
25 Ibid., para. 21.
26 Ibid., para. 26.
27 Ibid., para. 29. *Cf.* The financial threat in DES Circular 10/66, *School Building Programmes*, 10 March 1966, para. 5.
28 Cf. the means used by the DES to impose comprehensive reorganisation on some unwilling LEAs in the 1960s: see R. Buxton, *Local Government*, 2nd ed. Harmondsworth, Penguin, 1973, ch. 8.
29 *Statutory Proposals for Secondary Schools and Falling Rolls*, 8 June 1982.
30 Ibid., para. 2.
31 Ibid., para. 3.
32 Ibid., para. 4.

33 See Paul Meredith, 'Falling Rolls and the Reorganisation of Schools' (1984) *Journal of Social Welfare Law* 208 at p. 215; see also M. Loughlin, *Local Government in the Modern State*, London, Sweet & Maxwell, 1986 at p. 129.
34 See *R.* v. *Secretary of State for Education and Science, ex parte Avon County Council* (1990) 88 LGR 716 (Divisional Court) and 737 (No. 2 – CA).
35 It also supersedes DES Circular 2/80, *Procedure Affecting Proposals Made Under Sections 12–16 of the Education Act 1980*, 14 July 1980 and DES Administrative Memorandum 4/84, *Proposals Made Under Sections 12–16 of the Education Act 1980*, 5 September 1984.
36 DES Circular 3/87, para. 1.
37 Ibid., para. 2.
38 Ibid., para. 4.
39 Ibid., paras 4–5; see also Annex 1, paras 2–4 on parental choice.
40 Ibid., para. 12.
41 Ibid., para. 16.
42 Education Act 1980, s. 12(1)(a).
43 Ibid., s. 12(1)(c).
44 This chapter deals with county schools. Voluntary schools are mentioned only incidentally.
45 S. 12(1)(d).
46 Education (Publication of School Proposals) (No. 2) Regls 1980, SI 1980 No. 658.
47 Or governors of any voluntary school affected, or any other LEA concerned.
48 Or all that were received being withdrawn.
49 A further case where the Secretary of State's approval is always required relates to closing a voluntary school or transferring a voluntary school to county school status: s. 12(4).
50 s. 12(6). The Minister's power of 'modification' is, however, a limited one: see *Legg* v. *Inner London Education Authority* [1972] 3 All ER 177.
51 LEAs are required in such cases within four months from submitting the proposals to the Secretary of State to make a formal determination either to implement or not to implement the proposals: s. 12(7).
52 This is intended to cover situations where detailed changes are found necessary, e.g. as to timing, but not major changes of mind. A major change of mind, as occurred, for instance, in Tameside Metropolitan Borough after the May 1976 local elections, would require an LEA to go back to square one with the submission of fresh proposals; but in the meantime, it would be legally bound to carry out those already approved (unlike the incoming Conservative LEA in Tameside in 1976): see *Secretary of State for Education and Science* v. *Tameside Metropolitan Borough Council* [1976] 3 All ER 665.
53 s. 73 now requires an LEA planning to submit reorganisation proposals to the Secretary of State first to consult the governors of any school involved which would be eligible for grant-maintained status (see chapter 6). The purpose of this is to ensure that governors are forewarned well in advance to enable them to consider 'opting out' of LEA control in good time.

54 Op. cit., n. 35, para. 5.1.
55 Op. cit., n. 35, paras 9 and 10.
56 See section on 'Legal challenge. . .' below.
57 Circular 3/87, Annex 1, para. 1.
58 The average length of time taken for consideration by the Secretary of State of reorganisation proposals in 1987 was 7.1 months: see HC Deb. Vol. 131, col. 14 (Written Answers) (12 April 1988).
59 Annex 1, para. 2.
60 Between 1980 and 1987 the Secretary of State for Education and Science rejected 150 LEA proposals for school closures – 57 primary schools and 93 secondary schools: see HC Deb. Vol. 131, col. 14 (Written Answers) (12 April 1988).
61 (1986) 84 LGR 168. See Paul Meredith, 'Legitimate Expectations and School Closures' (1988) *Public Law* 4.
62 Ibid., pp. 186–7.
63 Ibid., p. 178.
64 Ibid., p. 179.
65 Ibid., pp. 181–2.
66 Ibid., p. 186.
67 Ibid., p. 189.
68 Ibid., p. 190.
69 Ibid., p. 191.
70 Ibid.
71 Ibid., pp. 193–4.
72 Ibid., p. 195.
73 Op. cit., n. 35, para. 5.1.
74 Op. cit., n. 35, paras 9 and 10.
75 See *Council of Civil Service Unions* v. *Minister for the Civil Service* [1985] AC 374 (The 'GCHQ Case').
76 (1986) 84 LGR 168 at p. 187.
77 See *R.* v. *London Borough of Sutton, ex parte Hamlet* (Unreported) CO/1657/85; *R.* v. *Northampton County Council, ex parte Tebbutt* (Unreported), CO/322/86; *R.* v. *Gwent County Council and Secretary of State for Wales, ex parte Bryant, The Independent* Law Reports, 19 April 1988.
78 (1986) 84 LGR 168 at p. 189.
79 Ibid.
80 (1989) 87 LGR 435.
81 These alternative patterns included continuing with secondary schools catering for the whole 11 to 18 years age range; schools for children of 11 to 16 years with centralised sixth form provision; and schools for children of 11 to 16 years with centralised tertiary college provision.
82 Unreported at first instance: CO/535/86.
83 LEXIS transcript.
84 (1989) 87 LGR 435.
85 Ibid., p. 456.
86 Education (Publication of School Proposals) (No. 2) Regls 1980, SI 1980 No. 658.
87 Education Act 1944, Schedule I, Part II, para. 7.

88 Education Act 1944, Schedule I, Part II, para. 1.
89 See *R.* v. *Croydon London Borough Council, ex parte Leney*, *The Times* Law Reports, 27 November 1986.
90 (1988) 86 LGR 115.
91 Ibid., p. 123.
92 Ibid., pp. 123–4.
93 See ibid., p. 126.
94 See ibid., p. 125.
95 Education Act 1944, Schedule I, Part II, para. 7.
96 (1986) 84 LGR 168.
97 See ibid., pp. 184-5.
98 Ibid., p. 185.
99 (1989) 87 LGR 435.
100 Ibid., p. 450.
101 *R.* v. *Northamptonshire County Council, ex parte Tebbutt* (1986) CO/322/86 (Unreported).
102 For a wider discussion of sexual discrimination in education, but covering this particular issue among others, see D. Milman and K. de Gama, 'Sexual Discrimination in Education: One Step Forward, Two Steps Back?' (1989) *Journal of Social Welfare Law* 4, especially at pp. 14–17.
103 See chapter 6 below: *R.* v. *Secretary of State for Education and Science, ex parte Avon County Council* (1990) 88 LGR 716 (Divisional Court) and 737 (No. 2 – CA).
104 (1986) 84 LGR 469.
105 Ibid., p. 473–4.
106 Ibid., p. 476.
107 Ibid., p. 477.
108 Ibid., p. 480.
109 [1989] 1 All ER 769.
110 Ibid., p. 772.
111 Which places LEAs under their basic obligation to provide 'sufficient schools'.
112 [1989] 1 All ER 769, at p. 774.
113 Ibid., p. 774.
114 Ibid.,
115 See *Watt* v. *Kesteven County Council* [1955] 1 QB 408; *Cumings* v. *Birkenhead Corporation* [1972] 1 Ch. 12.
116 (1989) SLT 612.
117 See ibid., p. 615.
118 Ibid., p. 615.
119 Ibid.

6 GRANT-MAINTAINED SCHOOLS – A FURTHER DIMENSION TO REORGANISATION

1 (1990) 88 LGR 716 (Divisional Court) and 737 (No. 2 – Court of Appeal).

2 *DES News*, 11 July 1990.
3 See Paul Meredith, 'The Education Reform Act 1988: Grant-Maintained Schools' (1989) *Journal of Education and the Law* 95.
4 *Grant-Maintained Schools: Consultation Paper*, 1987, especially at paras 1–2.
5 Education Reform Act 1988, s. 58(5)(c).
6 Ibid., s. 106(1)–(2).
7 DES Circular 10/88, *Education Reform Act 1988: Grant-Maintained Schools*, 14 October 1988, para. 63.
8 See DES Press Notice 133/91, 25 April 1991; 'Schools that opt out "free to change character"', *The Independent*, 26 April 1991.
9 Education Reform Act 1988, s. 89(2). See discussion in the section below ('Particular considerations relating to governors . . .') concerning the Cardinal Vaughan dispute in London.
10 *Grant-Maintained Schools: Consultation Paper*, 1987, para. 8.
11 Education Reform Act 1988, s. 53(1).
12 Ibid., s. 53(2).
13 Ibid., s. 53(4).
14 Ibid., s. 53(5).
15 Ibid., s. 53(9).
16 Ibid., s. 53(10).
17 Ibid., s. 53(8).
18 Ibid., s. 53(6)(a).
19 Ibid., s. 53(6)(b).
20 Ibid., s. 56(1)(b).
21 Ibid., s. 56(4) and (6).
22 Ibid., s. 58.
23 Ibid., s. 83.
24 Ibid., ss. 26–32.
25 Ibid., s. 75.
26 Ibid., ss. 44–7 and Schedule 3.
27 See *School Teachers' Pay and Conditions Document 1989*.
28 Education Reform Act 1988, s. 74.
29 Ibid., s. 74(4).
30 Ibid., s. 197.
31 Ibid., s. 78.
32 Ibid., ss. 76 and 77.
33 The former Prime Minister, Mrs Thatcher, has suggested the possibility of poll tax cuts to act as an inducement to opt out, which would clearly run counter to these principles, but her proposals remain obscure and would require legislation.
34 Education Reform Act 1988, s. 79(1).
35 Ibid., s. 38(3)(a).
36 Ibid., s. 79(2); see Education (Grant-Maintained Schools) Finance Regls. 1991, SI 1991 No. 353.
37 Ibid., s. 81.
38 Ibid., s. 79(3)(a).
39 Ibid., s. 37(3)(b) and (5).
40 DES Circular 10/88, op. cit., n. 7, para. 59.

41 Ibid., para. 60.
42 See *The Independent*, 27 January 1990, 'Schools That Opt Out "Get More Cash"'; *The Independent on Sunday*, 4 February 1990, 'Extra Cash for Opt-out Schools'; *The Independent*, 24 January 1991, 'Straw Condemns Schools "bribery"'.
43 See *TES*, 28 September 1990, 'MacGregor Begs for Support over Opting Out'.
44 See *The Independent*, 29 September 1990, '"Sweeteners for Schools" Inquiry Call'.
45 ss. 6–8.
46 ss. 3–6.
47 ss. 18 and 19.
48 ss. 33–47.
49 *Grant-Maintained Schools: Consultation Paper*, 1987, para. 2.
50 Education Reform Act 1988, s. 52(5) and (6).
51 Ibid., s. 60(1)(a).
52 Ibid., s. 60(3).
53 Ibid., s. 60(2).
54 Ibid., s. 60(4).
55 Ibid., s. 60(1).
56 See Education (Parental Ballots for Acquisition of Grant-Maintained Status) (Prescribed Body) Regls 1988, SI 1988 No. 1474.
57 Education Reform Act 1988, s. 61(6) and (7); see DES Circular 10/88, op. cit., n. 7, and DES, *School Governors: How to Become a Grant-Maintained School*, Revised Edition, 1989.
58 Education Reform Act 1988, s. 61(14).
59 See Pupils' Registration (Amendment) Regls 1988, SI 1988 No. 1185.
60 See DES Administrative Memorandum 1/88, *The Amendment of Pupils' Registration Regulations 1956: Keeping Records*, July 1988.
61 Education Reform Act 1988, s. 61(15).
62 Education Act 1944, s. 114.
63 See DES, *School Governors: How to Become a Grant-Maintained School*, op. cit., n. 56, para. 12.
64 Education Reform Act 1988, s. 61(3)(a).
65 Ibid., s. 61(4)(a).
66 Ibid., s. 61(4)(b) and (c).
67 Ibid., s. 61(4)(f).
68 Ibid., s. 61(5).
69 Para. 20.
70 See *The Independent*, 23 February 1989, 'Tough Tactics in a Bitter Campaign'.
71 See *TES*, 5 February 1988, 'No Threshold'.
72 See Official Report, HC Standing Committee J, cols 1053–85 (2 February 1988).
73 See HL Deb. Vol. 496, cols 1224–44 (12 May 1988).
74 Education Reform Act 1988, s. 62(5)(c) and (d).
75 Ibid., s. 62(6) and (7).
76 Ibid., s. 62(7)(f)(i).
77 Ibid., s. 62(8).

78 Ibid., s. 62(10).
79 Ibid., s. 62(11).
80 Ibid., s. 73(4)(b).
81 Ibid., s. 73(5).
82 See now also *R.* v. *Secretary of State for Education and Science, ex parte Newham London Borough Council, The Times* Law Reports, 11 January 1991.
83 *R.* v. *Governors of Small Heath School, ex parte Birmingham City Council*; *R.* v. *Governors of Small Heath School, ex parte Khan, The Independent* Law Reports, 30 June 1989 (Divisional Court); *The Independent* Law Reports, 3 August 1989 (Court of Appeal). See Paul Meredith, 'Opting-out Litigation: the Birmingham Small Heath Experience' (1991) *Journal of Education and the Law* 19.
84 s. 45, Education (No. 2) Act 1986.
85 *The Independent*, 27 October 1988, p. 21.
86 Under Education Reform Act 1988, s. 60(1)(a).
87 Ibid.
88 Under s. 62.
89 Under s. 62(11).
90 As required by section 61(3) and (4).
91 Under s. 63(3)(a).
92 Between 28 and 42 days: s. 60(1)(a).
93 *Per* Lord Justice Woolf, LEXIS transcript.
94 Ibid.
95 SI 1987 No. 1359.
96 (1989) 87 LGR 583.
97 Ibid., p. 587.
98 Court of Appeal LEXIS transcript.
99 Education Reform Act 1988, s. 61(1).
100 Ibid., s. 61(3) and (4).
101 See DES, *School Governors: How to Become a Grant-Maintained School*, op. cit., n. 56.
102 Divisional Court LEXIS transcript.
103 Ibid.
104 See chapter 3 for a wider discussion.
105 For a recent example of a court refusing to quash a technically flawed decision to seek City Technology College status, see *R.* v. *Governors of John Bacon School, ex parte ILEA, The Independent* Law Reports, 29 March 1990.
106 Divisional Court LEXIS transcript.
107 (1990) 88 LGR 716 (Divisional Court) and 737 (No. 2 – Court of Appeal). References are to the LEXIS transcript. See Paul Meredith, 'Opting-out Litigation: the City of Bath Experience' (1991) *Journal of Education and the Law* 65.
108 Along with proposals by the governors of one voluntary school submitted under s. 13 of the 1980 Act.
109 On 13 November 1988 and 11 January 1989: Court of Appeal LEXIS transcript.
110 This assumes that the s. 12 proposals ranged more widely than the one

school to which grant-maintained status has been granted.
111 See *Legg* v. *ILEA* [1972] 3 All ER 177 at p. 188.
112 LEXIS transcript.
113 Para. 13 of decision letter: see LEXIS transcript.
114 LEXIS transcript.
115 This unusual course of action was adopted in order to expedite proceedings. It was taken with the consent of the parties, despite the fact that it involved the loss of one stage in the appellate process.
116 LEXIS transcript (emphasis added).
117 Ibid.
118 Ibid.
119 (1986) 84 LGR 469.
120 [1989] 1 All ER 769.
121 LEXIS transcript.
122 There were several other unsuccessful subsidiary grounds of challenge, including failure to take into account the consequences of delay, and uncertainty as to the future organisation of schools in the area; miscalculation of projected numbers of pupils in the 16–19 age group; and miscalculation of the level of reduction in surplus capacity the LEA proposals would have achieved.
123 LEXIS transcript. Lord Justice Nicholls expressed himself in similarly trenchant terms as to the limited role of the court.
124 [1989] 2 All ER 417.
125 Under s. 105, Education Reform Act 1988.
126 See [1989] 2 All ER 417 at pp. 419–20.
127 Ibid., p. 419.
128 Lord Justice Balcombe dissenting in the Court of Appeal.
129 See discussion by I. Cram, 'Dismissing Dissentient Governors: the Governors Triumphant' (1989) *Journal of Education and the Law* 119.
130 [1989] 2 All ER 417 at p. 420, *per* Lord Bridge of Harwich.
131 Ibid. (emphasis added).
132 s. 14 of the 1944 Act provides an alternative route to closure of a voluntary school to its closure by the LEA under s. 12, Education Act 1980.
133 (1988) 86 LGR 507 (Divisional Court).
134 *The Independent* Law Reports, 27 July 1989 (Court of Appeal).
135 (1988) 86 LGR 507 at p. 518.
136 Ibid.
137 [1989] 2 All ER 417.
138 *R.* v. *Westminster Roman Catholic Diocese Trustee, ex parte Andrews*, op. cit., n. 132.
139 s. 66(8), Education Reform Act 1988.
140 s. 99(2), Education Act 1944.
141 See 'Baker May Sidestep Archbishop's Defiance', *TES*, 26 May 1989; 'Hume Determined Not to Give Way', *TES*, 28 July 1989; 'Cardinal Accepts Vaughan Case Is Unwinnable', *TES*, 11 August 1989.
142 See 'Catholic College to Go Ahead', *TES*, 8 December 1989.
143 See now s. 8(5), Education (No. 2) Act 1986.
144 *The Times* Law Reports, 7 December 1990. See also *R.* v. *Greenwich*

London Borough Council, ex parte Lovelace, [1991] 3 All ER 511. See also the unsuccessful Education (School Governing Bodies) Bill 1990, a Bill proposed by Mr Jack Straw, Chief Opposition Spokesman on Education, to secure as far as possible that LEA nominees on governing bodies do reflect party representation on the LEA as a whole. Failure by some LEAs to secure balanced representation has caused considerable controversy.

145 By 16 July 1991, 100 schools had opted out: see DES Press Notice 238/91, 16 July 1991.

146 See *TES*, 5 October 1990, 'Opted-out Schools Will Be Forced Back into the Fold'.

147 s. 92.

148 DES Circular 10/88, op. cit., n. 7, para. 70.

INDEX